SENSIBLE CRUISING:
The Thoreau Approach

**A Philosophic and Practical
Approach to Cruising**

by

Don Casey   and   *Lew Hackler*

Illustrations by Bobby Basnight

INTERNATIONAL MARINE PUBLISHING
Camden, Maine

Library of Congress Catalog Card Number 86-60480
ISBN 0-87742-288-5

Published by International Marine Publishing,
an imprint of TAB BOOKS.
TAB BOOKS is a division of McGraw-Hill, Inc.

1st Printing, October 1986
2nd Printing, November 1986
3rd Printing, December 1986
4th Printing, March 1987
5th Printing, October 1988
6th Printing, June 1990
7th Printing, July 1991
8th Printing, April 1993
9th Printing, April 1995
10th Printing, December 1995
11th Printing, December 1996

No truer American existed than Thoreau . . . there was an excellent wisdom in him, proper to a rare class of men . . . [with] power of description and literary excellence . . . he chose to be rich by making his wants few, and supplying them himself . . .

—Ralph Waldo Emerson

I never would have imagined that Thoreau's philosophy could be so aptly applied to anything as disparate as cruising.

—Dr. Walter Harding, author and
Secretary of The Thoreau Society

At sea, I learned how little a person needs, not how much.

—Robin Lee Graham,
Circumnavigator and author
of *Dove*

One of the wonderful things about the cruising life is that it teaches you how little you can get along on, that to lead a fulfilling life it is not necessary to have a big pile of bucks. This may have been self-evident to Thoreau before the day of mass media, but in our modern environment it is a philosophy that is difficult to come by.

Your readers should be aware that being judicious in their purchases can be financially rewarding at the end. We have always treated our boats as investments, and made money on all of them.

—Steve Dashew, Circumnavigator, and
author of *Bluewater Handbook*, and
The Circumnavigators' Handbook

It does look sometimes as if the world were on its last legs. How many there are whose principal employment it is nowadays to eat their meals and go to the post-office.

—Henry David Thoreau

College of the Ouachitas

To Olga, who understands the dream and occasionally hears the drummer.

To Mom, who kept the faith, and to Janice, who was always ready when I said "ready about."

and to HDT, with whom we would like to have sailed.

The sail bends gently to the breeze, as swells some generous impulse of the heart, and anon flutters and flaps with a kind of human suspense. I could watch the motions of a sail forever, they are so rich and full of meaning. I watch the play of its pulse, as if it were my own blood beating there.

—Henry David Thoreau

CONTENTS

ILLUSTRATIONS

ACKNOWLEDGEMENTS

Each of the three contributors to this book was drawn to sailing by the beauty and simplicity of the pursuit. Influenced and inspired by the power and splendor of nature, we found sailing to be somehow harmonious with the environment. We could spend a day sailing in our corner of this watery world, harnessing nature to our conveyance, yet neither depleting our resources (natural or financial) nor leaving a trace of our passage.

It fell upon the "old man of the sea," Sir Francis Chichester, to expand our horizons. He captured the imagination of the world with his courage and zest and led many, including us, to realize what a large portion of the world is open to those fortunate enough to possess seaworthy sailboats. If Sir Francis could round the Horn, and circle the globe, surely we could get safely to the opposite shore of the bay. Since Chichester seemed so much larger than life, we each had difficulty with identification. For one of us, the motivations of Sterling Hayden struck a resonant chord; the other was inspired by Robin Lee Graham to cast off.

This book was the eventual result of these inspired yet timorous beginnings. Along the way we were influenced by sailors before us whose passages we could trace by their writings. Although innumerable names come to mind, some merit special notation: Eric and Susan Hiscock, Irving and Electa Johnson, Hal and Margaret Roth, Larry and Lin Pardey, Herb and Nancy Payson, Carelton Mitchell, and Donald Street.

Yet the business of cruising is best learned by doing. Our own experiences are reflected in this book, influenced by the counsel and experiences of others with whom we have sailed. Among our mentors are most notably Abner and Beverly, Dan, Dick, Joe and Helen, John, John and Barbera, Norman and Jane, Owen, Parker, and Steve.

As for the book itself, special appreciation goes to John Weber who first encouraged us to write about cruising; to Olga and Janice who provided daily support, criticism, tolerance, and encouragement; to Patricia Rychlik Blaszak whose red ink on the manuscript contributed immensely to its literacy; to Richard T. Betton whose laser eyes helped cross the "t's" and dot the "i's"; and, to Henry Wagner for his invaluable guidance on publishing and distribution.

And finally, we wish to acknowledge the profound influence of Henry David Thoreau, who stated our case so eloquently.

INTRODUCTION

If this book is called *Sensible Cruising: The Thoreau Approach,* why are the authors named Casey and Hackler? The answer to that is simple really. This is the 1980's. Mr. Thoreau died on May 6, 1862. Under the circumstances, we decided to write the book for him.

Well, actually we did not write it for him. We wrote it for you. We have seen too many perfectly good *little* cruisers sitting at the dock or on a mooring while the owner struggled and sweated to get the *right* boat for his dream cruise. More often than not, it is not the sea that beats back the would-be cruiser; it is his attitude. If more of us understood what Mr. Thoreau knew so well, there would be many more of us cruising.

That brings up an interesting question. Do those of us who cruise truly want more people *out there* crowding up what once were deserted anchorages? Not really, although there are still many deserted anchorages to be found if that is what you want. If we don't want more cruisers out there, why write this book? That's easy. We only want *you* to go cruising, not everyone. It is such a great experience that we just have to share it. Anyway, don't worry. Most of the people for whom this book is written will go right on working, waiting, wishing, but not changing.

The mass of men lead lives of quiet desperation.

Oh, that Thoreau. Absolutely! If you are unfamiliar with Mr. Thoreau, then you have missed a chapter of the American heritage no sailor should be without. Although his actual cruising experience was very narrow, he knew more about what cruising is than most of us will ever know. Equally as important, he knew how to express that knowledge in a way which grabs the reader and shakes him. Once exposed to the writings of Thoreau, the intrinsic wisdom of his words will be obvious.

Henry David Thoreau was born in Concord, Massachusetts, in 1817. He was a Harvard graduate who, at various times in his life, was a teacher, a surveyor, a laborer, a handyman, a pencilmaker, and a small-boat cruiser. In his own mind, however, Thoreau was a poet, meaning he lived as a poet, the highest representation of mankind in his judgement. He believed "The collector of facts must possess a perfect physical organization; the philosopher, a perfect intellectual organization. But in the true poet they are so fairly but mysteriously balanced, that we can see the results of both, and generalize even the widest deductions of philosophy." Thus he lived as a poet and wrote as a philosopher.

My life has been the poem I would have writ,
But I could not both live and utter it.

The applicability of the philosophy of Thoreau to the activity of cruising is surely one of the most perfect imaginable. The same values that send many cruising led Thoreau to the shore of Walden Pond, where he so skillfully recorded his philosophy.

This is a book about cruising, and we have said almost enough about Mr. Thoreau. We are more interested in what he had to say about us. However, one final comment about Mr. Thoreau is in order. He was thrifty.

. . . instead of studying how to make it worth men's while to buy my baskets, I studied rather how to avoid the necessity of selling them.

Few cruisers go sailing without a budget, often a very restrictive one. Mr. Thoreau often speaks of that situation, but it is not just his monetary thrift that is valuable to us. He is also thrifty with time, committed to getting the most out of life today rather than waiting for some vague tomorrow. And there is his thrift with the written word. He packs a great deal of thought into a very few words. No writer in the English language has ever excelled him in this art.

His commitment to thrift makes him an authority on "sensible cruising." As you will see as you read this book, Thoreau in a very real sense tells us if cruising is what we want, then it is what we should be doing. Take the boat you already have and go. If you do not have a boat, then buy one you can afford and go. Life is too short and too full of wonder to spend the mass of it:

> . . . *laying up treasures which moth and rust will corrupt and thieves break through and steal.*

And what about these other two guys, Casey and this Hackler fellow? Are they great philosophers? Ha. Famous sailors, right? Well . . . we know each other. We are just cruisers, nothing more, nothing less. We both own 30-foot boats of very different designs, we live in different states, and we cruise in different areas. But we cruise for exactly the same reasons. We find within practical limits, the smaller the boat the better it satisfies our essential reasons for sailing in the first place. Cruising in a smaller boat is not a deprivation. It puts one more in touch with the essence of cruising.

> *It is life near the bone where it is sweetest.*

Finally, there is the matter of the table of contents. If you have already browsed through it, you no doubt wonder about a cruising book with a chapter titled "The Bean Field" or "Baker Farm." Thoreau's best-known work, and the one most applicable to the cruising sailor, is *Walden*. Many of the quotations that you will encounter herein came from this single, wonderful work. Since we had already shamelessly borrowed so much other material from *Walden*, we decided to borrow the table of contents also. This, perhaps, is not the order in which we should have put the book, however we do not understand order as well as a poet. In this matter we defer to the judgement of Mr. Thoreau.

That should just about cover all of the necessary explanations. Now, come cruising with us . . . perhaps you too will find the way.

WALDEN

Near the end of March, 1845, I borrowed an axe and went down to the woods by Walden Pond . . .

HUS Henry David Thoreau began an experiment in essential living that lasted more than two years and resulted in his most famous work, *Walden*. Cruising is also an experiment in essential living, and Thoreau's discoveries are of great value to anyone contemplating a cruise in a small boat.

ESSENTIAL LIVING

Walden Pond was hardly a cruising lake. No more than a half mile across, it offered no exotic ports. Yet the setting was one of exceptional beauty and serenity, one in which Thoreau, the philosopher, was able to accomplish much.

> *My purpose in going to Walden Pond was not to live cheaply nor to live dearly there, but to transact some private business with the fewest obstacles . . .*

Cruising is like that. It is essentially a natural thing, perhaps even a spiritual thing. Romance is the word most often coupled with the concept. Like Walden Pond, it offers the promise of exceptional beauty and serenity. And like going to the woods, it is an activity within the reach of the "common man."

Perhaps going to the woods in 1845 does not seem all that relevant to going cruising today. For the moment, let's stay with the woods, but move forward to today. Consider the situation of our friend, Bob.

Bob had a month's vacation available. His spouse was between jobs. For more than ten years Bob had talked about taking a trip to the magnificent national parks in the west and northwest portions of the United States. Repeatedly the matchless photography of *National Geographic* had fired his imagination: the early morning colors of the Grand Canyon, the gossamer falls of Yosemite Valley, trees 3,000 years old and 100 feet in circumference in Sequoia National Park, and the geysers of Yellowstone. He wanted to experience these sights for himself.

Now he had the opportunity and everything was perfect—except for one thing. In his mind's eye, Bob had made this trip a hundred times, but always in a top-of-the-line, 28-foot motor home. His camper-converted Volkswagen bus sat willingly in the driveway, a veteran of many weekends in regional parks, but it did not have a shower, nor a microwave oven, not even a real sofa. "No way," said Bob. "Not in the Volkswagen. Maybe in a few more years we can afford a *bigger* camper and then we will make the trip." So he stayed home.

Sound ridiculous? We hope so, yet thousands of sailors are deterred from cruising every year by the very same logic. Visit any large marina, talk to boat owners there, and you will hear over and over again, "In a couple of years we're going to buy a larger boat and go cruising." The speaker will be sitting atop a salty-looking and quite capable 25-footer.

THE 40-FOOT MYTH

Why does he equate cruising with a larger boat? Is a larger boat indicated for reasons of safety? Probably not. Comfort? Not really. Status? Perhaps. Contemporary opinion? Far too often. This is a question each must answer for himself. Its answer will determine when, or even if, he, or you, will actually go cruising.

This is an instructional book, but also a philosophical one. Its message is quite simple. If you wish to go cruising, go. If you subscribe to the school of thought that says a proper cruising boat must be at least 40 feet in length and you can afford a 40-footer, and your means of affording it does not conspire to prevent you from cruising it, then it is not our intent to discourage you from the purchase of such a yacht.

I do not speak to those who are well employed, in whatever circumstances, and they know whether they are well employed or not;—but mainly to the mass of men who are discontented, and idly complaining of the hardness of their lot or of the times, when they might improve them.

If you want a 40-footer and cannot afford it, or can only afford it by committing yourself to some unrelenting shore-side activity for the next ten years, we think there is a better way.

Cruising is a lifestyle, an attitude, a state of mind. Contrary to contemporary wisdom, a cruise can be just as successful in a 20-footer as a 40-footer, most likely more successful. Almost all of the current books written on cruising were written by blue-water cruisers, circumnavigators most. It is this accomplishment that makes them expert and their advice is good, valid, and deserves our consideration. However, most cruisers do not require the kind of capability suggested by these experts. Before committing yourself and your life savings to a big, heavy "world cruiser," consider the alternatives.

We do not advocate an around-the-world voyage in a cockleshell, but we do point out that many successful cruises have been accomplished in relatively small vessels. Some well-known cruises are briefly reviewed in a later chapter. However, most cruising is a private thing and the oceans and waterways of the world are loaded with competent skippers going about the business of cruising in small boats. Whether you join them or not is entirely up to you.

THE SENSIBLE BOAT

Although we are primarily listening to the counsel of Thoreau, we

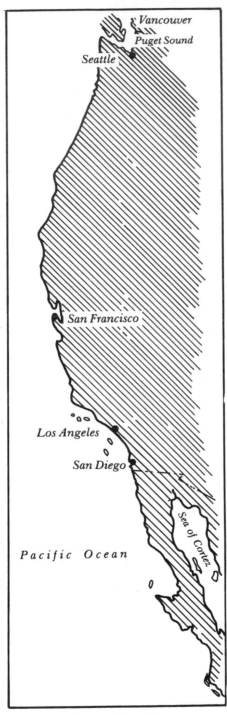

West Coast cruising areas.

are not above borrowing wisdom from someone else. In this case, we would like to quote Robin Lee Graham who successfully took his 24-foot sloop, *Dove*, three-quarters of the way around the world. Upon the completion of his five-year voyage, Graham wrote, "At sea, I learned how *little* a person needs, not how much."

Cruising almost always teaches that. Unfortunately the first-time cruiser must speculate on how *much* he needs for a successful cruise and obtain an appropriate vessel based upon such speculation. This chapter and the ones that follow will give the would-be cruiser valuable guidance in boat selection and outfitting.

A single gentle rain makes the grass many shades greener. So our prospects brighten on the influx of better thoughts.

The first step in boat selection is to define your cruising area and understand your objectives. Few of us set out to cross an entire ocean on a first cruise. More often our objective is to cross a small part of it. West Coast sailors may think in terms of a Mexican cruise or Puget Sound; East Coast sailors the Chesapeake, the Bahamas, or the Caribbean. Those bent toward bluer water may consider

4

Bermuda or perhaps even Hawaii.

The *big cruise* is usually down the road after we see how we like cruising. Even so, there is an almost irresistible temptation to try to purchase a boat capable of rounding Cape Horn despite knowledge that, at least in the foreseeable future, cruises will be limited to no more than a month, perhaps two. Time restrictions often define the outer boundaries of our particular cruising area. It is important to resist this temptation to search for the *ultimate boat*. A boat should be selected to satisfy cruising for the next two or three years. For the novice cruiser, there is far too much uncertainty to plan beyond that.

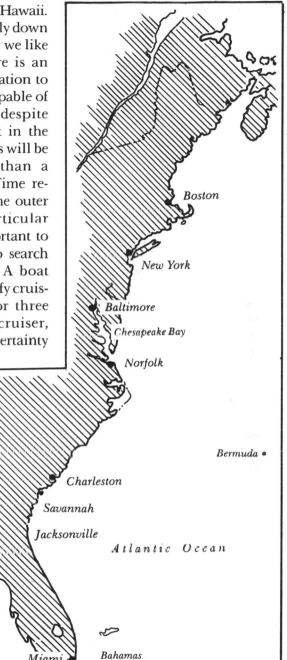

East Coast cruising areas.

Each new year is a surprise to us.

If you want to go cruising, the boat should facilitate that objective, not hinder it. The boat should not be too large to handle, too complex to maintain, or too expensive to afford. Of all the cruises made each year, there is little doubt 95% could be made in a boat of no more than 30 feet in length, most in a boat much smaller. Most of us run a far greater risk of buying a boat too large for our needs than getting one too small.

SAGE COUNSEL

In the following chapters, we will look at the specific advantages and disadvantages of the small cruiser. We will suggest how to select it, how to outfit it, and where to take it. We will examine guests and crew. We will assist you in the arrangements necessary for leaving, the adjustments necessary for returning.

Returning is a key word. This is not a book about unlimited cruising; few choose that course. Most are willing to allocate only a specific amount of time, able to allocate only a specific amount of money. If this is your situation, you will find assistance in the pages that follow.

I trust that none will stretch the seams in putting on the coat,
for it may do good service to him whom it fits.

Thoreau's discoveries at Walden will show you the way to change a wishful "someday" to an emphatic "now."

than one cruised primarily by two people. The proper boat for a six-month cruise is not necessarily the proper boat for a one-month cruise. A boat intended for gunkholing in shallow bays probably will not also be the best design for crossing oceans.

The vast majority of cruising is a two-person activity. Among the cruising boats in any harbor, the cruising couple is dominant. If comments concerning cruising are not valid for the cruising couple, they are of little use to the cruising community as a whole. In light of this, we can reconsider the opinion of the experts that a proper cruising boat must be 40 feet in length. That simply is not true.

It is never too late to give up our prejudices. No way of thinking or doing, however ancient, can be trusted without proof.

DEFINING TERMS

In this chapter, we propose to evaluate the strengths and weaknesses of the two different classes of cruising boats, those below an upper limit of 35 feet which we will call *pocket cruiser,* and those larger than 35 feet which we will call *world cruiser.* There are two important points to remember about our selection of names.

First, we do not intend to give the impression that a boat under 35 feet is not capable of ocean voyaging. Nothing could be farther from the truth. Our purpose in naming the classes of boats is to avoid repeatedly stating "the big boat this," or "the small boat that." The term *world cruiser* conjures up an image of a large, heavily-built, heavily-rigged sailboat, not a 25-footer. The *pocket cruiser* suggests a compact, easily-handled sailboat with, at a minimum, basic accommodations. Both images are appropriate for our purposes.

Secondly, there can be a great deal of difference between a 25-footer and a 35-footer although we refer to both as pocket cruisers. The same applies to the world cruiser category. To simplify comparisons, unless otherwise indicated, when we talk of a pocket cruiser, we will be referring to a boat of around 30 feet; for the world cruiser, 40 feet. If your cruiser is a 25-footer, differences between your pocket cruiser and our world cruiser will be more pronounced; for a 35-footer, somewhat less. Do not let this confuse you. The general conclusions will be more important than the specifics anyway.

In our examination, we have set the lower limit of the pocket cruiser category at 25 feet. Many exceptionally enjoyable cruises have been made in boats well under this arbitrary 25-foot threshold but, with some notable exceptions, few boats under 25 feet in length are designed with lengthy cruising in mind. For this reason we concentrate on boats slightly larger. If, for preferential or financial reasons, a 20-footer seems appropriate for your cruising plans, our discourse on boat size is not directed at you as you are probably already in touch with your own cruising needs.

We should also comment on the increasingly popular *beach cruiser,* a very small, often open boat with no built-in accommodations, which, with a boom tent or sleeping bags may be used for overnight or weekend cruising.

Consider first how slight a shelter is absolutely necessary.

While cruising is possible in a beach cruiser, except for the hardiest and boldest, it is very limited. When we talk of cruising, we mean sailing and living aboard for an extended period of time with a high degree of safety and comfort. For most of us, the *beach cruiser* is not consistent with that definition, and consequently is not included here.

THE SELECTION PROCESS

Certainly for coastal cruising, and even where some ocean voyaging is contemplated, a very strong case can be made for selecting a pocket cruiser, a boat of about 30 feet in length. A cruise should be fun. If it is not, what is the point? A cruising boat should also be fun. If it is not, it is not a good cruising boat. A boat too large for your available time and money can place a substantial strain on the joy of cruising.

The typical selection process for a first cruising boat is less than ideal. A couple, dreaming of extended cruising, begins by reading advertising copy in the major sailing magazines. Books are consulted regarding boat design and construction. Charts are purchased and the proposed cruise outlined. The need for true blue-water capability is evaluated, as are sailing abilities, anticipated crew or guests, and myriad other serious considerations. After careful research and agonizing soul searching, the results are disregarded and the couple simply *buys the largest boat they can afford,* or one a little larger.

Far too many cruising boats are selected based not upon suitability, but upon affordability—the largest boat that can be afforded. The first question asked of the new boat owner is invariably, "How big is it?" The larger the boat, the greater the respect shown by others.

. . . perhaps we are led oftener by the love of novelty and a regard for the opinions of men, in procuring it, than by a

true utility.

This aspect of human nature is a real obstacle to realizing a dream of cruising, the selection process it dictates is almost invariably a mistake. We run a far greater risk of buying a boat too large for our needs than getting one too small!

COST

The case for the small cruiser is very strong, beginning with cost. Even if one finds a 40-footer affordable, undoubtedly a boat of 30 feet will be even more affordable. The relationship between length and cost is not linear. The difference between a 25-foot boat and a 50-footer is two times in length, ten times in cost. More pertinent, a 40-footer is only one third longer than a 30-footer, but its cost, even in the used market, may well be three times as much. If a used 30-footer may be purchased for $30,000, an equivalent (in design and quality of construction) 40-footer will cost close to $90,000.

WITH $90,000 TO SPEND:

[10% Down — 10% Interest — 10-Year Loan]

30-FOOT	*40-FOOT*
POCKET CRUISER	*WORLD CRUISER*

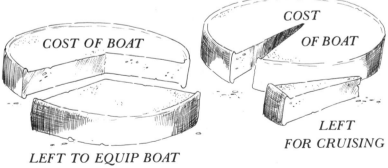

Relative costs with $90,000 to spend for everything.

Look at it another way: imagine two would-be cruising sailors, each with access to $90,000; one purchases a pocket cruiser while the other purchases a world cruiser; their situations become dramatically different. The purchaser of the 40-footer has a boat capable of accomplishing his cruise, but having spent all available funds on its purchase, can neither outfit it properly nor afford to cruise in it.

> *With consummate skill he has set his trap with a hair spring*
> *to catch comfort and independence, and then, as he turned*
> *away, got his own leg into it.*

The purchaser of the 30-footer also has a boat capable of accomplishing his cruise. In addition, he still has $60,000 in available funds with which to outfit his cruising boat in any way he may deem appropriate and will still have sufficient funds left over to support an extended cruise.

OTHER EXPENSES

Beyond the initial purchase cost, there are many other cost considerations. A new suit of sails for the larger boat will cost more than twice as much as a suit for a pocket cruiser. Even if you do not need new working sails, adding a sail to your inventory, such as a light air drifter, can easily be as much as $1,000 more expensive for the larger boat. The same relationship applies to standing and running rigging. Ground tackle will cost almost 50% more. Fuel consumption for the engine will be more than double. Slip fees are higher. It will take twice as much antifouling paint to cover the bottom of a 40-footer, and quality antifouling paint costs close to $150 per gallon. The list is endless. And maintenance requirements, in time as well as money, become increasingly oppressive.

> *I can impose upon myself tasks which will crush me for life*
> *and prevent all expansion, and this I am but too inclined*
> *to do.*

DRAFT

The concept of cruising is one of intense freedom. Owning a sailboat of significant capability literally opens the world to anyone so inclined to sail it. The sense of unlimited freedom, perhaps the romance of a tradewind passage to the South Seas, is what initially attracts many to cruising, but here an economy of thought is required.

ECONOMY

The reality is that cruising is usually done in shallow coastal waters, in lakes, across bays and up estuaries. You need cruise only for a short time to recognize that, given seaworthiness, a smaller boat with its shallower draft actually opens up more of the world to the cruiser than the larger boat.

Many of the world's best cruising areas can be fully explored only with a shallow draft. A notable example is the Bahama Islands. With a clarity unsurpassed anywhere else in the world, the water covering the vast banks is often less than six feet deep. Many of the anchorages are inaccessible to boats with a draft of five feet. In fact, if Bahama cruising is the prime goal, draft may well be the prime consideration. Shallow draft is perhaps the most formidable argument for the multihull cruiser. Having cruised the Bahamas extensively, we have often envied friends on trimarans and catamarans, sometimes drawing less than two feet and thus able to enter many areas from which we were excluded.

Where the cruising area is shallow, those on smaller boats will have the option of anchoring with the crowd if they choose, or slipping off to the tranquility of a secluded shallow cove. Those aboard larger yachts will not enjoy that option. Even when the cruiser is feeling gregarious and decides to anchor with the fleet, the smaller boat again shows its utility. No matter how crowded the anchorage, a shoal draft boat can almost always find a shallow spot, inaccessible to the larger boats, but providing ample depth and swinging room.

HANDLING

Consider also the economy of energy consumption. Sailing is supposed to be a relaxing pastime, but hoisting a huge mainsail or winching in an acre of wind-filled genoa is anything but relaxing. Just retrieving the requisite anchor and chain for a world cruiser can easily provide 100% of the daily adult exercise requirement, necessitating (expensive) mechanical or perhaps (more expensive) medical assistance.

The term "handy" appropriately equates with a small cruiser. It will turn a tighter radius; it can be tacked into and out of a narrow channel; it can be brought alongside the dock much more easily under sail. In the latter case, the consequences of a judgement error in a 5-ton boat will be considerably less than the same lapse committed in one of 15 tons or more.

An unfortunate aspect of cruising is grounding. Eventually it happens to everyone who sails very far from his home dock. With a 20-foot boat, a grounding means jumping into the water and pushing off.

Except for the most serious grounding, a 30-footer with a dinghy and good sheet winches can usually kedge off without difficulty. The larger the boat, the more difficult this process becomes. As grounding becomes a fearsome event, it detracts significantly from one's ability to relax when sailing in thin waters.

COMFORT

There are points of comparison in which the larger boat will enjoy the advantage. The most often mentioned, that larger boats are more comfortable for living aboard, is entirely true. Accommodations are more spacious and the inventory of luxury equipment (microwave, generator, air conditioning) is usually more extensive. When full time living aboard is contemplated, i.e., tied to a dock with shore-side responsibilities, a boat larger and more complex than would otherwise be chosen for cruising may be appropriate. For cruising, however, the cost of such comforts may be far greater than their value.

> *Most of the luxuries, and many of the so-called comforts of life, are not only not indispensable, but positive hindrances . . .*

Another common argument for purchasing a larger boat is that it will be more sea-kindly. It is true that, given equivalent designs, the bigger, heavier, deeper boat will have an easier motion in a seaway than the smaller, lighter, shallower one. However, this is a boat-by-boat characteristic, and size alone is no guarantee of sea-kindliness.

SEAWORTHINESS

Some will also argue that the larger boat is more seaworthy. There is a big difference between *sea-kindly* and *seaworthy,* and no evidence at all to substantiate that ten additional feet in length will make a boat more seaworthy. Seaworthiness is determined by design and construction. In almost all cases, the boat can tolerate adverse conditions far longer than the crew. This means seaworthiness, beyond a certain basic requirement, is more a matter of the crew's ability to handle the boat.

There is a strong counter argument that with a two-man crew, the smaller boat is less likely to get into trouble.

> *What you consider my disadvantage, I consider my advantage.*

ECONOMY

The gear is lighter and easier to manage. In storm conditions at anchor, the ground tackle can be more easily handled. At sea, the sails can be doused or reefed more easily. By virtue of its smaller size, there is less danger of being thrown across the boat and injured in rough seas.

Unexpected gear failure is easier for the cruising couple to deal with on a smaller boat. The second most feared gear failure, after sinking, is dismasting. Stroll through a marina and look at the mast on a typical 30-footer. Imagine losing it over the side in a near gale and having to either cut it loose or bring it back aboard to prevent it from holing the hull (causing the most feared emergency). Difficult and dangerous, but you could do it. Now look at the stick and rigging on a 40-footer and imagine the same circumstances!

STOWAGE

Another argument that is often made for a larger boat is stowage. There is more stowage space on a 40-foot boat, but a well-designed, medium-displacement 30-footer will have sufficient stowage to accommodate six months cruising supplies for two. Unless your cruising plans call for more than six months between supply ports, the additional stowage space is of little value.

A notable exception to this statement is dinghy stowage. A hard dinghy of generous size is a definite stowage problem on a small cruiser. For coastal cruising, towing provides a workable solution, but for offshore work, the dinghy must come aboard. The standard solution is the inflatable; other solutions are covered in a subsequent chapter.

SPEED

Cruising should be done on "island time," meaning a much more relaxed pace than most of us find ashore.

*A boatman stretched on the deck of his craft and dallying
with the noon would be as apt an emblem of eternity for me
as the serpent with his tail in his mouth.*

This means, theoretically, that it should not matter whether you get there today, tomorrow, or sometime next week. In reality it does matter, and a boat that sails well makes a much better cruising boat than one which does not. Boat speed is important. If it was not, cruising boats would all look like big, square barges (some do) with enormous lockers and prodigious accommodations.

In any comparison of boat speed, the larger boat has a decided advantage. However, boat speed is not a function of overall length, but one of sail area and waterline length. Given sufficient sail area for the wind conditions, maximum hull speed for a displacement hull is normally calculated using the formula: 1.34 times the square root of the waterline length in feet.

The table below provides comparative data on boats of 25, 30, 35, and 40 feet in overall length. Ten boats of each length were selected randomly, their waterline lengths averaged. The table indicates that the average difference between a 30-foot cruising boat and a 40-footer is less than 0.9 knots. This means that on a typical island-hopping cruise, you could cover an additional ten miles in the larger boat during daylight hours.

Where passage-making is contemplated, maximum speed comparisons are not very useful. A good sailing vessel will do well to average 1 times the square root of the waterline; most vessels will average about .8 times the square root. That means that our typical pocket cruiser will average 97 miles a day passagemaking, the world cruiser 110. As conditions become more ideal, the larger boat would lengthen its advantage. Still, considering the enormous cost differential, the incremental speed difference seems rather insignificant.

		SAILBOAT LENGTHS (LOA)			
		25 FT.	**30 FT.**	**35 FT.**	**40 FT.**
	1.	18' 6"	25' 0"	28' 0"	30'10"
	2.	21' 0"	24' 0"	28' 7"	32' 4"
Waterline	3.	22' 2"	24' 0"	26' 9"	34' 0"
Lengths (LWL)	4.	19' 0"	25' 5"	27' 7"	32' 0"
of ten	5.	20' 8"	25' 5"	26' 6"	33' 0"
Modern	6.	22' 0"	24' 0"	28' 9"	31' 0"
Sailboats	7.	23' 0"	24' 1"	26' 7"	33' 4"
(typical)	8.	21'10"	22' 0"	27'10"	35' 0"
	9.	23' 0"	22'10"	29' 6"	27' 6"
	10.	22' 1"	25' 4"	30' 0"	31' 4"
Average LWL:		21' 4"	24' 2"	28' 0"	32' 0"
Speed: (max. theoretical)		**6.18**	**6.59**	**7.09**	**7.47**

Comparison of boat speeds for various size boats.

HULL CONFIGURATION

Other factors besides waterline length determine whether a particular boat sails well or not. Boat performance is inextricably tied to rig and hull configuration.

ECONOMY

> *If rightly made, a boat would be . . . a creature of two elements, related by one half of its structure to some swift and shapely fish, and by the other to some strong-winged and graceful bird.*

As we have already mentioned, a hull shaped like a barge would have distinct advantages for just living aboard. For fast passages, however, the hull should resemble that of a 12-meter racer. The best hull shape for a cruising yacht is somewhere in between these two. There is little agreement, even among cruisers, about exactly what shape is ideal. Most cruisers will agree that neither the barge nor the 12-meter are satisfactory.

If you are purchasing your cruiser without prejudice, you will be well advised to select a hull configuration in the middle of these two extremes. In decidedly oversimplified terms, you will be looking for either a full keel design with a cut-away forefoot or a fin keel design in which the fin is carried well aft and the spade rudder is mounted to a skeg. We ask the hull of a cruising boat to provide speed, windward ability, maneuverability, directional stability, and easy motion. No single hull will perform better than all others in each of these categories, but either of the two hull configurations recommended above should perform satisfactorily in all areas.

RIG

What about the rig? The preponderance of sailboats in the 25- to 35-foot range will have single masts. Most will be sloop rigged although some will have inner stays and thus be considered cutters. A few small ketches are around, fewer still small yawls; you may even find a schooner or two. Every one of these rigs has distinct advantages; each also has disadvantages. Without exception they are all quite capable of propelling a cruising boat to any port the owner may desire to visit. The concept of an ideal rig, like that of an ideal cruising boat, is nonsense. Traditional wisdom is that below 40 feet there is little justification for a split rig, its major advantage being smaller and more easily handled sails. However, if the largest person aboard weighs 98 pounds, a 25-footer may advantageously be rigged as a ketch.

On a small cruiser, most sailors will be satisfied with a single mast rigged either as a sloop or a cutter. Almost any rig can be cruised successfully, the type of rig is not nearly as important as recognizing its advantages and disadvantages and learning to make the best use of those characteristics. When you are anchored in some faraway cove, it

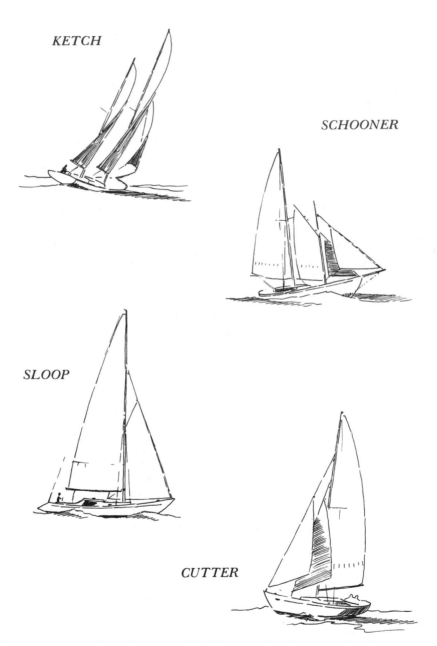

KETCH

SCHOONER

SLOOP

CUTTER

Almost any rig can be cruised successfully. The type of rig is not nearly as important as recognizing its advantages and disadvantages and learning to make the best use of those characteristics.

ECONOMY

is of little consequence whether you sailed there aboard a sleek little sloop, a sturdy little ketch, or a classic little schooner.

THE PERFECT BOAT

We have no guarantee of tomorrow. If you dream of cruising, start today. Take the small cruiser you have now and go cruising. Buy the small cruiser you can afford now and go cruising.

> *No wealth can buy the requisite leisure, freedom, and independence which are the capital in this profession.*

The perfect boat is not the one you dream about. It is the boat that takes you cruising.

WHERE I LIVED,
AND
WHAT I LIVED FOR

One farmer says to me, "You cannot live on vegetable food solely, for it furnishes nothing to make bones with;" and so he religiously devotes a part of his day to supplying his system with the raw material of bones; walking all the while he talks behind his oxen, which, with vegetable-made bones, jerk him and his lumbering plow along in spite of every obstacle.

NE sailor says to me, "You cannot cruise in the boat I own, for it is not big enough for such a voyage;" and so he religiously devotes his days to supplying his bank account with the raw material of a larger boat, and all the while he works, sister ships plow along through the oceans of the world in spite of every obstacle.

THE "RIGHT" BOAT

So often we hear sailors say, "If I just had the *right* boat, I would go cruising." Some eventually do. Most do not. Take a walk through a large marina. Look at all the "right" boats sitting neglected in their slips. Dream makers, all of them, yet they sit year after year tied to the dock, perhaps occasionally taken out on a weekend.

Why is that? Their owners would certainly not have committed so much money to their purchase unless planning to sail the boat. Why did they buy a 40-foot ocean-going sailboat? Because they like to sail? A Laser or a Hobie delivers more exciting sailing at a fraction of the cost. As a status symbol? Maybe. As an alternative to a weekend cabin in the mountains? Sometimes.

Getting away for a weekend or a week at a time is the objective of some. More often, the owner has cruising in mind. If you see the owner of just the boat you want checking on his investment one weekend, stop and ask him why he bought her. Chances are he will tell you that someday he is going to resign, retire, or sell out, and go cruising. As he caresses the teak handrail, he will tell you what a great boat she is, how many like her have gone around the world, how sturdy her construction is, or what famous sailor has a boat by the same architect. At least while he is talking to you, he really believes he will go, someday.

Don't you believe it. If he has had the boat for two weeks, maybe he will go; but if she has been at the dock for five years, the chances are very remote. It just doesn't work like that.

> *We seem to linger in manhood to tell the dreams of our childhood, and they vanish out of memory ere we learn the language.*

Think of cruising sailors you have read about. How many bought a boat, then waited five years to go cruising? The dream is difficult to sustain for that long. If you wait too long, you will never go. It is as simple as that. If you want to go cruising, find a way to *do it now*.

> *This is the only way, we say; but there are as many ways as there can be drawn radii from one centre.*

Forget about buying a 40-footer; cruise the pocket cruiser you own or buy one you *can* afford. Forget about a new boat; an old one will serve as well and may already be "equipped." Forget about Tahiti; try the Baja first. If the cruising life is for you, you will find out for sure, and then you can expand your cruising horizons. If you discover it is not for you, you will not have wasted years of your life in preparation for that lesson.

THE DRUMMER YOU HEAR

Cruising is not for everyone. In almost every major port around the world forlorn cruising boats sit neglected, "For Sale" signs in the portholes, their owners having simply walked away. Most knew the truth before they got to such a faraway port, but dreams die hard. Some among them have given up voyaging only, choosing to sail the worlds protected waterways, leaving blue water to those more bold.

A man has not every thing to do, but something; and because he cannot do every thing, it is not necessary that he should do something wrong.

Your kind of cruising should be right for you.

What is cruising like? That is a difficult question. Cruising is taking your son or daughter and an open 14-foot daysailer and, with a boom tent and canned heat, spending a week gunkholing behind barrier islands. It is selling your home and taking your 35-foot sloop to the Caribbean for a couple of years. It is leaving someone else in charge and going on a four-week charter aboard a 70-footer among the Greek islands. Each of these is different, yet they are all the same.

Cruising is a face-to-face encounter with nature. It is sunrises and sunsets. It is a million twinkling stars, undiminished by city lights. It is a giant silver tuna on the line, or a tiny blue chromis on the reef. It is a cobalt sea, a cerulean sky. It is beaches and bikinis. It is independence yet shared concerns. It is self-sufficiency yet camaraderie.

It is also bugs and bottom paint. It is storms at sea, swells in the anchorage. It is seasickness, sun poisoning, and sleepless nights. It is fog, waterspouts, and uncharted rocks. It is responsibility. It is never-ending maintenance, never-ending vigilance.

Cruising can be all of these things, both good and bad, regardless of the timidity or grandeur of your cruise. If there is no guarantee that a cruise will be fun, why do it? First, on balance, it probably will be fun. Good preparation and good planning can avoid most of the problems. But even if it turns out not to be idyllic, it will still be one of your most worthwhile experiences.

Why? Because the experiences of cruising are somehow more vivid than those typically found ashore.

> *We live but a fraction of our life. Why do we not let on the flood, raise the gates, and set all our wheels in motion?*

When things go badly, the depression you can experience is at the very bottom of the scale. But *it is the highs we cruise for.* Few experiences can match the satisfaction of a voyage safely completed or the beauty of the sunrise after a long night's sail. Even the bad times provide a base from which the good seems that much better.

Cruising provides the opportunity for uninhibited introspection and self-determination. As children, our parents tell us to behave, defining that term for us. In school our behavior is influenced, in some cases dictated, by our teachers and our peers. Then we go out into the "real" world. Earning a living becomes our need, success our objective. We go to work at a certain time, quit at a certain time. We defer to the dictates of the organization in behavior and dress. There is pressure on us to own the right car, live in the right neighborhood, even to buy the latest electronic gadget. We are inundated.

To those of us weary of social pressures, perhaps cruising is an escape. If so, it is without negative connotation. To the contrary, it forces us to enter ourselves, not run away.

> *Why should we be in such desperate haste to succeed and in such desperate enterprises? If a man does not keep pace with his companions, perhaps it is because he hears a different drummer. Let him step to the music which he hears, however measured or far away.*

Cruising is a way of stepping to the drummer you hear. It need not be a total commitment. Nowhere is it written you must give up everything to go cruising; nor is it written you may not.

It is an individual thing. The best counsel is to read about it, then try a short cruise before you consider throwing your life into a general upheaval and telling your friends you are off to sail around the world. If it is something you really want to do, you will know soon enough.

MAKING THE BREAK

And if it is? Then we are back to our original premise. It is such a fantastic experience that you should not let time and procrastination rob you of it. Make your plans and go cruising now. If what you have ashore is keeping you from going, store it, sell it, or give it away.

*I see young men, my townsmen, whose misfortune it is to
have inherited farms, houses, barns, cattle, and farming tools;
for these are more easily acquired than got rid of.*

Possessions have a way of owning you instead of the other way around;
it is a difficult bond to break.

A house is the most possessive. If you plan a short cruise, just close
the house and ask your neighbor to look after it. There may be some
expense, but consider it part of the cost of cruising. For a longer cruise,
renting your house may be the best option. You may be tempted to sell
the house to finance the boat and reverse the transaction upon your
return. Unless you also want to sell the house for some other reason,
this is probably not a wise approach. Only in the case of a truly open-
ended cruise, or where there is simply no other alternative available, do
we recommend effectively exchanging your house for your boat. Remember, this is a book about sensible approaches. Until you have some
cruising time behind you, we caution against burning too many bridges.

But burn a few. What about cars and furniture? If you are planning
a long cruise, get rid of them, all of them. *Nobody* out there cruising
hangs onto lamps and end tables.

*"But what shall I do with my furniture?" My gay butterfly is
entangled in a spider's web then. Even those who seem for a
long while not to have any, if you inquire more narrowly you
will find have some stored in somebody's barn.*

Well excuse us. Maybe you should store yours too. The point is not to
let such temporary things as a house, cars, or furniture keep you from
what will likely be one of your most lasting experiences.

FINANCIAL REALITIES

Cruising sounds great, and you agree that waiting around for just
the right boat when you already have a boat capable of taking you
cruising puts *ever* cruising in question. And despite our cautions, you
would sell your house in a minute to buy a cruising boat, if you had a
house. But you don't have a house. You don't have a boat. In fact, you
hardly have a pot.

*I have no doubt that some of you who read this book are
unable to pay for all the dinners which you have actually
eaten, or for the coats or shoes which are fast wearing or are
already worn out, and have come to this page to spend
borrowed or stolen time, robbing your creditors of an hour.*

25

Still, you want to go cruising. If you have nothing for lack of trying, forget cruising. It will require far greater effort than you can muster. There are a few "boat bums" around, but very few of them are cruising. They are just hanging out on some derelict of a boat until it sinks beneath them, garbaging up the harbor, both before and after their boats sink. They are not welcome in the cruising community, and you will not be either.

That is not to say all cruising sailors have money. They do not. In fact, many are constantly on the brink of financial disaster. Put another way, cruisers are often broke. But they are not "boat bums"; they pay their own way. They have some kind of periodic income; they have savings somewhere to draw on; they stop cruising to work periodically, or they stop working periodically to cruise.

So how do you start with nothing and go cruising? You cannot. You have to start with dedication, the single-minded kind that borders on the fanatical.

> *That aim in life is highest which requires the highest and finest discipline.*

If you have no assets to trade for a boat, you will have to somehow accumulate them, and quickly enough not to lose interest in the enterprise. How much will depend upon you and your cruising aspirations. If you are penniless, we do not recommend setting your sights on an around-the-world voyage. Temper your dreams with reality. A three-month or even a six-month cruise should not be that hard to achieve, if you want it badly enough.

The trick is to earn as much as you can and spend as little as you can. Can you work overtime? What about a second job? Are we crazy? No, and we do not work two jobs either, but you may have to. It comes down to how badly you want to go cruising. You are your only obstacle.

What do you have to give up? No new car. No cable T.V. Do you smoke? Quit. No eating out. No movies. No beer. Wait a minute, you're not becoming a monk. How about *less* beer? The point is that every decision you make must be made with the cruise in mind.

> *Be preoccupied with this, devoted to it, and no accident can befall you, no idle engagements distract you.*

As soon as you can, buy your boat, the least expensive boat you can find consistent with your cruising objectives. If cruising is what interests you, go cruising. If it is boat ownership that interests you, then forget the cruise for a while and just plan the boat. But do so with the knowledge that the cruise is at risk.

If you rent an apartment or own a home, if you can afford to live relatively comfortably every day, then you can already afford to go cruising. The day-to-day cost of cruising is no more, often a lot less, than the day-to-day cost of living ashore.

Why do you stay here and live this mean moiling life, when a glorious existence is possible for you? Those same stars twinkle over other fields than these.

Wait a minute—not everyone talking at once. We realize such comfortable living is predicated on a day-to-day income covering your expenses ashore (more or less). Without that income, you cannot afford to eat, much less go cruising.

Cold and hunger seem more friendly to my nature than those methods which men have adopted and advise to ward them off.

Excuse us, Mr. Thoreau. With all due respect, sir, we agreed at the outset we would illuminate a sensible approach. Our readers are not going to equate *cold and hunger* with *sensible*. But there are alternatives.

First, before we look too deeply for a more palatable solution, we need to establish if the cruise you have in mind will indeed cost you your income.

If your cruising plans are for a vacation cruise, or an approved sabbatical—a cruise having no significant implications on your income—then quit talking about it and get on with it. Take your pocket cruiser and go.

No boat? Then buy one—on credit if you must. Remember, we are talking about a sensible approach to cruising. There is no need to buy a boat costing more than your home, even if your credit rating will allow it. A capable little cruiser need not cost much more than a new car and will last infinitely longer. Most of us can qualify for that size loan.

Thoreau would not approve of the indebtedness, but times have changed. You can redeem yourself by selling it when you retire from cruising. If you buy and sell wisely, the use of the boat can actually be free. He would approve of that.

Drain the cup of inspiration to its last dregs. Fear no intemperance in that, for the years will come when otherwise thou wilt regret opportunities unimproved.

See.

That is not the kind of cruising you dream about. You want to go on a *real* cruise, you know, like for six months or a year or something. Like forever maybe. Fine. One cruise is no more "real" than another, but if you want to do a long cruise, then do it. Calculate the cost of the cruise you have in mind—sensibly—then dedicate yourself to earning and saving. When the bank account hits the magic number, do not delay another day. Load the boat and go.

THE BUSINESS TRAP

We often hear sailors say, "When business improves (or, alternatively, falls off) we are going to make that long cruise we have been planning." It is to us a sad fact that most never will.

There is no glory so bright but the veil of business can hide it effectually. With most men life is postponed to some trivial business . . .

Their job or business is too important to them. Inherently there is nothing wrong with this attitude and we have great respect for those who find complete satisfaction in their employment. For them, business is not trivial and it is not to them we speak. Rather, we address ourselves to those who would prefer cruising to business, at least for a time, but are fearful of making the break.

Generally, they fall into two categories. The first is afraid if he "drops out" for any length of time, his career will suffer irreparable damage or he will be unable to find employment upon his return. Thus he finds himself:

. . . the slave and prisoner of his own opinion of himself . . .

We can only suggest that the independence and self-sufficiency, not to mention organization and courage, displayed by the successful execution of a cruise are traits employers and business associates alike will respect. Besides, you might meet someone on the cruise who will lead you into a more satisfactory career. It happens.

The second type is worried about the actual cost. When he considers the expenses he projects for the cruise, and adds the amount of money he might earn during the period of time when he is cruising, the total gives him cause to ponder. Subtract from that number the expenses that accrue as a result of employment and shore life, i.e. housing costs, transportation, clothing, entertainment, taxes, anything, and the new lower number will more accurately reflect the cost of cruising. Still, when it comes right down to it and our worrier has the necessary funds, he begins to doubt the wisdom of spending this hard-earned money on something as seemingly frivolous as cruising.

Let us consider the way in which we spend our lives.

Enrichment has nothing to do with dollars and cents.

THE FAMILY OBSTACLE

Sometimes the obstacle is closer to home. Many would-be cruisers see family as a problem. Children are rarely a major obstacle. There are many boats making successful cruises, both short and extended, with children aboard. A reluctant spouse, however, can sink the cruise before it ever leaves the dock.

Quite often cruising is the dream of only one half of a couple. One partner dreams of selling everything and sailing to the South Seas; the other partner thinks such thoughts are hairbrained. If this is your situation, you do have a problem. You might try convincing your spouse that, as a disciple of Thoreau, you have seen a better way which the masses are unable to recognize.

The man of genius knows what he is aiming at; nobody else knows.

Never mind that it is true. If your spouse still thinks you are simply irresponsible, then another tack is required.

Cruising is an exciting pastime. If properly seduced, only the most hardcore can resist an offer of excitement in his life. Few will see mowing the lawn or shoveling snow as a more desirable activity than beachcombing on a deserted pink sand beach, or even ducking the jewels of spray accompanying a spanking reach across the bay. Would you rather have a new station wagon, or a new yacht? Such a nice word—yacht. Station wagon is so, you know, dull.

There is an incessant influx of novelty into the world, and yet we tolerate incredible dullness.

College of the Ouachitas

Let's not get away from this subject too quickly. Cruising is most often a couple activity, one of the best we think. Nothing can bring a couple closer together, can enhance mutual respect any faster than the

interdependence required of a couple to handle a sailboat smartly. In addition, cruising offers such a wide array of possible activities that both partners can satisfy their expectations of a cruise even when the expectations are quite different.

It is those expectations that determine whether or not the couple ever unites behind the goal of cruising, or whether one half simply derails the plans of the other. Typically, the romance of the cruise appeals to the male member while the wife is initially skeptical. We know of several cases in which the roles are reversed, but they appear to be sufficiently rare that addressing our comments to the hot-dog husband, recalcitrant wife will have the widest application.

Okay guys, listen up. If you want your wife to go along with this enterprise, you had better learn right now to look at it from her point of view. For yourself, you see the prestige of captaining your own ship, the macho romance of battling the elements (highly overrated), and perhaps in those darkest recesses of your mind the lure of topless

Polynesian girls. Your wife is relegated to a subservient role; she knows you will expect from her cooking, cleaning, laundering, even varnishing the teak and hoisting the anchor. And she has heard about those girls, too. No wonder she is not ecstatic about your hairbrained scheme to quit your jobs and sail off into the blue.

You had better reevaluate duty assignments: plan to spend as much time in the galley as she does and to share equally in the cleaning and laundry. It does not matter if she does all those things at home (except, presumably, hoisting the anchor). At home her kitchen is not the size of one made by Playskool; she does not clean on her knees, or do her laundry in a bucket. And she is in charge of the house, not you. You can skipper it when it moves. The prospect of living on a small boat is a heck of a setback.

What is to be done? Aside from swearing on a stack of Bibles that you will return from the cruise with dishwater hands and callused knees, you can alter the program some. While sailing is somewhat esoteric, travel seems to have an almost universal appeal.

A traveller! I love his title. A traveller is to be reverenced as such. His profession is the best symbol of our life.

Concentrate on the travel aspect of a cruise. Hold passages to a minimum. Plan in terms of a floating motor home. Plan stays at marinas where there are showers, laundromats, and restaurants. Include inland sightseeing trips, an occasional car rental. Cannot afford such luxuries? Luxuries? You are not paying attention. *If she does not want to go, you are not going at all.* If your wife is cool on the whole idea, then you better find a way to include these things.

What about passage-making? What about battling the elements? My gosh, what about the Polynesian girls? Relax. We have a plan. Unless she has a certain inclination, you will never convince your wife she wants to cross oceans; and this Polynesian girl stuff is not helping your case at all. Your best hope is other cruising couples, particularly other cruising women. Scale down and go cruising the way she wants to. You will meet other cruisers and she may get infected with the same fever you have. Don't push it. Just keep the environment right. If it is going to happen, it will.

THE FINAL OBSTACLE

If cruising is something you really want, then there is little reason not to experience it in some way. Reading about cruising is both enjoyable and informative, but reading lacks the texture of personal experience.

A man has not seen a thing who has not felt it.

And there is little reason for anyone to be denied that experience.

It does not take a large boat to go cruising; in fact a small boat will usually serve better. It does not take a great deal of money to go cruising. Almost everyone can afford the expense of a modest cruise. You can plan it around a vacation, or you can trade your shore life for it, but either way, a sensible cruise is affordable. A break from your employment or business might be unexpectedly beneficial, both to your health and to your esteem. Cruising is a family activity; couples draw closer as do parents and children. It is also a solo activity if that is your inclination.

If you want to sample the world of the cruiser, we cannot think of a single reason why you cannot, and we have already defused all the reasons you thought of. Something is still holding you back. You are just not sure. You have heard the old saw that the happiest two days in the life of a boat owner are when he buys the boat and when he sells it. What if that happens to you? What if you find out you don't really like cruising?

Hey, come on. Somewhere we've got to quit analyzing this thing and just go with it. Statistically, marriage is not such a good bet either, but that does not keep those of us in love from tying the knot.

We must walk consciously only part way toward our goal,
and then leap in the dark to our success.

Go ahead, take the leap.

READING

If you would really take a position outside the street and daily life of men, you must have deliberately planned your course, you must have business which is not your neighbors' business, which they cannot understand.

HE necessary financial arrangements have been well thought out, your pocket cruiser tugs anxiously at her mooring, and you are indeed poised to make the leap. Not so fast. How far can you swim? There is still much to be done before putting to sea. I know we said not to let anything get in your way. I know we said not to wait too long, but if you expect to succeed, preparation is everything. This chapter is required reading.

DEFINING YOUR REQUIREMENTS

We have been extolling the virtues of the moderate sized yacht. Does that mean any boat between 25 and 35 feet long will do? No. Seaworthiness is an imperative. Beyond basic seaworthiness and basic accommodations, additional requirements are minimal. Some boats will obviously be more suitable than others, but not to the extent that some builders would have you believe. In this chapter we will try to point out those characteristics most desirable in a sensible cruiser. If you have yet to buy your cruiser, you can look for these characteristics during your search. If you already own the boat, then this information will assist you in evaluating your boat's particular strengths and weaknesses. In both cases we will suggest configurations and equipment that will enhance your boat's cruising capabilities.

First, we need to review our definition of cruising. We find those accounts of the suburban couple selling all, buying a boat, and sailing around the world, or the middle-aged couple who have adopted the cruising lifestyle and lived and cruised aboard for the last twenty years just as exciting as the next sailor. There are some riveting cruising narratives in print today, and most conclude with the advice that if you want to do the same thing, you can. We do not take issue with this advice. If your heart is set on floating around the world for the next dozen years, and it is a goal that you can accomplish with no regrets, we encourage you, perhaps we even envy you. But that is not the only way to experience the delights of cruising.

In fact, there is the real risk of setting your goals too high and missing the cruising experience altogether. We have already devoted a whole chapter to this concept as it applies to boat selection. Just because you cannot afford a $150,000 boat does not mean you cannot experience cruising. Buy a $15,000 boat, or even a $1,500 boat. Your view of the world from the deck will be exactly the same as from the gold-plater, and you will probably have more free time available to be on deck.

Money is not required to buy one necessary of the soul.

Radar and electric toilets do not make the cruising experience one bit better.

The same applies to the cruise itself. If you are unwilling to settle for anything less than a circumnavigation, or Polynesia at the very least, you may never experience cruising at all. Life has a way of conspiring to get us to put off plans for another day. The most grandiose generally succumb first to this lack of attention. Do not get caught in that trap. We have cruised for thousands of miles, and enjoyed those faraway ports immensely, but some of our very best times aboard have been less than 20 miles from the home dock.

We are wont to imagine rare and delectable places in some remote and more celestial corner of the system, behind the constellation of Cassiopeia's Chair, far from noise and disturbance. I discovered that my house actually had its site in such a withdrawn, but forever new and unprofaned, part of the universe.

Remember, this book is about sensible cruising. It is not that we think circumnavigating is not sensible. But we know that the pleasures of cruising are just as exciting to the thousands of individuals, couples, and families who find the time, or make it, to go on shorter cruises.

Sensible cruising is the kind of cruising *you can do.* Eventually it may be a circumnavigation, but even a circumnavigation starts with a sail down the bay. Whether that sail is only the beginning of the cruise or all of the cruise, the pleasures of that particular sail are the same. First take that sail down the bay, then decide which way to point the bow.

This chapter concerns itself with the basics, the bare necessities of preparing the boat to go cruising. Subsequent chapters deal in greater depth with safety, comfort, electronics, and the galley. We have also planted a few seeds in "The Bean Field." What we have in mind as we compile this chapter is an initial cruise, one of several weeks or months, perhaps a year. Primarily you will be engaged in coastal cruising, with an occasional fair-weather passage. If, after that initial cruise, you decide to head for Tierra del Fuego, you will know more about preparation of your boat than we. Just don't forget we got you started.

The first thing to do after you have determined the seaworthiness of your chosen vessel is to inventory the equipment aboard. Is it sufficient to sustain a comfortable cruise and of high enough quality not to fail while you are "out there"? Let's take a stroll around the deck and see what we discover.

SAILS

The term "sailboat" suggests there are sails aboard although if you bought the boat new you may have discovered that this is not necessarily so. In any case, you are going to need sails.

What sails? You will need all *plain* sails. And what exactly does that mean? All plain sail for a catboat is a mainsail—period. For a sloop, plain sail means a mainsail and a jib. With the ketch or yawl, add a mizzen. A cutter rig will require a staysail, flown inside of the jib.

Also called working sails, these should be aboard and in good condition. That means going over every stitch carefully, from both sides of the sail. A single broken or chafed stitch should cause you to re-stitch that area of that seam. "A stitch in time . . . " and all that.

With the pocket cruiser, the need for a few stitches need not send you to the sailmaker. Almost any domestic machine with a heavy needle and polyester thread will do a good seam repair. Just roll the sail up from both sides, like a scroll, with the suspect seam between the two rolls. This will allow you to get the excess material under the arm of the machine and, with a little help from the mate in controlling the sail, you should have little problem.

For most of us, larger repairs, or those to a sail with a wire luff, are best left to the sailmaker. Also, if the sails are quite old and have been exposed to the sun a lot, you should ask a sailmaker to examine the sail and give you his opinion of the strength of the cloth. Polyester is subject to weakening from exposure to the sun's ultraviolet rays. A shredded sail during a cruise is like a blown engine in the car while away on vacation, with one big difference: AAA is not going to come out to tow you in. Look carefully at those sails.

Working sails are sufficient for a nice breezy day, but what about light air? Most pocket cruisers are sloop rigged and the trick to making a sloop go is the headsail. When the wind gets lighter, the headsail should get larger. You can cruise with just the main and jib, but we think a genoa is an essential sail for cruising. The size will depend upon the boat and your cruising area, but usually one of at least 150% is indicated.

If you cruise in an area of frequent very light air, a light air sail will be a worthwhile addition to your sail inventory.

> *I have spliced my old sail to a new one, and now go out to try it in a sail to Baker Farm. I like it much. It pulls like an ox and makes me think there's more wind abroad than there is.*

You might choose a spinnaker although if you do, you will have to learn how to handle this unruly sail carefully. It can be a real handful on a short-handed boat. A more sensible choice for a light air sail is the drifter. This sail is easy to control and while it will not pull like a spinnaker in the very light stuff—

The boat is like a plow drawn by a winged bull.

—it can be carried longer when the wind picks up and is an easily handled sail. In addition, a well-cut drifter can be used for sailing far closer to the wind than can the spinnaker.

For the heavier stuff, particularly if you contemplate any offshore passages, a storm jib is a good addition to the inventory. It is inexpensive, not very bulky, and if maintained will last indefinitely. As long as the main can be deeply reefed, the combination of reefed main and storm jib should competently handle any heavy weather you are likely to encounter. If you are going to Tierra del Fuego this summer, then put a storm trysail aboard, but not for a cruise of the Chesapeake.

"No problem," you say. The cruiser you bought belonged to a club racer and came with 13 sails. There is a problem. In whose attic are you going to store those extra eight bags of sail? Successful cruising in a pocket cruiser means carrying only those items essential to the operation and safety of the vessel. This especially applies to bulky items like sails. We do not care what they cost, or how nicely they set. Leave them behind.

It is so hard to forget what it is worse than useless to remember!

You can put the space to better use.

For just the five sails we have listed, stowage deserves our consideration. The main can be furled on the boom when it is not in use. It should always be covered. A loose-fitting mainsail cover of a durable acrylic fiber not only enhances the beauty of the boat, but will protect the sail from the sun, adding years to the life of the main. When the sail is down, it should be covered.

The genoa may be configured as a roller furler. If it is, it too is self-stowing. We like the roller-furling genoa for safety and convenience. Pull on the sheet and you are sailing. When it is time to get the sail in, you do that from the security of the cockpit also. The rap (no pun intended) on roller-furling headsails used to be that they sagged off to leeward and did not set well. The new generation of roller-furling gear generally uses a grooved extrusion around (or in place of) the headstay.

Consequently, a modern roller-furling headsail sags no more than a hank-on and in moderate conditions is infinitely more convenient, and it resolves genoa stowage.

But it is not necessary. If your sails are all hank-on, do not put off cruising until you can afford a roller-furling rig. First, there are a lot of knowledgeable sailors out there who would not have the rig on their boats. You cannot overlook the fact that you might find you agree with them. Second, even if you wish you had roller furling, hank-on headsails are the norm and are more than adequate for any cruise you might contemplate. The sail can be removed and bagged to be stored below or on deck. It can be left hanked on and bagged. The best solution is a jib cover, much like the cover on the mainsail, but enclosing the jib and attaching around the headstay.

With either type genoa, you are left with three other sails to stow. The working jib and the drifter, if you have one, should be stowed where they are easily accessible. The storm jib need not be quite so accessible, but when it is needed, conditions will be at their worst so it should not be impossible to retrieve either. A net bag against the underside of the deck in the forepeak, or a similar arrangement in an out-of-the-way place in the cockpit locker is ideal. If the weather begins to deteriorate, get the sail out before you need it. Try to avoid stowing the other two sails below. Not only do sails clutter up the cabin and make the boat feel smaller, but they often come in wet and salty, both conditions undesirable for below. Make room in the cockpit lockers.

Allow us one final comment on sails, and then we will move on.

> *Say what you have to say, not what you ought. Any truth is better than make-believe. Tom Hyde, the tinker, standing on the gallows, was asked if he had anything to say. "Tell the tailors," said he, "to remember to make a knot in their thread before they make the first stitch."*

We cruised quite contentedly for more than ten years with nothing larger than a 160% genoa aboard. There were many times when we wished for a big, light drifter, but we would not have put off cruising to own one. This worked for us partly because we cruised in areas where very light air was not prevalent, and partly because we had refrigeration aboard. Sounds nuts, but it is true. We considered light air an opportunity to run the engine with more purpose than simply running the refrigeration compressor. It salved our conscience.

Also during that time, the storm jib only saw the light of day for its annual checkup. We account for the lack of need for the storm jib because we did our best to stay anchored when bad weather was around. You cannot do that when making a passage. Consequently, for an offshore passage this sail should be aboard. For coastal cruising or island hopping, it is not as essential. The point is, beyond a good sized genoa, extra sails may not be an imperative. Your cruise plans, the prevailing weather in your selected cruising ground, the ease with which your boat moves in light air, and the amount of time you want to run the engine are the determinants. Take every sail you will need, but no more.

RUNNING RIGGING

While we are looking at the sails, let's look at how we will control them. The various control lines are known collectively as the running rigging. Running rigging wears out, so examine it carefully. Pay particular attention to lines where they pass over sheaves or through blocks. Examine wire halyards from end to end for broken strands. One way to do that is to slide the halyard through your hand from one end to the other, but if it does have any broken strands, it will become painfully apparent to you why those little culprits are called meat hooks. Use a big wad of bathroom tissue instead, and any broken strands will be marked with a little white flag instead of a red one. See why we have *sensible* in the title?

Some of the cruising books devote a page or two to the issue of external halyards versus internal halyards. Which kind does your boat have? *Those are the ones for you.*

We cannot be quite so glib with sheeting arrangements. There are some aspects that deserve consideration. Main boom sheeting arrangements are varied. Typically, the sheet is a multi-part purchase, attached to the boom either at its aft end or somewhere in mid-boom and to the boat at a fixed point or to a car on a boom traveller. We can look at each of these variables individually.

The multi-part purchase is to reduce the effort required in sheeting in the main. Whatever the boat is equipped with is probably fine. However, if you have difficulty pulling the main in tight in a strong breeze, you should consider increasing the power of the mainsheet by changing the blocks to add more falls. Conversely, with a very powerful mainsheet, sheeting may be very slow and a reduction in the number of falls might be advantageous. A cam cleat on the lower block of the mainsheet tackle greatly simplifies sheeting adjustments.

The attachment point on the boom is really not that important on a cruising boat. Anyway it may be determined for you by the type of reefing you have. For a number of years, roller reefing enjoyed great popularity. If your boat has roller reefing, the main sheet is attached to the end of the boom. Do not even think about moving it. With slab or "jiffy" reefing, the attachment point on the boom may be anywhere from the extreme aft end to near the center of the boom. Sometimes the sheet attaches in two or even three different places, not a very good cruising arrangement since it creates almost a net that sweeps the cockpit every time the boat is tacked or jibed. Often the sheet is attached toward the center of the boom, usually in concert with a traveller on the boat, either across the bridge deck or across the cabin top.

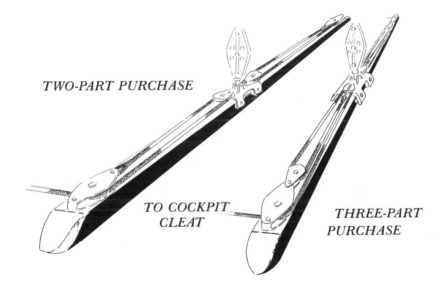

Two examples of mid-cabin travellers. The three-part purchase is much easier to trim than the two-part purchase.

The bridge deck traveller can be inconvenient since it will inhibit passage through the companionway. It may also prohibit the installation of a spray dodger. The mid-cabin traveller is a much better arrangement on a cruising boat, unless you intend to carry a hard dinghy on the cabin top. Such a plan may force you into a boom-end attachment and a traveller across the after part of the cockpit.

There is no question that the traveller allows for more efficient mainsail trim on the wind, but the cruising boat can get along quite well with no traveller at all, particularly if equipped with a boom vang.

So, if your boat has a single-point deck attachment for your mainsheet, do not run out to buy traveller track and a car. Spend your money on a vang instead. Once off the wind, the traveller has no effect, but the vang can be used to advantage on all points of sail.

Headsail sheeting is also subject to some variables. On the wind, the sheeting angle needs to be sufficiently narrow for the boat to perform to windward. This is usually between 12 and 15 degrees. To accommodate this requirement for different sails, the jib and the genoa for example, many beamy boats will provide for an inboard attachment point for the jib, while the fairlead block for the genoa typically attaches along the rail. Proper trim also requires some fore and aft positioning of the headsail fairlead. This may be accommodated with genoa track and movable cars although on many new boats a perforated toerail has become quite popular.

Your boat's sheeting arrangement will probably be satisfactory unless no provision is made for the narrower sheeting required with the working jib. If not, you should consider attaching a short length of track to the deck on either side, sufficiently backed to take the strain. Consult your sailmaker or a good book on sails for assistance in determining the exact location of the track. A less expensive alternative is attaching a pad-eye to the deck. This may be satisfactory, but will not allow for any fore and aft adjustment of the fairlead. Proper placement of the pad-eye will be essential.

As you pay off the wind, the headsail can become unruly. A quality, *strong* whisker pole can tame that obstinate sail, soothing your jagged nerves and saving the sail from self-destruction. If you are going to try to save a few bucks by buying a smaller pole than you need, save a few more and don't buy the thing at all. Otherwise, you will be deep-sixing a buckled pole on your first ocean run. Either way, you end up cruising without it, but one approach is cheaper. The best approach is to buy a pole strong enough for your sail area. The manufacturers provide sage counsel here. If you cruise very long, the pole will provide ample return just in extended sail life, and you will go faster to boot.

Most newer boats will be equipped with at least one set of sheet winches. Powerful winches make the control of a big headsail in a breeze much easier. For cruising, one set is ample, and the winches that the boat is equipped with, assuming they are of good quality, will probably handle your largest sail easily. If not, you need more powerful sheet winches. The greater power may also help you when you eventually go aground and try winching yourself off that "uncharted" bar. If you do need to replace winches, you may be able to find excellent values in used winches (racer discards), particularly in the sizes appropriate for the pocket cruiser. If you opt for new ones, look carefully at bottom-action winches. A number of cruisers recommend them highly for convenience and sail handling ease.

SNATCH BLOCK
FOR JIB SHEET

VANG

A perforated toerail has many uses for the cruising sailor.

Take a look at the sheets. They should be braided polyester to minimize stretch or tangling. On a pocket cruiser, strength is not usually the determining criteria in the selection of rope to be used for sheets. You could lift a 25-foot boat right out of the water with ⅜-inch braided polyester lines attached to the bow and stern, certainly ample strength for controlling the jib. In fact a smaller line could do the job, but it is difficult to grip. For this reason we recommend that all the sheets aboard a pocket cruiser, except those for your light air sail (drifter), should be at least ½ inch in diameter and all of the same diameter. This allows you to carry a length of spare rope which can be cut into lines as needed. We are not recommending that you throw away all those ⅜- or 7/16-inch sheets and go buy new ½-inch ones. Be sensible! What we are suggesting is that as sheets require replacement, replace them with ½-inch or heavier lines. Before you follow this advice, be sure all your blocks and cleats will accommodate the larger line.

STANDING RIGGING

While you are looking at rigging, examine the standing rigging carefully also. Meat hooks, broken strands at the fittings, or cracked swage fittings dictate replacement of that particular stay or shroud. Examine them very slowly and *very carefully*. Look especially closely at the swage fitting. A magnifying glass is a good idea, and a mirror will be useful to locate problems on the back side of fittings attached to the mast.

> *All this is perfectly distinct to an observant eye, and yet could easily pass unnoticed by most.*

If they show any signs of weakness, replace them. Do not fool around.

We strongly recommend that if you replace some (or all) of the standing rigging, you do not use swage fittings. They may give excellent service (we have some aboard more than 15 years old), but are only as good as the operator and the equipment that was used to install them. Far too often they fail unexpectedly. A better option is one of the mechanical end fittings, either Sta-Loks or Norseman. These you can install yourself and if you do it properly they are virtually 100% secure. They cost little more than swage terminals and can be reused when it is time to replace the wire. All you will need is the very inexpensive compression cone. If you have them aboard, you can do rigging repair anywhere.

Also examine all the tangs and chainplates carefully for wear, especially around the pin hole. Examine the clevis pins for wear as well. Be certain all pins are properly secured with either a cotter key or a split ring. Sails will need to be protected from the cotter key or other sharp metal. Taping the fitting is normal, but in some cases trapped salt and moisture may encourage corrosion in the fitting. A loose fitting boot is a better option.

There should be—no—there *must* be a toggle between every turnbuckle and its corresponding chainplate; otherwise you are courting rigging failure. Likewise, in addition to the toggle at the bottom, a toggle is needed between the fitting and the tang at the top of the headstay—the staysail stay as well if you have one —to accommodate the movement of these stays under the press of sail.

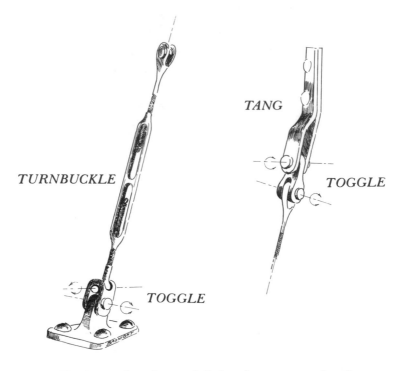

TANG

TURNBUCKLE

TOGGLE

TOGGLE

Toggles must be used to permit flexing of components under sail.

ANCHORS

Once you have determined that the necessary equipment is aboard to keep the boat moving in a breeze, you need to be sure you can also keep it *from* moving. Almost every cruiser will agree that the single most important category of cruising gear is ground tackle and you should not even think of sailing without being certain effective ground tackle is aboard.

The ground tackle of a boat is made up of the anchor and the rode attaching it to the boat. We will also examine the ways of getting the ground tackle back aboard and of stowing it. Let's look at anchors first.

An institutional size pork and beans can filled with concrete and attached to the rode with an eyebolt can be an anchor. Don't laugh; we have seen it. Anchors that depend upon weight are not very effective until they get *very* heavy. Old automobile engines are often used for a mooring, but you would not want to carry one around on the bow of a 25-footer. As an alternative to brute weight, we *hook* ourselves to the bottom. The better the anchor attaches to the bottom, the more secure the boat.

There are a wide variety of anchors on the market, but virtually every cruising boat you will encounter will have one or more of three types of anchors. By type or name, they are the fisherman or Herreshoff, the lightweight or Danforth, and the plow or CQR. Some boats carry all three. The type of anchor you select depends upon the types of bottoms you expect to encounter and the size of the anchor depends upon the size, displacement, and windage of your chosen vessel.

The lightweight anchor, universally called the Danforth, is undoubtedly the most popular anchor among the weekend boating set. It does not, however, enjoy such universal acclaim in the cruising community. It is a popular anchor because it is effective in a wide variety of bottoms. With its broad, flat flukes, it holds well in sand, is the best anchor for mud, and will often set even on a rocky bottom. It comes aboard fairly easily, stores flat, and has enormous holding power relative to its weight. Amazingly, Danforth recommends for boats up to 25 feet in up to 30 knots of wind only a five-pound anchor (high tensile).

So why aren't cruisers sold on it? Aha! Because if it does not absolutely love you, it can be downright deceitful.

> *I am sorry to think that you do not get a man's most effective criticism until you provoke him. Severe truth is expressed with some bitterness.*

We have seen a boat sit rock solid to a Danforth through a 50-knot squall and 20 minutes later, in a breeze of under five knots, drift right up on the beach as though it had no anchor out at all. How can this be, you may ask; and well you should. What happened was simply a *change in wind direction.*

In a good, clear, sandy bottom, the lightweight anchor trips, the flukes drop to the other side, and the anchor resets. No problem. But if the bottom is grassy, rocky, scattered with coral, or made up of sticky mud or clay, a different scenario is played out below the surface. As the wind changes direction, so does the pull on the anchor. Even if the breeze is light, a left over chop or a slight swell will be enough to work the anchor out of the bottom. As the lightweight anchor flips over to align itself with the pull of the rode, the flukes are supposed to drop to the bottom, poised for that powerful bite. Instead, clay, a rock, or a big clump of eel grass (the culprit in the above story) is wedged or packed between the flukes and the shank, so that the flukes point toward the surface instead of the bottom. Get the kids off the beach; here we come.

The partridge loves peas, but not those that go with her into the pot.

So throw out the Danforths, right? Of course not. It is a great anchor, just not perfect. How long do you think your marriage would last if your spouse adopted that attitude about you? You're right, that's probably a bad example. Anyway, if your boat is married to a Danforth, be sure she does not turn her back on it, or the relationship could end up on the rocks.

One way to avoid this heartbreak is to set a second anchor astern, leading from the bow. In the event of a wind shift, the boat simply fetches up on the stern anchor with a fair lead rather than tripping the bow anchor. If the wind clocks on around, you are still in good shape.

The lightweight Danforth. Effectiveness is improved by using more chain.

Another way is to use a plow instead of the lightweight anchor. Specifically, we recommend the British-made CQR. Shaped like a farming implement, the CQR wants to bury almost without regard to what direction it is pulled. In a wind shift, it rarely breaks out, choosing to turn instead. In the event it does break out, there is nothing to keep it from resetting, short of a beer can impaled on the point. There are not any beer cans in the anchorages in paradise . . . not that many anyway.

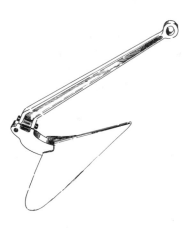

The British-made CQR plow.

The CQR is undoubtedly the most versatile anchor in common use among cruising boats. In a power test, the CQR may not hold as well in sand as a Danforth, but it will hold better than the fisherman. It may not hold as well as the fisherman in rock, but it will hold better than the Danforth. In most other bottoms, with the exception of soft mud, it will hold better than either anchor. Power tests aside, a CQR of the appropriate size will hold your boat securely in sand or rock, or almost any other bottom you might encounter. We have used CQR's primarily for many years with great success.

> *I was never cast away nor distressed in any weather, though*
> *I encountered some severe storms.*

Sometimes cruisers carry only plow anchors aboard. We like the plow as a primary anchor, and it will set and hold 99% of the time, but occasionally you will come across an anchorage where the plow just will not bury. One such anchorage is Black Sound at Green Turtle Cay in the Bahamas. Tall and extremely thick grass refused to allow the plow to penetrate. The Danforth would be worse so we did not even try it. The long, narrow fluke of the fisherman went right through the weeds into the sand bottom on our first attempt with it. If you only carry one type of anchor, make it a plow, but a cruising boat should have at least three anchors aboard, and there is no reason they should not be of various types.

One problem with plow anchors is that all plows are not genuine CQR's. We are not trying to plug a particular manufacturer, but the CQR has been much copied, often badly. The CQR is drop forged for strength, and apparently the fluke angle is critical to the holding power of the anchor. Many of the imitations are significantly weaker castings and, we have heard often, do not hold as well. If we had known we were going to write this book, maybe we would have bought someone else's plow

The fisherman may be the most secure anchor you could choose in some situations, but is difficult to get aboard and to stow. Also note that the exposed fluke can foul the rode with a change of tide or wind.

and then we could have told you first hand whether it dragged or not; that is, if it did not drag at a bad time. Come to think of it, we still would have bought the CQR. Let someone else experiment. We prefer

47

to sleep nights.

A second problem is stowage. A plow can be quite awkward on deck. The solution is a stem roller, preferably on a small sprit. Aside from providing perfect stowage for the CQR (or the Bruce), the roller greatly simplifies both deployment and retrieval of the anchor, any anchor, and is easier on the rode than chocks.

There is a whole generation of sailors today who have never been shipmates with the venerable fisherman anchor and scoff at it as old-fashioned and inefficient.

> *Every generation laughs at the old fashions, but follows religiously the new.*

That is too bad, because in some situations, the fisherman may well be the most secure you could choose. Its versatility depends upon the shape and area of the flukes. Old fisherman types often had small flukes with shoulders on the inner end of the fluke, like a small shovel—a poor design. The Herreshoff and Yachtsman versions have much larger diamond-shaped palms which give them greater versatility. They are excellent in rock or coral and have enough fluke area to be effective in sand and mud.

One reason for the lack of popularity of the fisherman is that, because of its shape, it can be a bear to get aboard. For most of us, a fisherman of more than about 50 pounds will require specialized gear to get it aboard without leaving a permanent signature on the bow. The smaller fisherman, with care, is not too difficult to handle, but the smaller sizes, while still effective in rock, have less holding power in sand and mud, strikingly less than the Danforth and CQR.

The Yachtsman anchor, like the Herreshoff, has larger fluke areas which are effective in mud or sand.

Another drawback is their difficulty to stow. To simplify stowage, most newer fisherman anchors have a removable or folding stock, allowing the anchor to lie flat on deck. We have one aboard of unknown pedigree; both the stock and the arms fold against the shank. The Herreshoff can be dismantled into three pieces, greatly facilitating

48

its stowage, but in its dismantled state it is not ready for quick deployment.

A final caution about the fisherman has to do with the way it lies on the bottom. One arm is buried, the other stands proud above the bottom. If the tide turns or the wind changes, the rode could foul the exposed arm and trip the anchor. Diamond-shaped flukes reduce this risk, but do not eliminate it. Because of this difficulty and the others mentioned above, we do not recommend the fisherman as a primary anchor, or even necessarily as a secondary anchor, but it is an excellent choice as a third anchor. If your cruising area includes rocky bottom, a well-designed fisherman is a good anchor to have aboard.

There are, of course, other anchors. It is not our intention to evaluate all anchors, but only to provide guidance for initial anchor selection. When you actually sail, other cruisers you meet will be very generous with their opinions of all types of anchors, including the three we have listed. If you have a preference for some other type with which you have had good experience, fine. If you are not experienced, you will not go wrong with the anchors described above.

One new anchor that merits mention because of its increasing popularity is the Bruce.

> *The head monkey at Paris puts on a traveller's cap, and all the monkeys in America do the same.*

Perhaps it is just fashionable, but the design is so simple and clean it merits watching. On one of our boats, we replaced the plows with Bruce anchors and have been very satisfied; despite some very nasty conditions, there is not a single incidence of dragging to report. For the most part, other Bruce users we have talked with have been enthusiastic about the holding power and simplicity of this design. We do know that in some bottoms, the anchor does not hold well (just like every other anchor) and it does

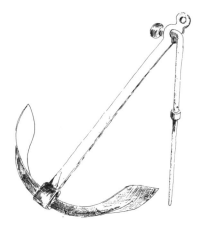

The Herreshoff anchor stows in three pieces.

not penetrate weed and kelp easily. If you are the "cutting edge" type, you may want to give the Bruce a try. Those of you who are more conservative should stick with the CQR until more comprehensive data is available.

RODES

Once we are satisfied we have anchors aboard that will cling tenaciously to the bottom in almost all conditions, then we need to look carefully at how we fix the boat to the anchor. There are only two possibilities for anchor rode on a cruising yacht: chain or nylon rope. Often both are combined in a single rode.

We will consider all chain first. The circumnavigators like all chain. They often cite a number of reasons for this preference, but the only valid reason is chain's resistance to chafe and abrasion. A circumnavigation will likely take you into some marginal anchorages where the bottom is primarily coral and in such circumstances chain is clearly superior. The successful circumnavigation by a number of boats without all-chain rode suggests chain is not absolutely required.

Another advantage of chain claimed by its proponents is its weight, which must be lifted by the vessel before any appreciable strain comes on the anchor. This catenary action minimizes the actual pull on the anchor and is said to result in a more horizontal pull on the anchor for a given scope. The heavier the chain, the more pronounced will be the catenary effect. This is all fine in moderate conditions, but deserves a closer look in storm conditions.

Why level downward to our dullest perception always, and praise that as common sense?

Where wind and windage combine to put sufficient strain on the ground tackle to straighten out the rode, the direction of pull on the anchor will be exactly the same regardless of the type of rode used. Additionally, in such conditions, where the shock-absorbing quality of a catenary would be most beneficial, there is no catenary and as the chain has no elasticity, it will try to jerk the anchor right out of the bottom, or, failing that, to jerk the bow right off the boat. Even the most devoted users of all chain recognize this characteristic and often rig a shock absorber by attaching a length of *nylon* line between the chain and the vessel, then letting slack in the chain so that the line absorbs the jerks.

A third advantage purported for chain is that it is self-stowing. With a properly designed chain locker, as the chain is fed below, either by hand or directly off the windlass, it stacks itself neatly awaiting its next use. Unfortunately boats with a well-designed chain locker are rare. We do not know anyone who does not have to occasionally go below to straighten out the chain locker. Most find that once more than ten fathoms of chain is pulled up through the deck pipe, a person is required below to help the "stacking" process as the chain is returned to the locker. Self-stowing depends on the locker, not the chain.

What about the disadvantages? They are numerous. Next to inelasticity, the most significant is weight. If your boat is designed so the chain locker is low and in the center of the boat, chain is nothing more than additional ballast and will have little effect on the performance of the boat. If all-chain rode is specified at the inception of such a design, the architect could take that into account in calculating ballast so that stowing the chain would actually put the vessel on her lines.

Most cruising boats are mass-produced sailboats adapted for cruising. Almost to a boat, the chain locker is right up in the eyes of the boat, often actually above the waterline. For boat performance there can be no worse place than high and forward to carry excess weight. How much weight are we talking about? The minimum size chain any cruising boat should consider is 5/16 inch. Even this size minimizes the catenary advantage and ⅜ inch is more often recommended for pocket cruisers up to around 10 tons displacement. The recommended scope of chain is usually five to one. If the anchorage is ever 50 feet deep, you will need 250 feet of chain. Assuming a minimum of two anchors, we are talking about 500 feet of chain. Three-eighths-inch BBB chain weighs about 170 pounds per hundred feet or 850 pounds for our 500 feet, more than 900 pounds with the anchors.

A boat with 3,000 pounds of ballast cannot afford this kind of weight in the bow. It will prevent the bow from rising to oncoming waves and will cause an otherwise sea-kindly boat to pitch markedly. Sometimes the recommendation is for only one all-chain rode, carried in two sections to be shackled together as necessary. To limit the weight carried forward, half of the rode is carried separately in the center of the boat. Even with this more sensible arrangement, allowing for 20 feet of chain on the second anchor, you will still be carrying 300 pounds or more at the bow. That is unacceptable on a 25-footer and undesirable on a 35-footer.

A second problem with the weight of chain is handling it. In a 50-foot deep anchorage, assuming a 35-pound anchor, when the anchor clears the bottom, you will have 120 pounds of dead weight hanging straight down. You will either need a strong back or a windlass. The windlass will add to the already substantial weight at the bow and simultaneously lighten your wallet.

Chain also is abrasive, scratching the deck if it is given a chance. In a tidal anchorage, when the wind opposes the tide, the chain will try to take the paint or gelcoat off the bow of the boat. It usually comes aboard dirty, requiring either a deck hose or a bucket and brush before it can be stowed below. If it is allowed to dry on deck, it invariably leaves rust stains. It is fine for ships designed to handle it, but on the typical pocket cruiser, chain is not user friendly.

The only other acceptable rode material is nylon rope. We have a cruising friend whose seamanship otherwise is excellent, but his nylon rodes are tied directly to his anchors. No. No. No! All nylon is not a good choice. Nylon rope is a terrific product and has a very high tensile strength. It would probably pull the anchor out of the bottom before it would break, but run that line over a coral head and the equation changes. Just sliding back and forth across a nice sandy bottom will do the fibers no good. To deliver its rated strength, a nylon line must be protected from chafe.

Not all chain, and now not all nylon. What does that leave? For the pocket cruiser on a six-month cruise, the anchor rode of choice is a combination of chain and nylon. All anchors should be shackled to a length of chain, and not the little six-foot, vinyl-covered chains marketed in many marine stores. Three fathoms is the minimum amount of chain; 30 feet would be better. The reason for the chain is to try to strike a workable compromise between an all-chain rode which is resistant to chafe, and an all-nylon rode which is elastic and easy to transport and handle. By shackling a reasonable length of chain between the anchor and the line, the chain absorbs most of the chafe while the nylon line will be clear of the bottom except in calm conditions, and even then will be subjected to minimum chafe.

Unless your pocket cruiser is of extremely heavy displacement or unusually high windage, ⅜-inch chain will be adequate in size. The choice of rope size need not be complicated either. For ease of handling, ½ inch appears to be the smallest size to consider. With a tensile strength of around 6,000 pounds, ½-inch line may seem to be overkill on a pocket cruiser. However, the U. S. Navy recommends that the working load of a rope should never exceed 40% of its tensile strength. For a ½-inch nylon line, this yields a working strength of 2,400 pounds, almost exactly the same as ⅜-inch proof-coil chain. As displacement and windage increase, both chain and rope sizes must be correspondingly increased. You

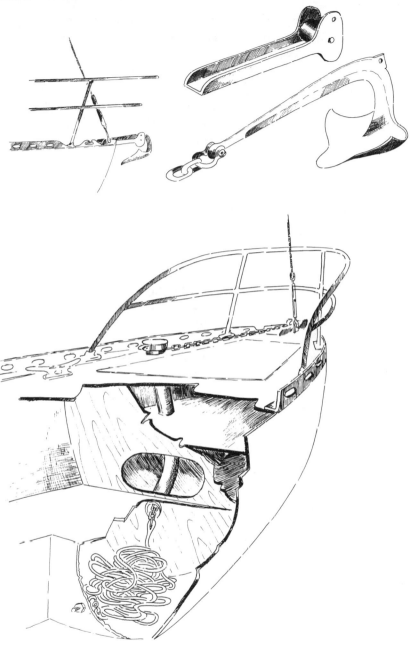

Extended stem roller, Bruce anchor, and chain locker. PVC pipe was fitted to bypass the on-deck anchor locker. This guides the rode (and it's weight) below the V-berth.

might select a larger size of rope for insurance, but you will give up elasticity in the bargain, and elasticity is one of the major advantages of a nylon anchor rode.

Stowage of nylon anchor rode merits a short aside. Traditional stowage involves feeding the line through a chain pipe (or sometimes a cowl ventilator) into a forepeak chain locker. Newer boats often have an anchor locker under a hatch on the foredeck. If the locker is not large enough to accommodate all necessary cruising ground tackle, or if you wish to use it for some other purpose (e.g. propane stowage), a modification similar to the one shown might be considered. The PVC pipe allows the rode to be passed through the anchor locker into the forepeak locker below. For below deck stowage, braided nylon self-stows more readily and is less likely to tangle in the locker.

AUXILIARY POWER

When the wind blows, you have the equipment aboard to make the boat move or to keep it from moving, whichever is your pleasure. What if it does not blow? For most of the history of sailing, this was a pointless question. If the wind did not blow, a vessel dependent upon the wind for power did not move. Despite its extreme rarity, there is still a great deal to be said for cruising in a pure sailing vessel.

> *Keep the time, observe the hours of the universe, not of the cars. What are three score years and ten hurriedly and coarsely lived to moments of divine leisure in which your life is coincident with the life of the universe?*

Such an approach to cruising surely puts you more in touch with nature. Dependent upon the vagaries of the wind, you become a student of the wind. The effect of tides and currents must be understood intimately. You will, no doubt, become more proficient at handling your vessel under sail. In calm conditions, you will hear only your own thoughts.

Perhaps these are romantic notions. If so, there is surely a practical side to cruising purely under sail. More than any other piece of equipment that can be brought aboard, the marine engine complicates cruising. It is expensive to own, expensive to operate, and will require more time in maintenance than all the other equipment aboard combined. It attracts additional equipment, hence additional expenses, like a magnet: alternators, refrigerators, electronics of all types.

An engine also reduces the carrying capacity of the vessel. In a pocket cruiser, it may occupy an inordinate amount of space. It is often dirty, sometimes dangerous, and, when it is running, usually annoying.

Do we cruise with an engine? Yes, and probably so will you. We have included the above only to encourage those of you who may be inclined to try cruising without an engine. There are those who will tell you that you cannot successfully cruise without an engine aboard.

. . . they honestly think there is no choice left.

They are wrong. Lin and Larry Pardey sailed for 11 years all over the world in *Seraffyn* powered only by sails or a single 14-foot oar. We personally know others who have cruised quite successfully without an engine, more successfully perhaps than those around them with an engine, us included. If you are capable and so inclined, then the engine does not belong in your list of essential gear.

On the other hand, this book purports a "sensible" approach to cruising. For the person planning a cruise for a definite time frame, for the person with limited sailing background, for the person trying to convince his spouse of the merits of the cruising life, an engine will undoubtedly be an essential piece of gear. Not to worry. Almost every boat suitable for cruising has an engine already. Just as we previously pointed out about types of rigs, it is possible to cruise successfully with almost any type engine, except one that is undependable.

We cannot overlook the possibility that you may be purchasing a new boat and have some input into the type of engine aboard or that you may be planning to repower the boat you already own. In both of these cases, our comments on engines should assist. The rest of you are going to cruise with the engine you have, but some of the information below may still be helpful.

The requirements of a good engine for a cruising boat are not very exotic. We want it to be safe, reliable, economical, and to require a minimum of attention. To simplify our selection even further, there are only three basic possibilities: the diesel-powered inboard, the gasoline-powered inboard, and the gasoline-powered outboard. For your particular boat, there may be only one sensible option. Still, we will consider each of the three basic types of engines individually.

DIESEL

By far, the biggest share of modern sailboats are equipped with diesel engines. As little as ten years ago, the gasoline engine was the standard for inboard-equipped sailboats. Usually a diesel was offered as an option, at a $2,000 to $4,000 tariff. Today, through a lack of public demand, almost no manufacturers even offer a gasoline inboard engine. There are three reasons for this rapid evolution.

The first is the volatility of gasoline. Highly explosive, gasoline is an inherently dangerous shipboard fuel. If it drips from an automobile engine onto the ground, no big deal. If it leaks from a marine engine inside of the hull, it is a very big deal. Horror stories abound of explosions scattering bits and pieces of boat and crew all over an otherwise serene harbor. A cup full of gasoline in the bilge has a lethal explosive power. Hit the starter button, and ka-BOOM.

A period—a semicolon, at least—is put to my previous and habitual ways of viewing things.

More and more new boat purchasers decided it was easily worth an additional $30 per month on their note not to risk untimely demise. After all, cruising was supposed to deliver peace 'n rest, not rest in peace.

The second reason was that purchasers were becoming increasingly sophisticated in financial matters. Saving two or three thousand dollars at the time of purchase was false economy. When the time came for resale, a diesel-equipped boat would easily recover the initial price difference, and diesel power was much easier to sell in the used market. Even if long-term ownership was contemplated, the gasoline engine had a very limited life expectancy relative to the diesel.

The third reason was a dramatic increase in availability of small, lightweight diesel engines suitable for marine installations. There are small diesels available today weighing less than 150 pounds. Where diesel engines had been notoriously heavy, they now compare favorably in weight with a gasoline engine of equivalent usable power.

There is very little debate, if any, that the engine of choice for the cruising boat is the diesel inboard. It offers numerous advantages over the other two normal alternatives. We have already mentioned that diesel is a vastly safer fuel than gasoline. We have also suggested higher resale value and longer engine life. The other advantages have to do with reliability and ease of maintenance. A gasoline engine requires an electrical system, a constant source of problems when the engine spends its life in the damp bilge of a sailboat. A diesel has no electrics and is consequently infinitely more reliable. In addition, there are no adjustments to make on a diesel, no points, no plugs, no ignition timing, no carburetor setting. Other than changing oil and filters and keeping the fuel clean through good filtration, the engine requires very little attention. An added benefit is that, in the smaller sizes and with adequate access, diesel engines may be hand started.

What were the four qualities we said we were looking for when we started this section? Safe, reliable, economical, and requiring a minimum of attention. Sounds like the diesel just about covers them all. Yes, it does, but not without a price.

You never gain something but that you lose something.

Besides the initial expense, there are some other drawbacks to diesel power. The most noticeable one is vibration. Small diesels are essentially unbalanced, depending upon a very heavy flywheel to smooth out the power strokes. This design is only partially effective. New soft engine mounts are now available that do wonders for minimizing the amount of vibration transmitted to the boat, but they must only be used in concert with a flexible shaft coupling. However, once you price this alteration, you may decide you find the vibration to be restful, like having a vibrating massage in every bunk.

Due to their high compression, diesels are notoriously noisy also. The noise can be reduced substantially by lining the engine compartment with sound deadening insulation. The only kinds really effective are the multilayered types: a cleanable layer toward the engine, flame-retardant acoustical foam, a lead barrier, and another layer of flame-retardant foam. Completely lining the engine compartment will result in the most effective noise reduction, but this type of insulation is not inexpensive. If, at a minimum, it is used on all bulkheads between the engine and the cabin, it will make the cabin habitable while the diesel engine is running. You will no longer feel as if someone aboard is breaking concrete with a jack hammer, but do not expect the silence of a cathedral either.

Starting a diesel engine generally requires plenty of battery power, so a diesel-powered vessel will usually be fitted with a couple of heavy-duty batteries. While undoubtedly representing an initial expense, high quality, heavy-duty batteries are, we think, advantageous for other reasons we will cover in a subsequent chapter.

Although repairs are required far less often by a diesel engine than its gasoline-fed cousin, when repairs are required, they may be notoriously expensive. And, with the wide variety of small diesels in use, parts are sometimes difficult to obtain. We cannot list this as a disadvantage without pointing out that a quality diesel engine, religiously cared for, may reasonably be expected to run for 5,000 engine hours, or more, before any major repair work is required. At five knots, that is enough for a circumnavigation under power alone. The key to such longevity is conscientiously following a program of periodic maintenance and keeping the fuel clean and free of water, i.e. using an effective fuel filtering system with the regular filter replacement.

While it is not true of everyone, many find the odor of diesel exhaust objectionable. There is nothing like being out of sight of land and motoring with three or four knots of following breeze, just enough to keep the exhaust fumes in the cockpit. The sensation of following a bus in rush hour traffic is overwhelming. With a little left-over swell, you may find yourself lunging for the rail. The good news is that with a diesel, there is little danger of carbon monoxide poisoning. You will undoubtedly survive although you may be hard to convince of that fact while you are feeding the fish.

If we are really dying, let us hear the rattle in our throats and feel cold in the extremities; if we are alive, let us go about our business.

Good advice, but hard to follow in the grip of seasickness.

GASOLINE

A lot of older sailboats are outfitted with gasoline inboards. While not as safe, as dependable, or as long lived as diesel engines, many have given great service over a long period of years in less than ideal circumstances. If your boat has a gasoline engine in good condition aboard, its replacement should not be a reason to delay your cruise. If the appropriate precautions are followed, danger can be minimized. We know skippers that have been shipmates all their lives (long lives we might add) with gasoline engines and have never had a serious safety problem. Vigilance seems to be the key.

If you have a gasoline engine aboard, it is not without merit. It is smoother and quieter than the diesel; fuel is readily available everywhere; its principle of operation is probably more familiar to you, certainly more familiar to most mechanics; and the biggest advantage of all, it is already aboard, running and paid for.

OUTBOARD

Few pocket cruisers above 30 feet are not inboard powered. Under that length, it is not uncommon to encounter outboard power. If you think you cannot cruise on a boat that is outboard powered, you are wrong. "Sure," you say. "If you can cruise without an engine, it follows that you can cruise with one, no matter how unsuitable."

That is not what we mean. There is no question that in some circumstances, the outboard is a most unsuitable power plant for a sailboat. This becomes particularly apparent if you use the outboard to try to push through moderate sea conditions. As the boat pitches to the wave action, the transom-mounted outboard alternately tries to submerge or to pull the prop clear of the water. The solution to this is to avoid using the engine in such circumstances, not as unlikely as it seems since waves are indicative of wind. It is a sailboat, you know. When there is no wind and the engine is required to move the boat, the outboard will function much more efficiently, even in mid-ocean.

In many ways, particularly for a smaller cruiser, the outboard offers some advantages neither of the other options can match. First, it is the least expensive option at about 25% or less of the cost of a small diesel inboard installation. Second, it is portable, meaning if it requires service, it can be removed and taken to the mechanic at a significant savings. Outboards are the most common small marine engines everywhere in the world and consequently if you have a major brand, parts and mechanics are available in the globe's most remote corners. In the worst case, repowering is a matter of unclamping the bad motor and clamping on a good one, even one of different power and manufacture.

There is another advantage. One of the biggest drags on the performance of an inboard-powered cruising sailboat is the typical big three-blade prop. A folding prop is an improvement, but an outboard on a lift bracket eliminates the drag altogether. If you are a real hot dog, you can even remove the motor to get the weight away from the stern.

> But the eyes, though they are no sailors, will never be satisfied
> with any model, however fashionable, which does not answer
> all the requisitions of art.

Okay, fine. So it is ugly hanging out on the transom like that. If we were talking about windvanes, you wouldn't be complaining like this, and there is nothing uglier than the typical windvane framework. If your sensibilities are affronted, you have three options. You can pay the big bucks for an inboard installation. You can store the motor below in a locker, putting it on only when you need it. Or you can pull a really slick trick that we have seen a number of pocket cruisers do. You can select an outboard that can be used for propulsion of your cruiser when underway and can be used on the dinghy when at anchor. If you plan to have an outboard for your dinghy, when underway the engine will be aboard on a stern bracket anyway; it may as well do double duty.

We cruised for several years aboard 26- and 27-footers powered by 9.9 horsepower outboards. Our cruising included some offshore sailing, several crossings of the Gulf Stream, and some memorable cruises through the Bahamas. We carried aboard only six gallons of gas, yet never failed to go anywhere we chose. The only serious shortcoming recalled was the fact that the ship's battery had to be taken ashore for charging; otherwise we were without the electric cabin lights or the running lights for frequent night passages. Fortunately, the current generation (no pun intended) of outboards are available with alternators. While not very powerful, 50, 60, or 80 watts most common, they will keep the running lights burning or light your way through the last 100 pages of *Moby Dick*.

SPARE PARTS

All engines are subject to unexpected failures. Drive by the Mercedes Benz dealership if you want evidence. Engine failure need not be catastrophic. An engine has only the importance to your cruise that you assign it. Regardless of whether you have a four horsepower outboard or 40 horsepower diesel, if you use it only to get in and out of creeks or alongside docks, engine failure will not ruin your cruise.

More often, potential cruisers cannot imagine cruising without a certain level of comfort. We have often heard, "Warm rum and Tang. Yech! There is no way I am going to cruise without refrigeration. No way!" Refrigeration is not a necessity for cruising (nor pressure water, nor powerful radios), yet many will insist on putting these items aboard, the lack of them perceived as a barrier to the cruise. Just keep in mind that if you have mechanical refrigeration and electric everything else, powered by the engine's alternator, you have assigned the engine an inordinate amount of power over the success of your cruise.

> *Thus I am a helpless prisoner, and these chains I have no skill to break. While I think I have broken one link, I have been forging another.*

This risk can be minimized by taking aboard spare parts for any item likely to fail and the necessary tools to effect the repair. If you have the mechanical know-how to do the repair yourself, all the better. If you do not, that does not relieve you from the need to have parts and tools aboard. While cruising, a mechanic can often be found, either ashore or aboard a neighboring boat. But without the tools to fit your engine and the necessary parts to make the repair, sharing the anchorage with Mario Andretti's pit crew will not get you running.

Spare part selection is very dependent upon your engine. The best approach is to talk to a mechanic familiar with your engine to find out what the common problems are and what parts should be aboard to rectify those problems. In most cases, your spare parts inventory will not be very extensive. Typically, for an outboard you will need little more than spare spark plugs, shear pins, a new fuel filter, lubrication for the lower end, a few gaskets, maybe a pump diaphragm, perhaps a spare prop and nut.

The gasoline inboard will primarily require ignition parts, points, plugs, ignition wires, a coil, a distributor cap, plus perhaps a carburetor rebuild kit. The diesel inboard has no ignition system. Problems are usually associated with the fuel system. Spares might include injector nozzles, a transfer pump (or kit), gaskets and seals, replacement fuel filters. Sometimes cruisers carry a spare alternator aboard. Bushings and brushes for the starter are not a bad choice either. For either engine, you should have lubrication and filters for routine maintenance.

The most often repaired item on every inboard engine, and on many outboards as well, is the water pump. Neoprene impellers are used universally and they wear out and are subject to damage if for any reason the water flow is restricted. Spare impellers should always be aboard as well as the necessary gaskets and O-rings for their proper installation.

Your particular engine may be prone to an idiosyncratic failure. A mechanic familiar with the engine can forewarn you so that you can be forearmed. Draw on your own experience also, if you have any. For example, we have never owned an engine for a long time (auto or marine) without the oil sending switch eventually beginning to leak. This is a tiny problem, but it can quickly ruin a $4,000 engine. A spare is always aboard.

Having plowed a far longer furrow through the water than we three, some very well-known cruising sailors recommend that if you cannot fix it yourself, it should not be aboard. Modify to "if you cannot fix it or do without it, it should not be aboard," and we are compelled to agree. To an extent, this applies as well to the engine. There is nothing mysterious about engines and every skipper should make the effort to learn to do regular maintenance and at least minor repair.

*He gets more out of any enterprise than his neighbors, for he
helps himself more and hires less.*

Even if you are not Thoreauvian by nature and would prefer to hire the
work done, there are far more places *where you cannot* than places
where you can.

If you have a mechanical inclination, a good service manual may be
sufficient. If you have no idea how the internal combustion engine
works, enroll in a course in a nearby technical school. With the parts,
tools, and knowledge, most problems can be quickly rectified and the
cruise continued with little delay. Without them, you may find yourself
killing time in some undesirable port, awaiting a parts shipment.

As if you could kill time without injuring eternity.

Remember that Federal Express probably does not go where you are
going. If there is any part you anticipate needing, take it with you. The
need for spare parts is not limited to the engine, but applies as well to
other gear and equipment aboard the boat.

TOOLS

Having the necessary tools aboard to perform maintenance and
repair fits right in with a chapter on necessities.

*. . . and hearing me complain of the want of tools, he said
that I ought to have a chest of tools. But I said it was not
worth the while. I should not use them enough to pay for
them. "You would use them more, if you had them," said he.*

A selection of basic tools is required: wrenches, screwdrivers, a
socket set, pliers, a chisel or two. Do not overlook specialized tools. For
example, when the water pump fails, there is little consolation in
knowing you were clever enough to have spare impellers aboard when
you discover the pump body is held together with Allen-head machine
screws and you have no Allen wrenches aboard.

You can avoid this embarrassment by spending a couple of hours
going around the boat with your toolbox in hand. Make sure that you
have a tool to fit every fastener and adjustment aboard. If the water
pump does not, do the stanchion base attachments require hex
wrenches? Are ring-clip pliers required to dismantle the winches? Does
the foreign-built engine require metric wrenches or sockets? The prop-
shaft stuffing box typically requires two large wrenches for periodic

maintenance. Are they aboard? What about a filter wrench, a plug-gap gauge, feeler gauges for point or valve setting? Can you actually get to all bolts or are extensions and universals required for your socket set? Can you retrieve a dropped wrench from the bilge? Is a puller required to remove the prop? Will you need gauges to service the refrigerator? We are sure that you get the picture. Consider the requirements of your toolbox carefully.

And sensibly. Tools can be either inexpensive insurance or very expensive ballast. Selection is the difference. You should have every tool aboard that is necessary, but aboard a pocket cruiser, there is no space for useless tools (a level, for example) or excessively redundant tools (e.g. 30 screwdrivers). Every tool aboard must have earned its space with its usefulness.

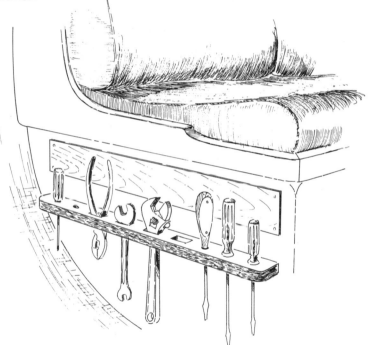

Hand tools can be located quickly from this wooden rack.

Keep in mind your potential need to go aloft. A boatswain's chair should be aboard. The canvas type offers the best security; a board in the bottom will make it vastly more comfortable.

Even new sails can get torn so sail repair could be required. Make up a sail repair kit (ditty bag) with needles, heavy polyester thread, sailcloth, repair tape, and perhaps a leather palm.

Unless you anticipate major repairs or modifications, power tools are best left ashore. Hand saws and drills will satisfy most requirements. If you already own a quality, cordless drill, you may find it convenient to have aboard. You can carry it ashore to charge it.

We cannot leave the subject of tools without a brief mention of quality. We have recently seen some very high-priced hand tool sets marketed as "marine grade." It is undoubtedly true that aboard a cruising sailboat, particularly one used in a salt water environment, the tools chosen should be of good quality. It is pointless to buy pliers from the 99-cent counter at Woolworth's and put them in the ship's toolbox. The first time you want to use them, they will be frozen completely shut. But any forged steel, nickel-chrome plated, *quality* tools will hold up well. For hand tools, we prefer Craftsman because of their availability and lifetime warranty. There are others just as good. The point is that there is little need to pay a premium price for "marine" tools. If a standard Craftsman tool will last "forever," how do marine tools improve upon that?

THE COMPASS

Another item included in the necessity list is a first quality compass. It is *the* essential piece of navigational gear. Compasses come in all sizes and all price ranges. Within reason, the larger the compass is, the easier it will be to read. Also, the closer it is placed to the helm, the more functional it will be. The effectiveness of the compass installation depends upon its visibility from the helm.

With wheel steering, the compass is usually mounted in a binnacle atop the pedestal. With the helmsman standing at the wheel, this installation affords good visibility, but if the helmsman is seated (cruising helmsmen are always seated), the compass may be too high for easy viewing. The problem is compounded when the helmsman sits to one side or the other of the wheel. The compass must be mounted low enough to be comfortably visible to the seated helmsman, and lubber lines are a distinct advantage. If you are purchasing a compass for a boat with wheel steering and you have a choice, select one with lubber lines at 45° and beam bearings. They will make holding a compass course much easier, no matter where around the wheel you may be seated.

On a boat with tiller steering, compass mount is a bit more difficult. The ketch rig offers the not inconsequential advantage of having a conveniently located mizzen mast for mounting the compass close to the helmsman and equally visible on either tack. With the more common sloop rig, the compass is most often mounted on the after side of the cabin bulkhead. If the cockpit is not too long, this position theoretically gives the helmsman a clear view of the compass on one tack. In reality, the entire crew is probably sitting on the windward side between the helmsman and the compass. On the opposite tack, the helmsman's distance from the compass and his angle of view are not ideal. Sometimes skippers mount dual compasses, one on either side to minimize this difficulty. Dual compasses are rarely necessary, but a bulkhead compass should be mounted as close to the center of the cockpit as possible. An offset companionway will determine on which side of the companionway to mount the compass.

We have seen boats with compasses mounted in the bridge deck or in the floor of the cockpit in an attempt to get a more central mount. Both locations are extremely vulnerable to damage and not particularly easy to view. Unless your boat is already rigged this way and you love it, we see little to recommend it.

Any compass purchased for cruising should be illuminated. Care should be taken to make sure that the light is sturdy and well protected, and that it does not, at any angle of viewing, show a white light around the red filter. Even a little reflected white light will destroy your night vision.

The compass is such an essential piece of equipment that we think it merits some type of redundancy. A good hand-bearing compass can get you home if you drop a winch handle on the main one. We have mixed thoughts on hand-bearing compasses. For accuracy and ease of use, we like the rubber-coated hockey puck type very much. It is very convenient, requires little space, and, with tritium gas lighting, is just as useful at night. However, if you wear metal-framed eyeglasses (or, we suppose, have a mouthful of braces) this compass may be influenced into erroneous readings. And, as a back-up compass, it leaves much to be desired.

The arms-length type is neither as convenient nor as accurate for hand bearing, but if you purchase one with mounting brackets, such as the Swedish-built Silva, it can easily convert to a back-up to the ship's compass. Mounted below, over the skipper's bunk, this type also makes a good telltale compass. It is also about half the price of the hockey puck. You really only need one aboard, and this one is the most versatile, hence the sensible choice. If you use a hand-bearing compass a lot, maybe you can talk someone into buying you a hockey puck for Christmas, unless we get you underway before then.

An automotive-type compass can serve as a telltale compass.

STEERING SYSTEMS

We have already mentioned steering as it relates to compass placement. Often steering is discussed in a more fundamental way, a discussion of whether wheel steering or tiller steering is better. We do not perceive one as better than the other. Each has advantages and the choice is usually nothing more than a matter of preference.

The tiller offers foolproof simplicity. The only possible malfunction is breaking the tiller and, even then, repair would be relatively easy to effect. Another advantage of the tiller is that it provides positive feedback to the helmsman, signalling through feel what helm actions are required to maintain course. On the debit side, a long tiller dominates the cockpit, sometimes making a large portion untenable.

Wheel steering, on the other hand, offers the benefit of usually occupying less of the cockpit. However, it trades that benefit for complexity and generally is considerably more prone to failure than the tiller. Most types of wheel steering provide much less rudder feedback, but with a long trick at the wheel this can be an advantage, the lower level of effort required postponing fatigue.

Our only intent in including the above material is to justify our recommendation that you make the first cruise with whatever steering system the boat is already equipped with. Until you have spent some time with it, there is no way of knowing whether you or your crew will be content with the system. Changing based on others recommendations is not a sensible course of action.

> *Public opinion is a weak tyrant compared with our own private opinion.*

For those of you still looking for the sensible pocket cruiser, unless you have experience based prejudices, steering should not be a selection criteria. We vividly recall looking for a cruiser some years back armed with a list of "requirements," one of which was tiller steering. We had a tiller on a previous boat and liked the feedback and the simplicity. The boat we ultimately purchased had a wheel commanding the rudder through a geared quadrant. We were disappointed, but boat purchase is always a compromise. A decade later we still have the same steering system and we would not select any other.

BASIC ACCOMMODATIONS

At this point, we have established that the boat is seaworthy, we can make it go, we can stop it, we can point it in any direction, and we can determine what direction that is. Are those all of the necessities? Not quite. What delineates a cruising boat from other sailboats is that in addition to being our means of transportation, it is where we live.

> *As I understand it, that was a valid objection urged by Momus against the house which Minerva made, that she "had not made it movable, by which means a bad neighborhood might be avoided,"* . . .

And a good neighborhood might be embraced.

As a house, our cruising boat must fill some basic requirements. It must have ample sleeping accommodations. There is a fascination among the general public with how many people can sleep aboard a sailboat. Name your boat *Sleeps Six* and you would put an end to a lot of dockside conversation. If it is a 30-footer, better to call it *Six-Pack*. We will discuss bunks more fully in a later chapter. Under the heading of necessities, it will be enough to say that the boat must provide a dry bunk for every crew member.

An occasional hot meal will also go a long way toward making a cruise successful. Just kidding. There is no doubt that most members of the cruising community eat better than they did ashore. This is due in part to the healthful environment which is conducive to good appetites; in part to the general healthiness of a diet centered around seafood; and finally because considerably more time is spent in meal preparation aboard the cruising boat than ashore. This additional food preparation time is not drudgery, but choice. Food takes on new significance in the cruising lifestyle. Consequently, the cruising boat requires a workable galley. We will be devoting an entire chapter to a discussion of what makes a galley "workable."

HEAD

Beyond bunks and the galley, the only other necessity is the head, in one form or another. In today's legal environment, we find it very difficult to include a discussion of marine toilets in a book called *Sensible Cruising*. There is not a shred of sensibleness to be found in any treatment of this subject. We thought about just recommending a cedar bucket as the only sensible solution, but the first time the boat lurches as you are carefully trying to lift the bucket out through the companionway, our credibility might *also* be besmirched.

We want to begin our discussion with assurances that we are environmentally conscious. We are infuriated when we see someone toss a beer can or a bag of garbage over the side. We are as interested in the protection of the earth's waters as the next person, *more interested*. We regularly cruise in areas where we swim in the water, bathe in it, snorkel in it, even wash our dishes in it. It should go without saying that we do not want to see those waters polluted.

So what is so wrong with marine discharge prohibitions aimed at protecting these waters? Plenty. It is not unusual to hear old timers tell us how clear the water used to be in various stateside cruising areas and wonder why we cannot see the bottom when our keel is firmly stuck in the mud. How did it get this way?

To oppose *marine sanitation device* (MSD) regulations almost seems against motherhood and apple pie, but the issue is not so clear cut. Although the current law has been on the books since 1976, there is little evidence that pleasure boat effluent ever represented a significant pollution concern (except in highly populated marinas), particularly in tidal waters. Pollution is a matter of concentration. Human waste is not a pollutant until you have a high concentration like, for example, a city outfall. Even if the MSD laws were effective, which they are not, the logic of beginning clean-up efforts with relatively insignificant pleasure boat discharge while industries and municipalities continue to belch tremendous amounts of chemical and fecal pollutants into the waterways of the nation is obviously faulty.

Okay, you're right. We are incensed that the politicians have used the "rich" yachtsmen as a decoy to draw attention away from the politically powerful real sources of pollution. In our naiveté, we were also shocked at the effectiveness of the blatant self-serving lobbying of MSD manufacturers.

> *But I have since learned that trade curses everything it handles; and though you trade in messages from heaven, the whole curse of trade attaches to the business.*

So have we.

Doesn't every little bit help anyway? That is a question you will have to answer for yourself. W. C. Fields decried drinking water because, he said (in a somewhat more earthy manner), "fish procreate in it." They also evacuate in it, W. C. We wonder if Congress knows. Consider the whale population for a moment. *National Geographic* has reported that scientists conservatively estimate that commercial whaling has decreased the population of whales worldwide by more than 1,200,000. Makes you proud, doesn't it? Just the blue whale population is down by almost 200,000. These are animals that weigh up to 200 tons, each digesting as much as eight tons of food per day. It seems as if the natural cleansing ability of the world's oceans has some excess capacity, not for chemical effluent or city outfalls, but surely for the wandering boatman.

Maybe we should have stopped with the cedar bucket! Of course, rinsing it overboard after use is still technically illegal (though very hard to enforce), and we are reluctant to encourage civil disobedience. Mr. Thoreau does not share that reluctance:

Must the citizen ever for a moment, or in the least degree, resign his conscience to the legislator? Why has every man a conscience, then? . . . It is not desirable to cultivate a respect for the law, so much as for the right. The only obligation which I have a right to assume, is to do at any time what I think right.

Legally (in coastal waters), you have two options: you can retain waste on board, or you can treat it and pump it overboard. Practically, you have only one choice for compliance because treatment systems are not legal in some areas through which your cruise may take you, because treatment systems typically require 50 amps of power for the treatment cycle (a completely separate battery is necessary just for this function), and because few of us "rich" yachtsmen are going to spring the $1,000 necessary for a complex piece of equipment of questionable environmental value and no practical improvement over the bucket.

Retention systems take two forms. One uses a standard, through-hull discharge head connected to a holding tank. With this type, emptying requires a shore-side pump out station. You must locate a pump out station, usually impossible, and then take the boat to the dock. There is often a charge for this service, and as likely as not the sewage still ends up in the ocean through the municipal outfall. Many owners see little benefit in the charge or the circuitous routing and use a "cheater" pump to empty the tank directly overboard. Even more common is the use of a *Y-valve* which allows the effluent to be directed overboard rather than into the holding tank to begin with. This is a perfectly legal configuration to allow overboard discharge offshore where MSD regulations do not apply. Pumping untreated effluent over the side in coastal waters by either method is illegal (although the "outfall" method is not).

The other form is the *portable head*. This consists of a bowl sitting on top of a small holding tank. Flushing the head merely drops the contents, along with a small amount of water to rinse the bowl, into the tank. When the tank is full, it is removed from the bowl and carried ashore to be emptied into a shore-side toilet, a disgusting chore. Since portables require emptying every two or three days, they may be the best compromise for the weekend sailor but are not a good choice for cruising. Besides, generically speaking, they leak and they stink. So do the regulations.

The only sensible way to comply is with a holding tank. Manufacturers are required to provide only legal installations (if any at all), and generally agree with our assessment. While many of the

70

smaller cruisers are outfitted with portable heads, on new boats large enough to have a head compartment, you will usually find a holding tank installation. If a Y-valve is not already installed, there is much to recommend it. There was a time, before the bureaucratic term MSD found its way into the sailors' lexicon, when the only discussion necessary about heads could be summed up by saying buy a good quality one, do not put anything in it that has not been eaten first, keep it scrupulously clean, replace the valves and leathers annually, and double clamp the hoses to the sea-cock. Outside of the regulated areas, the Y-valve allows us to return to those good old days.

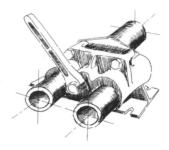

Y-valve.

The world and my life are simplified.

DOCKING

Even if you manage to avoid going to the dock to pump out your holding tank, there will undoubtedly be times when you will want or need to go alongside. For such occurrences you will need a minimum of four dock lines. They should be nylon for the same reason that anchor lines should be nylon and they should be at least as large in diameter as the anchor lines. Since they will often be exposed to chafe, you may decide to select a larger line. Each dock line should be about as long as the boat so they may be used for spring lines as well as bow and stern lines, and we prefer a large eye spliced in one end only. The eye makes it easy for an inexperienced dockside volunteer to slip the line over the piling you specify while you make all adjustments aboard. We have seen numerous occasions when a fifth line, twice as long as the others (perhaps smaller in diameter), has been very handy to have aboard.

The biggest concern with going alongside is the potential for damage to the boat. A minimum of two *large* fenders should be aboard. Smaller fenders simply will not do the job. Recognizing the limited stowage space aboard a pocket cruiser, we recommend two fenders;

three or four would, of course, be better. Nevertheless, it has been our experience that with careful adjustment of dock lines and proper fender placement, the hull can normally be protected with two fenders. Protection can be vastly improved with a fender board.

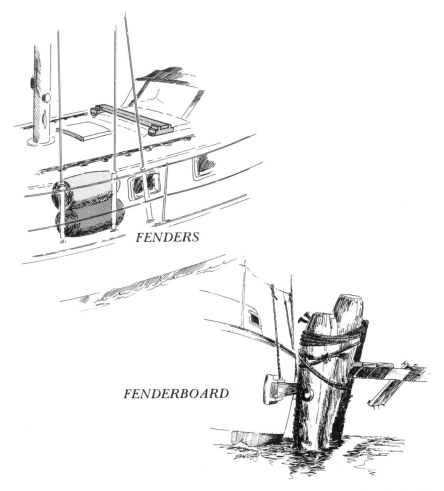

FENDERS

FENDERBOARD

With limited locker space, large fenders and fenderboards may be stowed on deck. The fenderboard shown was cut to fit a convenient stowage place.

DINGHY SELECTION

We believe the term "sensible cruising" presupposes that the amount of time spent at a dock will be proportionally small compared to the amount of time spent at anchor. If the boat is self-contained, there is little reason to incur the expense of dockage charges even where docks are available. At most cruising destinations there are no docks. When you are tied to a dock, it is a simple matter to step ashore. It is quite another matter when the vessel is anchored.

Getting to and from shore requires some kind of dinghy. On a cruising boat, the dinghy is used for more than just ferrying the crew to shore, much more. Dinghy selection can be one of the most important decisions you will make in readying your boat for a cruise. There are two questions you must answer before you select the proper dinghy for you: how will you use the dinghy and how will you carry it?

We will look at the second question first, since it may represent a limiting factor. Of course, any dinghy can be towed, and if your cruising plans call for strictly protected waters, towing may be the easiest way to handle the dinghy. If any offshore work is planned, then the dinghy must come aboard. This is not optional. In a quartering or following sea, the dinghy may come careening down the face of waves, slamming into the transom. You can lower this risk by towing with a very long painter, but it is disconcerting to have your painter disappear into a wave behind you, then seconds later watch as the dinghy is literally jerked off the top of the wave, sailing through the air until it lands in the trough rather like a pelican, only to disappear again. Both the drag and the strain are tremendous. As a result of such poor judgement, we lost a favorite sailing dinghy one night in a blow when the painter snapped under the load. If you plan to go offshore, the size and deck layout of your boat will be important to your selection of a dinghy, particularly if you choose a rigid dinghy.

We see a lot of sailors carry the dinghy on the foredeck but we generally consider this to be a poor practice. Foredeck work is already dangerous enough without the additional hazard of a dinghy occupying 90% of the deck space and the dinghy itself quite exposed in rough conditions. If you plan to carry a dinghy on the deck of a pocket cruiser, it belongs on the cabin top, abaft the mast. With an aft cockpit, this generally means that the absolute maximum length that can be accommodated is the distance from the mast to the aft end of the cabin, and even that makes the cabin accessible only through contortion. A spray dodger will shorten the available cabin top space.

A center cockpit boat might allow for dinghy stowage on top of the aft cabin, if the cabin is of sufficient size. Stern davits are seen on larger cruisers but we have seldom seen a successful installation on a pocket cruiser. This option should only be considered for a boat in the upper range of pocket cruisers, and then only for a heavy boat with a fat (and buoyant) stern.

The ideal rigid dinghy rows easily, tows lightly, moves well under power; many also sail nicely. Unfortunately, it is almost impossible to build a versatile rigid dinghy under about nine feet. Below this length, it lacks carrying capacity in both senses of the word: it does not carry well between pulls on the oars and it will not safely carry more than three people or a large load of equipment or supplies.

> *Our boat, which had cost us a week's labor in the spring, was in form like a fisherman's dory, fifteen feet long by three and a half in breadth at the widest part, painted green below, with a border of blue, with reference to the two elements in which it was to spend its existence.*

Virtually any cruising boat can carry a good sized inflatable aboard, but the disparity between the maximum cabin top space available for storage and the minimum ideal hard dinghy size may suggest that smaller cruiser owners simply cannot consider the rigid dinghy as a viable option. This need not be the case. There are some nesting dinghies around that may satisfy a preference for a hard dinghy and at the same time fit aboard in limited space. Such a dinghy, in a nine-foot length, can be separated into two halves of about four and a half feet, one of which fits inside the other. We have even run across a 12-footer which breaks into three nesting sections.

Once you have in mind what limitations your ability to carry the dinghy place upon you, you can make your selection from dinghies that accommodate those limitations. In making that selection, you need to determine how you are going to use the dinghy—what you expect from it. If your preferences parallel those of Thoreau, placing a premium on serenity and solitude, and you like to explore every anchorage and creek in the cool morning hours without disturbing your neighbors, you may choose a good rowing dinghy. Perhaps you are more Hemingway, thrilling to the click of the drag and the power of a finned competitor at the other end of a line: consider a small, flat-bottomed power skiff. Those following the lead of Cousteau will choose the inflatable, the ideal diving platform. With children aboard, the small sailing dinghy is worth its weight in gold. You have to consider how many people are aboard, how often you expect to have guests, and what range you want from the dinghy.

Do not overlook the utility of the dinghy in handling ground tackle. You should be able to take out a kedge quickly in case of accidental grounding. You should also have the capacity to lay out a second (or third) anchor by dinghy into the teeth of a rising gale. This can be accomplished in an inflatable, but only with an outboard. It can also be done in almost anything before the wind gets up, but sometimes what appears to be a harmless shower turns into a localized storm without much warning. As an alternative to rowing out an anchor, it is

A sailing dinghy can be used for recreation, instruction, handling anchors, or as a tender.

possible to float the anchor with a fender or life jacket and swim it out. This works fine for an afternoon storm in the tropics, but do not expect to enjoy yourself in the middle of the night in cold water with lightning above and who knows what below. For this reason only, many cruising sailors insist upon having a good-rowing, hard dinghy. We used to share this philosophy, but having seen the job done more often, quicker, and with less hesitation with outboard-powered inflatables, we no longer view the rigid dinghy as imperative.

Things do not change; we change. Sell your clothes and keep your thoughts.

The rigid dinghy that rows, sails, and powers well does offer wide versatility. Hard dinghies typically tow *very lightly* compared to inflatables. A quality hard dinghy stands up to the hard knocks of cruising very well. Without complaint, it will absorb the punishment of landing on a rocky beach, lying against a seawall, or banging against the other dinghies at the dock in a chop. On the negative, particularly in the sizes appropriate for a pocket cruiser, hard dinghies are tipsy, are difficult to board from the water, have less carrying capacity than inflatables, have a penchant for banging into the hull, are hard to bring aboard, and are both ugly and in the way when carried on deck.

Things are not all rosy with inflatables either. They are very susceptible to wear and chafe, not to mention punctures. They are also susceptible to theft, a very serious problem for inflatable owners. If not stolen, they still have a limited life although, with care, much longer than you might expect. They tow very heavily, although this can be improved if the motor is removed and the bow lifted clear of the water, attached right against the stern rail. They give a very wet ride in a chop. They are relatively expensive and require an outboard. We see nothing at all to recommend the small rowing inflatables and do not know a single owner who has been satisfied with this type of dinghy. We do not even recommend the inflatables with a motor bracket. If an inflatable is selected, the reasons for that selection will generally indicate an inflatable with a transom, the so-called sport dinghy. A rigid floor complicates packing and unpacking but makes the boat much more satisfying to use. The greatest attraction of the inflatable is its speed and range, significantly broadening the cruising horizon. Its stability and tremendous carrying capacity, and its usefulness as a diving platform are also common reasons for its selection.

Choosing between a rigid dinghy and an inflatable is not always an easy decision. Perhaps you should not choose.

> *While one of us landed not far from this island to forage for provisions among the farmhouses whose roofs we saw—for our supply was now exhausted—the other, sitting in the boat, which was moored to the shore, was left alone to his reflections.*

Sounds nice, unless "the other" is reflecting on going ashore. We are seeing more and more cruising couples with two dinghies. As often as not, one is a rigid, rowing (and usually sailing) dinghy and the other is a well-powered inflatable. The inflatable stays in its bag while the boat is on the move and in larger ports where theft is a problem. At other times, both dinks are available to do what each does best.

We are not suggesting that two dinghies are necessary. One is, but two are not. Still, it has become a popular option and one that might work for you if your circumstances are appropriate.

OTHER CHOICES

Except for safety equipment which we will examine in depth in a chapter called "Higher Laws," we have just about covered the necessities for a successful cruise. If our approach thus far seems Spartan, do not worry. Even Thoreau acknowledged the need for a warm coat in the winter. We will devote several chapters to gear and equipment that can make your cruise more comfortable and correspondingly more enjoyable. We will only cover sensible options, and even then we will emphasize the fact that they are options.

When authors suggest that the minimum size for a proper cruising boat must be 50 feet or state that a piece of specialized equipment is "inexpensive," then tell you in the next sentence that it costs $3,000, we think they fail if they are trying to encourage cruising. The "common man" does not buy a 50-footer or the "inexpensive" equipment recommended. Those with less determination are put off by the suggestion that such are the requirements of cruising. Bunk!

> *I think I will not trouble myself for any wealth, when I can be so cheaply enriched.*

Cruising is about independence, accomplishment, and self-esteem. It is about new friends, broadened perspective, and relevance. It is also about crystalline waters, infinite skies, and the green flash. The richness of the experience does not equate with the wealth of the participant. Concentrate on the necessities and you will be cruising far sooner than you ever imagined.

SOUNDS

. . . for a man is rich in proportion to the number of things which he can afford to let alone.

HIS chapter should be called "Sounds and Lights" but unfortunately Mr. Thoreau left us when Mr. Edison was only 15 and had not yet converted electricity into light. Mr. Thoreau can thus be forgiven for this oversight. We cannot. We will cover in this chapter many of the wonderful things that electricity and its modern cousin, electronics, can do for us. We will remain true to our premise, however, in trying to keep even this potentially obsessive aspect of cruising as sensible as possible.

After reading the chapter on necessities, the first question, appropriately or otherwise, is likely to be, "What about electronics?" This preoccupation with marine electronics is understandable. We are a society fascinated with electronics, stemming from our long-term love affair with electricity. Let Con-Ed shut off the power to New York City for five minutes and it will make the national news; shut it off for an hour, and it will be the top story; shut it off for a day and it will be the *only* story. Without electricity, elevators stop, traffic lights do not work, the subway is paralyzed. At home, our food spoils, our televisions are dark, our stereos are silent, the microwave oven does not work, nor does the VCR. Even otherwise industrious writers sit in front of blank screens. We fill our homes with electric and electronic gadgetry; it should surprise no one that we fill our boats with them also. This tendency deserves an objective look.

There is no such thing as pure objective observation. Your observation, to be interesting, i.e. to be significant, must be subjective.

We certainly want this to be interesting. Let's take a subjective look.

ELECTRICITY AFLOAT

Ashore, electronics present few problems. We have a readily available, seemingly inexhaustible, and relatively cheap power source. Buy a home computer, set it on the desk, plug it into the wall and you are up and running. The plug is already there, the desk is not likely to move, and unless you gargle over the keyboard, salt water corrosion is unlikely. If it quits on its own, repair is probably only minutes away.

Attempt to install the same system aboard a 25-foot sailboat and you are courting disaster. The power source is limited at best, probably erratic. The "desk" shakes, pounds, and rolls. The salt air will do the circuits in soon enough; one unfortunate dollop will finish the job instantly. Forget finding a repairman.

This is not to suggest that electronics cannot survive on board. Some of the newer marine electronics are amazingly robust, seemingly unaffected by the marine environment. That is not our point. What we are suggesting is that ashore we see all new electric and electronic products as a new "convenience," as often as not a reasonably inexpensive one. We do not have to consider wiring it, providing the power to run it, protecting it from a hostile environment, or repairing it ourselves. Such considerations should raise questions about the applicability of the term "convenience."

Our homes ashore are also filled with a lot of electrical "necessities." Are you paying attention? A cruising sailboat does not need a single electric or electronic item aboard. Let's restate that: For a perfectly safe and eminently enjoyable cruise, *not a single wire nor a sole electronic marvel needs to be aboard.*

Are we advocating cruising without any electrical power? Absolutely not. Look at our title. We are advocating a *sensible* approach to cruising. Too many come to their first cruising boat with a conception that the boat is not fully found until at least $5,000 in electronics are aboard.

When any real progress is made, we unlearn and learn anew what we thought we knew before.

Before you can evaluate your own electrical needs, you must abandon that prejudice totally. The sensible approach to electronics is that none are required. *None.* When you believe something is a necessity, you do not compare its cost to its benefit. Any cost comparisons are only with other items that fill the same need. We cannot draw sensible conclusions about even the desirability of electrics and electronics if we have such a predisposition.

We have arranged this chapter to discuss types of electrical equipment in *loosely* their order of importance to us. Beyond the first few items, there is little reason to conclude that there is any universal significance to this sequence. Each item we discuss should go aboard *in the order of its importance to you.*

BATTERIES

Any discussion of on-board electrical systems must begin with the power source. On larger yachts, it is common to find a small generating plant aboard, providing 12-volt, 110-volt, and sometimes 220-volt power. The generator runs much of the time, providing power for an all-electric kitchen, air conditioning, washer and dryer, electric heads, television, and most of the lighting. Aboard the pocket cruiser, electrics are much simpler.

The power source we are concerned with is the battery. Away from the dock, all of the electrical equipment aboard a pocket cruiser will operate on 12 volts of direct current. There are 110-volt powered items that make living aboard at the dock much more palatable (sitting here in south Florida where the temperature today is 91°, the humidity higher, air conditioning comes to mind), but this is a book about cruising and we will limit our coverage to cruising electrics. On a pocket cruiser, they are 12-volt powered.

If you are going to have electrics aboard, you will need at least one 12-volt battery. If your cruiser is inboard powered, that battery is likely already aboard since it is a necessary component in an electric start system. If you have outboard power, a small battery may still be aboard for factory-installed cabin and running lights. In either case, if you plan to have more than a few lights aboard, you may have to improve the battery package.

Determining your battery needs depends upon what level of demand that you anticipate putting on them. Since we have yet to talk about what equipment you might put aboard, it is a bit early for specific calculations. Instead, we will provide some general comments about battery installations, regardless of ultimate capacity.

If you depend upon the battery to start your engine, you should not also use that battery for powering shipboard electrics such as lights, pumps, and radios. You will not "wear out" the battery by use, but it is easy to lose track of how much power you may have used and find yourself in a "catch 22" situation: a battery too low to start the engine and no way to charge it without the engine running.

There is an exception. A small diesel, accessibly installed and with a compression release, can be hand cranked. This can be a great advantage, taking the worry out of accidentally draining the battery too low to power the starter motor. Unfortunately, with many factory installations the engine is so inaccessible as to actually prohibit the swinging of the hand crank or to prevent a huddled attempt from generating enough force on the crank to keep the engine turning with compression. The only way to know for sure is to get down there and give it a spin.

Nevertheless, for most inboard installations, dual batteries are indicated. Manufacturers recognize this and most auxiliaries will be so equipped. If your boat does not have dual batteries (outboards excepted) and any of the equipment that follows in this chapter interests you, you will need to install a second battery.

Batteries need to be accessible so water levels can be regularly checked. The batteries should reside in acid-proof trays and should be firmly strapped in place. Quite heavy and filled with acid, they can do major damage if they come adrift in a seaway, not to mention the fact that you will be without electrical power. A cover is also required to keep stray items from shorting the terminals, but be sure that both the cover and the locker where the batteries are located are well vented. The charging process generates hydrogen gas, the same gas that was in the Hindenburg, so you want it to escape, not accumulate in a sealed locker.

For short cable runs, the battery locker should be close to the engine room, but not in it. Heat kills batteries. Despite the temptation to get the substantial weight of the batteries as low as possible, do not install them in the bilge. If they are already there, move them. The time may come when the bilge floods. When you see the battery cables disappear beneath a foot of bilge water, you will wish you had taken our advice.

There are basically two types of "wet charge" 12-volt batteries: the so-called automotive type and the deep-cycle type. The automotive type has a lot of initial power, "cold-cranking amps," and as long as it stays fully charged, it has a long life expectancy. It is designed for use in cars where it is called upon momentarily for starting and spends the rest of its time being charged. Subject an automotive battery to regular discharging and most will die young.

The deep-cycle battery is a different concept. It is designed to provide a lower peak power, but to provide that power over a long period of time before recharging is required. You may be familiar with this type of battery if you play golf since these batteries are used in the carts. You do not play any longer? What with dues, green fees, and cart rentals you had to give it up for a less expensive pastime—yachting, for example? Well anyway, if you remember, the carts were charged every night and then they were driven all over the course each day. They can handle this deep discharge cycle time after time without losing their ability to be fully recharged.

If you use the battery only for starting the engine, the automotive type will serve fine. For lights and accessories, a deep-cycle battery is required. In a two-battery installation, it is not uncommon to find both types of batteries for their respective specialties. However, many skippers prefer to install only deep-cycle batteries so that either battery can provide all battery functions in case of the failure of one. A deep-cycle battery can readily serve as a starting battery without injury but in the reverse situation, the automotive battery is damaged by each deep discharge.

Batteries are rated in ampere-hours. A battery rated at 100 ampere-hours can deliver 100 amperes of electrical current for one hour, or one ampere of current for 100 hours, or 50 amperes for two hours, or two amps for 50 hours, or any combination that adds up to 100 ampere-hours. That is *theoretically*. Practically, count on usable current being only 75% of the rating on a new battery, 50% on an older one. As the battery discharges, the voltage also drops until it is too low to operate equipment requiring 12 volts. Amperage is still available, but at an unusably low voltage. As the battery gets older, its ability to hold a charge deteriorates so that usable ampere-hours are even less.

CHARGING SYSTEMS

As we talk about equipment, we will provide the typical power requirements for each item which should enable you to determine daily power requirements and consequently the appropriate battery sizes. Even without that information, we can look at how we keep the battery charged. Typically, a marine engine has an alternator. This statement used to exclude outboards but, as we have already mentioned, many outboards are now available with alternators.

We do not see the need to go into the differences between generators and alternators. Most of you will already have an alternator aboard. If you have an older boat with a generator, replace it with an alternator. The alternator on a small marine engine will probably be rated at between 30 and 50 amps. This means that if we run the engine for one hour, a 50-amp alternator charging at capacity will put 50 ampere-hours of charge into our batteries. This may be ample for most cruisers. By contrast, even the largest alternator on a small outboard is rated at less than seven amperes. It would take more than seven hours of running to generate the same 50 amps.

At low demand levels, these two are not so far apart. Charging a battery is somewhat like filling a glass from a pitcher. If the glass is empty, we pour rapidly until the glass gets close to full, then we begin to pour more slowly. Just before the glass is full, we are pouring very slowly. If the charge on the battery is very low, a 50-amp alternator is putting up to 50 amps into the battery; as the battery approaches fully charged, the regulator reduces the charging rate until, at fully charged, it shuts off completely. On a boat where the only daily electrical demand is from the anchor light, running lights, or a few cabin lights, the large alternator will be called upon to deliver perhaps only 10 amps, not a great deal more than the outboard alternator can deliver.

On the other hand, if you have lights, fans, radios, and numerous electronics aboard and you use them often, the outboard alternator cannot keep up. With enough demand, the standard alternator will also fall short, requiring excess running time. There are three common solutions to this problem. The most obvious is to increase your charging capacity.

The first solution has two approaches. The first approach is to exchange your alternator for a larger one. Exchange the 35-amp

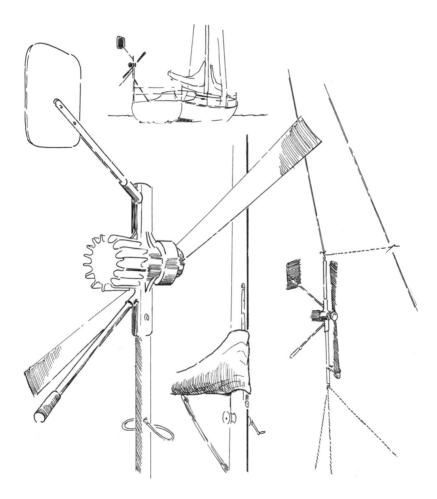

More and more crusing boats are using wind generators to recharge batteries.

alternator for a 50, or the 50 for a 70. We prefer this second approach. Even though alternators are amazingly trouble free, having a single source of power is like having all your eggs in one basket. Alternator failure is a major problem. A rebuilt alternator should cost under $50, and many cruisers *carry* a spare. A much better arrangement is to *mount* the spare alternator, giving you a back-up (already mounted and running) and at least doubling your charging capacity.

The second solution is what is known as a manual alternator control. This is a rheostat that by-passes the regulator, allowing you to select a higher input into the battery than the regulator would provide. There is some risk to the batteries in overheating or overcharging, but if manual control is carefully monitored, the risk is minimal. There have been numerous technical articles published that show how to assemble such controls. They are also commercially available. At least one manufacturer builds an automatic version which senses a full charge and switches off, eliminating the overcharge risk. We have had such a system aboard for several years with excellent results.

The third solution is to augment the engine-powered charging system. On larger boats, this is done with an auxiliary generator. We think a separately powered generator has limited applicability on a pocket cruiser. One alternative is the solar panel. Unfortunately, solar panels continue to be expensive, relatively fragile, and in the sizes appropriate for a pocket cruiser, provide only a modest current output. Wind generators, on the other hand, have improved significantly in recent years. A good wind generator may not just augment the alternator but, if current demand is modest, may supply all necessary charging power.

BATTERY SELECTOR SWITCH

With a dual-battery system, usually one battery is used for running the boat's electrics, the other only for starting the engine. Once the engine has been started, both batteries require charging. The way we handle the need for the batteries to be independent during use yet both charged by the same alternator is through the use of a battery selector switch. Typically a rotary switch, it has four settings as indicated below.

Without getting too technical, to deliver direct current, alternators depend upon diodes to block one side of the generated alternating current. It is imperative that, when it is charging, an alternator be connected to a load. With a diesel installation, that load is charging the battery. When the engine is running, the alternator must never be disconnected from the battery, not even instantaneously, or the alternator will be damaged (blown diode). That is why most texts recommend that you do not switch from one battery to the other when the engine is running. So how do you charge both batteries?

One way is to start the engine with the switch set on *Both* and leave it that way, not very satisfactory when only one battery needs charging. We have often seen the recommendation of starting the engine on *Battery 1*, charging it for a while, then stopping the engine, switching to *Battery 2*, and restarting the engine.

> *The greater part of what my neighbors call good, I believe in my soul to be bad, and if I repent anything, it is very likely to be my good behavior.*

Aside from the obvious complexity of this method, how in the world do you charge *Battery 2* if it is too discharged to even turn the starter? The solution to this problem is a battery selector switch that connects before it disconnects. In other words, when switching from *Battery 1* through *Both* to *Battery 2*, at no time is there even a momentary disconnection. With this type of switch, you can select either battery or both while the engine is running.

Battery selector switch.

Check with the manufacturer for this feature before you buy a battery selector switch. If one is already installed, you can check it by turning on a cabin light (with the engine not running) and very slowly rotate the switch from *Battery 1* to *Battery 2* through the *Both* setting. The light should never go out or even flicker. If it does, switching batteries with this switch while the engine is running will damage your alternator. No matter what kind of switch you have, damage will result if you pass through the *Off* selection when attempting to switch the batteries, so pay close attention when you do switch.

MONITORING THE CHARGE

If you do not plan to run the engine daily, keeping track of the level of charge in the batteries becomes important. The most reliable device is the battery hydrometer, that thing that looks like a big eye dropper with a tiny man-overboard pole floating inside it. But hydrometers are fragile, bothersome to use, and tend to drip highly corrosive acid. The expanded-scale voltmeter offers a simpler, though less accurate, method of monitoring battery levels. Sometimes called a battery condition indicator, the expanded-scale voltmeter is inexpensive and easy to install, and at the push of a button the meter will indicate the voltage of the battery in service. Rotating the main selector switch will allow checking of the other battery. Although referred to as a 12-volt battery, the battery will actually deliver over 14 volts fully charged. A reading of 13.5 volts would indicate about 25% discharged; a 12-volt reading may mean that the battery has insufficient power remaining to start the engine. What the meter lacks in accuracy, it makes up in convenience, lending itself to close monitoring of the batteries.

By now you may be wondering why bother. First, it takes a lot longer to write about batteries than it does to actually look after them. Second, an ample and reliable source of electrical power aboard provides you with the opportunity to select a number of items that may make your time afloat more enjoyable.

CABIN LIGHTING

We know many cruisers who rise with the sun and retire with it. Cabin lighting is not of vital importance to them. They may even be so bold as to suggest, as do some very well-known cruising authors, that the "best" cabin lighting is the kerosene lantern.

Truly they love darkness rather than light.

They must also like heat.

To be perfectly honest, one of the reasons we go cruising is so that we do not have to rise with the sun. On the other hand, the first wisps of morning grey may be on the horizon before we retire for the night. We enjoy the night every bit as much as the day. Swimming, diving, fishing, shelling, harbor watching—all the traditional cruising pastimes—we do in daylight. After dark, the anchorage becomes hushed—serene. We like to sit out and look at the magnificent sky or introspect quietly in the dark, but we do not want to be limited to that. We also like to entertain, read, write, consult the charts, play a game, or bake a cake if the mood strikes us. Good lighting is an imperative.

We cruised for several years without electricity. The lack of adequate lighting detracted from the cruise. As we shopped for a next boat, ample power for quality cabin lighting was the top item on our "must have" list.

Cabin lights come in two types, incandescent and fluorescent. The fluorescent delivers more light for the power consumed, almost four times as much. With fluorescent lighting, the cabin of a pocket cruiser can be brightly lighted using little more than two amps per hour. Some find fluorescent lighting harsh. Incandescent lighting is softer, warmer in the sense of atmosphere, but also warmer in the sense of heat generated, and requires four times the power for an equivalent amount of light.

Specialized cabin lighting is also worthy of consideration. While two or three 8-watt fluorescent cabin lights provide more than ample light for a party or a late-night discussion, their placement may make them somewhat less ideal for reading. Cruisers are a notoriously literate lot, devouring volume after volume. If there is a reader aboard, well-placed reading lights will be daily appreciated. We have been very

Oil lamp. No electrical power required.

happy with the small, high-intensity type. Mounted over a bunk, they allow one bunk mate to read without preventing the other from sleeping. They were so effective in easing eyestrain when we installed them over the bunks that we quickly added reading lights over the main settee in the main cabin where we often sit to read. They require about the same amount of power as the fluorescent but concentrate a softer light directly on the reading material. We, and your optometrist, highly recommend reading lights.

Another specialized light worthy of consideration, particularly if you have any night sailing in mind, is the chart light. Of low intensity, usually on a long gooseneck, the chart light will come with a red filter. The photo receptors of the human eye are insensitive to red light wavelengths, so you can drop below for a quick look at the chart without destroying your night vision. You could also dress to come on watch, grab your foul weather gear or a granola bar, or do anything else requiring light without affecting night vision. There is one drawback; any red markings on the chart will be invisible in red light.

RUNNING LIGHTS

Night sailing will also dictate running lights. The boat almost certainly was supplied with running lights by the manufacturer. The provided running lights will be adequate for sailing in confined waters but are almost sure to be ineffective offshore. A tricolor masthead light offers a much better likelihood of being seen offshore and since port, starboard, and stern lights share the same bulb, the tricolor uses less power. If you decide to install a tricolor light, do not disconnect the old running lights. Unfortunately, you cannot legally use the tricolor when under power. You will have to use the traditional running lights with a steaming light also showing—a white light above the port and starboard lights showing through the combined arc of both (240°).

ANCHOR LIGHT

Even if you avoid night sailing like the plague, and you should not, you will still need an anchor light. The masthead-mounted anchor light is very popular and if you decide to fit a tricolor, many are offered with a low wattage anchor light. But even drawing less than one amp, forget it and it can singlehandedly draw your battery flat in a couple of days. In deference to our late rising, we have used a kerosene anchor lamp for years. If we forget to turn it off, there is no harm done. We like it but readily admit that it is not as convenient as flipping a switch.

STROBE

For twice the cost of a masthead tricolor/anchor light, you can get one that incorporates a strobe also. Highly visible, the strobe is approved for distress situations only, not collision avoidance. This means that if you turn it on to let a freighter know where you are, you should attract him rather than cause him to turn away. Unfortunately, enough sailors use the strobe regularly for collision avoidance that, despite the regulations, shipping either ignores them or takes evasive action. If you install one on the premise that it will attract assistance should you require it, unless you use it in conjunction with your VHF or EPIRB, you are likely to be disappointed. Use the same money to buy a quality pocket strobe instead. It can always be hoisted if you want to try to obtain assistance.

HANDHELD LIGHTS

Independent of the ship's battery, at least two waterproof flashlights or lanterns should be aboard. We like to have one in the cockpit and one mounted just inside the companionway. We keep a penlight in the forward cabin. A lantern is also in the dinghy when we are on a night

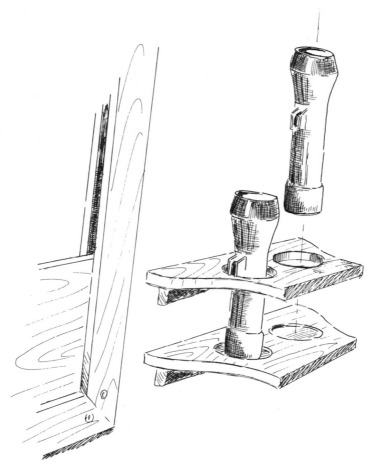

Flashlight holder mounted on the inside bulkhead. Flashlights can be reached from either the cockpit or the cabin.

excursion. If you have several flashlights aboard, buying ones that all use the same type of battery (D-cells, for example) will minimize the number of spares that will need to be aboard.

No matter how powerful your flashlights, they will have nowhere near the penetrating power of a 12-volt spotlight. Available in models up to 300,000 candlepower, a rugged spotlight is a tremendous aid to night navigation. The highest intensity ones draw almost 13 amps so if that is what you select, the electrical supply of most pocket cruisers will dictate judicious use.

SPREADER LIGHTS

If you are thinking about spreader lights, we have them but never use them. Underway at night, they will completely destroy the night vision of everyone aboard. Sail handling can be done very effectively without light after you become familiar with the vessel. If light is absolutely required, a small, red-lens flashlight is a better choice. In the event of a big snafu, a wrapped headsail for example, spreader lights might make recovery easier. Better to minimize the risk. One potential use for spreader lights is to secure sails and coil lines after the anchor is down when reaching an anchorage after dark. Do it by feel and save the money.

MARINE ELECTRONICS

Marine catalogs are filled with glossy color pictures of the latest in marine electronics. All of it is fascinating, much of it is useful, little of it is cheap, and none of it is required.

If there are any to whom it is no interruption to acquire these things, and who know how to use them when acquired, I relinquish to them the pursuit.

We are no more anti-electronic than we are anti-big boat. It is just that much of the current literature and all of the advertising copy would lead one to conclude that to leave the docks without a complete inventory of state-of-the-art electronics will subject the skipper and his "loved ones" to unspeakable risks. That simply is not true. The lead line is just as accurate as the electronic depth sounder and infinitely less expensive. An old-fashioned chip log will tell you your speed, and standing on deck will give you a good idea of wind conditions.

If you choose to take any electronics aboard, they should enhance your cruise, not prevent you from cruising. If you cannot afford any electronic gear and that is that, fine. Go cruising without it. If you can afford it, or at least some of it, then we want you to make a sensible selection based upon the equipment's value to you.

We will take a cursory look at the broad spectrum of marine electronics. There are items that obviously lack practicality for installation aboard a pocket cruiser, and we have omitted them. We have yet to see a 25-footer with radar mounted, nor are we likely to see it soon. On the other hand, few technologies are expanding as rapidly as the field of electronics. Who would have thought five years ago that you would be able to buy a television that can be carried in a shirt pocket, and for a hundred bucks, yet? Who is to say what type of radar might be available five years hence?

DEPTH SOUNDER

Some type of depth sounder is found aboard all cruising boats. The most elemental and most reliable is the lead line. With two people aboard, the lead can be used very effectively, especially in shallow water. In deep water, the lead is less effective and much more difficult to use accurately. Sensible cruisers have a lead line aboard; most also have an electronic depth sounder.

Depth sounders come in three basic types: flasher, digital, and chart recorder. The principle is sonar, sending out a pulse of ultra-high-frequency sound and then measuring the time it takes for the sound to be reflected back. The flasher type has a small light on a rotating arm. When the light is at zero (usually located at 12 o'clock on the dial), a sound pulse is transmitted and the light simultaneously flashes. When the echo returns from the bottom, it likewise causes a flash. Functioning like the second hand on a stop watch, the time between the signal and the echo is measured by the distance the arm has rotated which in turn has been calibrated into measured depth. The scale around the dial is in feet, fathoms, or meters. Sounding the depth as much as 30 times per second, the flasher appears to the observer as a fixed light, both at 0 and at the measured depth.

Older flasher sounders used a tiny neon light and were impossible to read in sunlight. In recent years, the neon flasher has been replaced with the light-emitting diode (LED), much better but still difficult to read on a bright day. The advantage of the flasher type is that if you know how to read it, it can tell you quite a bit about the bottom. A very narrow reading indicates a rock hard bottom; mud would give a broader, less distinct indication. Inconsistent flashes may indicate fish if they are well clear of the bottom, or coral outcroppings or rocks if they are close to the depth reading. Flashers are relatively inexpensive, eminently reliable, and have a large devoted following.

All depth sounders work on the same principle of timing the echo. The digital depth sounder does it electronically and uses a liquid crystal display (LCD) to provide numeric depth readings. The digital is the easiest to interpret. If it is reading in feet and the display shows 15, you can conclude that the water is 15 feet deep (or the bottom is 15 feet below the transducer if the unit has no provision for offset). It is visible in bright sunlight, but tells you nothing about the bottom. Some digitals regularly display false readings. If you are in 20 feet of water and a large fish passes just beneath the keel, the digital suddenly announces that the depth is only four feet, perhaps even sounding an alarm. In such circumstances they fail shallow, meaning that the water is deeper than the reading, so unless you have a weak heart no harm is done. Unless it happens often; then you will lose confidence in the instrument. Digitals are the most miserly with power at 0.05 amps or less although the flasher at 0.2 amps could hardly be called demanding.

Chart recorders, providing a graph of the bottom contour, are much more complex than the other two types. Rarely seen on cruising boats, chart recorders are used mostly by commercial and sport fisherman to examine the bottom for likely habitats for fish and often to locate the fish themselves.

The choice between a flasher or a digital depth sounder is personal preference. In either case, a transducer must be mounted. The unit will be most sensitive and read to greater depths if the transducer is mounted through the hull. On smaller boats with a solid (not cored) fiberglass hull, the transducer can *sometimes* be successfully mounted inside the hull, either in an oil-filled box or glued directly to the hull. The location will depend upon the hull configuration and to a lesser extent the cabinet work inside.

All depth sounders have one major drawback: they do not tell you what is in front of you, only what you have passed over. Consequently, they are not a substitute for diligent navigation and piloting. If viewed as an aid to piloting and used accordingly, a depth sounder offers numerous benefits and is a sensible option for any cruising boat.

LOG

For coastal navigation and dead reckoning (DR), the log is extremely helpful. Like the depth sounder, the log need not be electronic. The old Walker-type taffrail log has been used by voyagers for decades, although in restricted waters it is not very practical. The English-built, mechanical Sumlog is another non-electronic type, cable driven by a small, hull-mounted impeller. We used one for many years and found it both dependable and accurate.

Most logs available today are, however, electronic. Typical current consumption is almost negligible at about 0.01 amps or less. The log provides an accurate measure of distance run, greatly simplifying coastal navigation. There is no completely accurate way to determine distance run without the log. A chip log (dropping a wooden "chip" over the stern and measuring how far you sail away from it in a fixed amount of time, by means of an attached line) will yield the boat's current speed which, multiplied by the time you sail, will give an approximation of distance run. Unfortunately, the speed of the boat varies with the strength of the wind and the trim of the sails, introducing considerable potential for inaccuracy over any distance. The log, on the other hand, registers changes in speeds, giving a more accurate measure of distance run.

Taffrail logs are widely used by world voyagers. Electronic logs are more common today.

When combined with a knotmeter, the log is one of the most useful instruments aboard. A sensitive knotmeter can help with sail trim. It can also help in determining whether to run or to tack downwind. There is a psychological effect also to be considered.

. . . which we bounded merrily over before a smacking breeze,
with a devil-may-care look in our faces, and our boat a white
bone in its mouth, and a speed which greatly astonished some
scow boatmen whom we met.

Watching the needle oscillate between one and two knots can be disheartening, but on a sparkling broad reach we have found few things that get us as totally excited as seeing the knotmeter hit the peg as we surf down the face of a cobalt wave. If we had a very heavy displacement slow boat, I think we would choose a log without a knotmeter. If the boat is a good performer, the knotmeter will be a joy.

RDF

The radio direction finder (RDF) used to be a very popular choice for a cruising boat, particularly one doing coastal cruising. The RDF is nothing more than a radio with a directional antenna mounted on top. In theory, you simply identify from the chart a coastal radio beacon or the transmitting tower of an AM radio station, set the dial to the appropriate band and frequency to receive the transmission, then

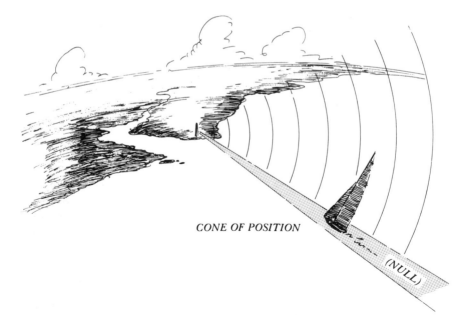

CONE OF POSITION

(NULL)

RDF "cone" of position as received from a transmitting station. The fix becomes more accurate at the narrow end of the "cone."

rotate the antenna on top until you find the null, the weakest signal. The null is determined audibly by a loss of sound and usually visually by a null meter which measures signal strength. Whichever direction the antenna points when the null is obtained is the direction to the beacon or tower. By obtaining a compass heading, you can plot a line of position on the chart. Using a second beacon, and crossing the second line of position with the first one, a fix is obtained. Homing is also possible. If there is a beacon at your inlet, you simply obtain a null on it, point the bow in that direction and look for the breakwater. That is the theory.

In actual practice the null itself is two or three degrees wide and, on a pitching and rolling boat, there will be some guesswork in locating the null. Realistically, an RDF bearing in anything other than perfect conditions can easily be erroneous by as much as ten degrees. Add the fact that the signal itself is sometimes bent by atmospheric or geographic conditions and you have a situation that might take you onto the breakwater.

We are not suggesting that the RDF is useless or dangerous. What we are suggesting is that what appears to be a line of position is really a "cone" of position, the cone being perhaps as much as 10° wide. Cross that with a second cone and you see that you do not have a fix but an approximate position. The area of that approximation depends upon how far from the beacons you are. As you get closer to the beacon, you approach the narrow end of the cone, improving the accuracy of an RDF bearing. If the deviation of the signal is known, you can use a coastal beacon quite accurately for homing since, as you approach the beacon, you will be working in the narrowest part of the cone.

We have had an RDF aboard for years. It is only rarely used. When crossing the Gulf Stream from Florida to the Bahamas, we dial up the aerobeacon on Bimini and determine whether we are north or south of the island as we approach it. Because of the unpredictability of the speed of the Gulf Stream, just this limited information can be very reassuring on a dark night. If you can put an RDF aboard inexpensively, you may also find it reassuring, particularly as you first begin cruising. One problem with RDF's is that in the face of increasingly cheaper electronics, they remain relatively expensive for what they are, a radio receiver with a directional antenna. And the manufacturers continue to make them bulky and complex. The most useful RDF we ever owned has doubled as a portable radio for going to the beach; complete with a carrying strap. It is completely independent of the boat's electrical system and cost only a few dollars more than a regular portable radio. Today it would be cheap indeed, but they are no longer manufactured. That is too bad.

VHF

Surely the most misunderstood of marine electronics is the radiotelephone. This is particularly true with the most common type of marine radio, the VHF. Skippers too often see the VHF as the most important piece of safety equipment aboard, assuring them that if they get into trouble they can summon assistance. We find this attitude abhorrent. In the first place, you made a conscious decision to challenge the elements, so what gives you the right to ask someone else to run a risk to save your hide? A sensible approach to cruising means going prepared to extract yourself from any unfortunate situation you may encounter.

In the second place, VHF is line-of-sight transmission with limited range, rarely more than 30 miles between cruising boats, probably no more than 50 to a typical Coast Guard antenna. How would you respond to your insurance man if he told you that your auto insurance was valid only as long as you never got more than 50 miles from his office?

Third, most emergencies require immediate action; some will wait for the cavalry to ride to the rescue, but they are rare. Finally, if you are cruising and you do manage to reach someone, unless it is the Coast Guard, that person is not likely to be any better equipped to deal with your emergency than you should be.

The VHF is *not* the most important piece of safety equipment aboard. It is still a very useful tool. It can be used to get draw bridges opened, to notify a supertanker of your insignificant presence, to reserve a marina slip where you plan to stop for the night, and to place a telephone call from 20 miles offshore. It can help you locate a specific boat in a large cruising area, provide a new recipe to a fellow wanderer, reserve a taxi to an island airport, and, along the coast, obtain a continuous weather forecast. As a last resort, it might, just might, get your fat out of the fire.

If you decide to put a VHF aboard, spend your money on power at the antenna, sensitivity, and water resistance, not on channels. There is nothing wrong with having 55 transmit channels and almost twice that many receive channels, but if you ever use more than six or eight, you will be unusual. The majority of channels are reserved for commercial applications and you are prohibited from using them anyway. You do want all the weather channels since they change as you move up and down the coast.

Most VHF radiotelephones draw about 6 amps during transmission. However, they are used only intermittently and usually for a short period of time. At one time marine radios placed a big demand on the batteries, but today the electrical system of almost any pocket cruiser should easily handle the demands of the VHF. If circumstances arise requiring the radio to be put to long-term continuous use, the considerable current drain should be kept in mind.

The depth sounder, the log, the RDF, and the VHF make up what we will call the basic cruising electronics.

> . . . I forsee that if my wants should be much increased the labor required to supply them would become a drudgery.

So do we. Still, if we can find a few extra bucks, some of the more "exotic" electronics offer capability and convenience not otherwise available.

SSB

Let us not immediately stray from the subject of marine radiotelephones. Everybody knows about ship-to-shore radio. With VHF limited to 50 miles, how is that accomplished? The answer is marine single sideband (SSB). Replacing double sideband in 1975, SSB is capable of long distance communications, commonly as far away as 6,000 miles. However, SSB is highly sensitive to atmospheric conditions. To use it successfully, you must pick the right band for the distance you want to communicate and transmit at the optimum time of the day. And there had better not be any electrical storms around either.

Once mastered, the SSB radiotelephone can be used quite successfully for long distance communications, if there is someone listening on the frequency you select. In many places there are commercial SSB operators, the so called high-seas operator, but the truth is that SSB is not very useful away from the United States or a few other highly industrialized countries, particularly in an emergency. The international call and distress frequency, 2182 kHz, has a maximum range of probably no more than 60 miles in the daylight hours although transmissions in the hours before dawn may reach 1,000 miles or more. (Have your emergencies at night?) This means that in remote areas you probably cannot reach home and no one nearby is likely to be listening.

HAM RADIO

Some cruisers either replace or augment the SSB unit with a Ham rig. Ham radio has become particularly popular with long distance cruisers; some estimate that 80% of this group now carry a Ham transceiver aboard. While technically not a marine radio, a mobile Ham rig works very well on a cruising vessel. To operate a Ham radio, you will need to have an amateur radio operators license, a challenge itself, but the number of cruising Hams attest to the fact that it is not prohibitively difficult. With a good transceiver and a bit of patience, the range of a Ham radio is unlimited. In addition, amateur networks operate daily at specified times on specified frequencies, assuring daily contacts, information about the next anchorage or port, and usually a willing relay for messages home. New equipment is not much larger than a VHF (a major change in recent years) and most boats will be able to handle the power requirements.

There are two risks to consider in putting a Ham rig aboard. First, despite the highly publicized assistance of ham radio operators in major disasters, it is not essentially an emergency radio. Someone is always monitoring VHF 16 or SSB 2.182 MHz and if you are in range, he will hear you. There may not be anyone listening on the frequency you select on the Ham rig. Even so, in remote areas it may still be your best bet. The second risk is that amateur radio is so addictive that you may decide to give up cruising to spend more time in the "shack." Even if you maintain your determination, you relinquish a degree of self-sufficiency or independence.

Perhaps I am more than usually jealous with respect to my freedom.

For us, it is a bit too much like having a telephone aboard. If you wish you could take the phone along with you, by all means take a close look at Ham radio.

AUTOPILOT

In our minds, there is no question that among the recent entries into the affordable marine electronics field, the electronic autopilot offers the most return on investment. We have yet to meet the autopilot owner who would willingly go back to pre-AP. Do not scoff and say, "But I *like* to steer." So do we, but not to excess.

The difference between weekend cruising and long-term cruising is duration, not just in the length of the cruise, but in the length of the passages. There is something very satisfying about the fatigue felt at a Saturday night anchorage after a boisterous, 30-mile sail. Plan any kind of offshore passage and the fatigue is not satisfying at all—it is just fatigue. No matter what kind of watch system you use, a couple on a passage splitting helm duties will each spend 12 hours of every 24 at the helm. Even if you are lucky enough that your shoulders do not tie up into searing knots, it is going to get boring.

Enter that wonder of modern electronics, the autopilot. It will do both tricks at the helm without the tiniest complaint. Freed from the tyranny of the helm, you will find yourself trimming sails, watching the bow wave, playing the stereo (stereo?), in short enjoying the sail, not just wishing it was over.

You may perceive windvane steering as an alternative to the electronic autopilot. It is not. Circumnavigators like windvane steering because it requires no electrical power. A rugged and dependable windvane can steer a boat on a 30-day passage as "naturally" as the sails power the boat. Some vanes have proven not to be all that rugged and, hanging out astern, they are very subject to damage. Some are not powerful enough to steer the boat in all conditions, and none will steer effectively downwind in light air (because of no apparent wind).

The autopilot, on the other hand, will steer in any conditions. We even use it to hold a course in the narrow confines of a channel, a practice that does not even merit consideration with a windvane. Once requiring a prohibitively large amount of electrical power, the newer autopilots use about 0.25 amps per hour, about 6 amps *per day*. Even many cruisers with a vane aboard have added an autopilot to the inventory for downwind or motoring. In many cases, the autopilot installation has been so successful that the vane has been abandoned altogether.

Unless you have an ocean crossing in mind, the sensible choice for self-steering is the electronic autopilot. It is versatile, compact, and about a third the price of a powerful vane. Even for an ocean crossing, you may want to follow the lead of the OSTAR racers who, in recent years, have all been using electronic autopilots.

LORAN

Traditionally, navigation aboard a small boat has been a highly respected skill. The tools of the navigator have been the compass and the chart for coastal piloting; the sextant, almanac, and appropriate tables for offshore work. We believe strongly that these skills and tools should still be aboard.

. . . he may have to steer his way home through the dark by the north star, and he will feel himself some degrees nearer to it for having lost his way on the earth.

However, on those nights when the north star is not visible, there are some new tools available to the navigator.

The most common electronic navigation aid is *Loran* (**LO**ng **R**ange **A**id to **N**avigation). Loran has been around a long time as the basic navigation system for commercial shipping, changing some years ago from Loran A to the current system, Loran C. Once little used on small sailboats because the receivers were bulky and difficult to use, and demanded significant electrical power, they have since become very popular. The latest generation of Loran receivers are little larger than an epic-length paperback book and may draw as little as 0.5 amps. With an educated press of a few buttons, the display provides the vessel's current latitude and longitude, a fix. It works day or night, in good weather or foul. It sounds perfect, doesn't it?

It isn't. Loran C is subject to a number of limitations. If the signal from any of the transmitters (the system uses three for each fix) passes over a land mass, the signal is slowed, distorting the accuracy of the fix. In bad weather, when you need it most, the radio waves are subject to atmospheric distortion. Background static, "noise", may prevent obtaining a fix. It is not unknown for a transmitter to fail; likewise the receiver. The biggest limitation, however, is that many parts of the world simply are not covered, or lie in fringe areas where the electronic fix will not be accurate. You need not go too far afield to find a fringe area. For example, Loran C is notoriously inaccurate in the Bahama Islands even though they lie only 50 miles offshore of Florida. Before you invest in Loran C, make sure that it will work where you plan to cruise.

SATNAV

SatNav (**SAT**ellite **NAV**igation) systems do not suffer from many of the limitations of Loran. SatNav is state-of-the-art electronic navigation. Based on a group of six satellites in near-polar orbits, the SatNav receiver, through electronic wizardry, can provide a fix every time a satellite passes overhead. Therein lies its one major limitation. Where Loran fixes are available continuously, it may be as long as five hours between fixes with SatNav. A fix every 90 minutes is probably average. Subject to few external influences, SatNav is accurate to within about 500 feet if the boat is motionless, within ½ mile if underway. The SatNav receiver is about the same size as a Loran unit and requires about the same amount of power.

A new generation of satellite navigation, called NAVSTAR GPS (Global Positioning System) is scheduled for full operation in this decade. It will provide those with a GPS receiver continuous electronic positioning with spectacular accuracy.

There is no reason to believe that you cannot cruise without these sophisticated aids to navigation. If you decide to put one of these "magic boxes" aboard, be sure you know how to navigate without it. If "it" is the only one aboard that knows where you are, you are playing a dangerous game. If the system fails for any reason, you are lost. The potential reasons for failure are numerous: a dead battery, alternator failure, engine failure, a short circuit, an electrical fire, failure of the receiver, failure of the transmitter, and others. Then there is every electronic sailor's nightmare, lightning. If you take a hit (trust us, it happens), how do the electronics fare?

They are puffballs filled with dust and ashes.

Sensible cruising does not necessarily mean getting there and back without electronic aids, but it does mean knowing how.

WIND INSTRUMENTS

Apparent-wind indicators were developed for yacht racing. They are of little relative value to the cruising sailor. A bit of yarn (or cassette tape) tied to the shrouds can be just as effective. Many cruising sailors find the masthead wind indicator, typified by the ubiquitous *Windex* windvane, useful and a good value.

The apparent-wind-speed indicator satisfies universal curiosity about wind speed and may be of some value in sail selection, but it is by no means required cruising gear. Experience will soon tell you if you have your boat over or under canvassed. If you feel the need to assign a number to the wind speed, you can buy a handheld unit for under ten dollars that is quite accurate and has only one moving part.

MAINTAINING PERSPECTIVE

Spend a little time with the marine equipment catalogs and you will see a number of other offerings. Radar is available in a portable version. Radar detectors have moved from the dashboard to the bridge, warning that you are within the radar sweep of another vessel. A sophisticated celestial calculator can work your sights for you

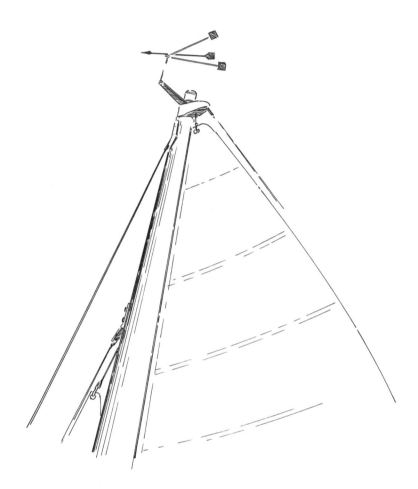

Masthead wind indicator. Useful for trimming sails, docking, or anchoring.

instantaneously without the need for tables or almanac. The handheld VHF is the latest effort to tempt you out of your cruising dollars. Resist. If you are serious in your wish to cruise, stick religiously to the basics. It is the surest, safest route through the shoals in your path.

We do not want to leave anyone with the impression that we see the inventory of electronics aboard as a continuum, with the sailor choosing the smallest inventory as "most sensible" and those loading the circuits as "least sensible." Those things absolutely required to satisfy your expectations from a cruise should be aboard. We would never again cruise without ample electric cabin lights; it would prevent us from doing many of the things we go cruising to do.

What we do see is a desire on the part of many for various pieces of electronic gear based on false perceptions of indispensability. Every item in this chapter is dispensable.

Shall we always study to obtain more of these things, and not sometimes to be content with less?

Weigh your selections carefully, particularly if your rich uncle of whom you are a favorite, is still hanging on. When he goes, you can buy all the other things you want—and have them shipped to you in St. Croix. For now, just put aboard what you need.

SOLITUDE

*There sits one by the shore who wishes to go with me, but
I cannot think of it. I must be fancy-free.*

E have already pointed out that most cruising is done by
couples. Why do we insert a chapter on sailing alone
at this point? Is it that we share Mr. Thoreau's penchant
for solitude; that we advocate single-handing? Yes.
And no.

Solitude is an integral part of cruising. There is no escaping this fact. We challenge any reader to find a single cruising narrative that does not at some point speak with reverence about solitude. Whether it is introspection on an uneventful dogwatch with the compass light as the only earthly reference or simply the delight in the absolute silence of a private anchorage, solitude is something that all cruisers experience. It is one of the things that cruising is about.

The cruising lifestyle is also about conviviality. We can promise you that on a cruise you will soon make new friends that will be friends for the rest of your life. Common interests, concerns, and perceptions of life will provide the basis for far closer relationships than was ever possible with your shoreside neighbors, those who thought your talk of cruising an indication of maladjustment.

> *I see that my neighbors look with compassion on me, that they think it is a mean and unfortunate destiny which makes me to . . . sail on this river alone.*

You will entertain and be entertained. You will join other cruisers for impromptu beach parties. You will likely fall in company with other boats, perhaps cruising together, certainly looking forward to meeting again at the next anchorage or the one after that. You will share books, recipes, information, and time. You will be a member of the community.

Few of us will have any serious concerns about the social side of cruising. As a member of "society", most of us have fairly well-developed social skills. In fact, we often reach a point of social saturation.

> *I feel the necessity of deepening the stream of my life; I must cultivate privacy. It is very dissipating to be with people too much. As C. says, it takes the edge off a man's thoughts to have been much in society.*

The concept of sailing "away from it all" periodically appeals to almost everyone. Solitude and the attending silence is a soothing change, like a warm bath to overworked muscles. Solitude is one of the reasons we choose to cruise.

It is also one of the reasons we do not. We can imagine any number of potential situations where the prospect of being alone fills us with apprehension. This anxiety is the primary reason that the overwhelming majority of cruisers take aboard a radio transmitter, often more than one. There is a fear of facing whatever comes alone.

SOLITUDE

It is a natural fear. We prefer to stay to the beaten path. No matter how deep in the woods, if we have a path to follow, we do not feel lost. It must lead somewhere. Cruising provides no paths. If 1,000 boats make the trip from Long Beach to Catalina on Sunday and you sail alone on Monday, there is no evidence of their passing, no path to follow. Because of the trackless nature of water, the solitude found in the ocean is probably the most complete to be found.

SELF-DEPENDENCY

Our purpose in this chapter is to attempt to resolve the dichotomy of solitude. It cannot both attract you and repel you. The attraction is real, the fear only imagined. Overcoming anxiety at the potential for facing a stressful situation completely alone depends upon your ability to develop a sense of self-dependency. We will examine both mental and physical preparation.

The need for self-dependency is not limited to the single-hand cruiser. It applies just as well to the cruising couple or family. If you doubt that, consider the following. What happens to the cruising couple if one falls overboard? Both are instantly alone, each with his or her distinct responsibilities, the competent performance of which will avert a disaster.

You are both too cautious to fall overboard? How about one ashore with the dinghy, the other aboard alone? Okay so far? An afternoon thunderstorm brings 50 knots of wind and the boat suddenly swings beam to the wind and stays there. Does the person aboard know what to do?

One more. The boat is close reaching in a moderate breeze. There are four aboard, but only one on watch. There is a tap and a splash as something falls to the deck and bounces overboard. Almost immediately, both windward lower shrouds collapse to the deck. This is no time for a committee decision.

A man thinking or working is always alone.

Dealing with these and other situations like them is what self-dependency is all about. There is no one around to give directions, no one to even ask an opinion, no one to provide physical assistance. You will be alone—the moment either saved or lost solely on your decision and action. And preparation.

PREPARATION

Preparation is a key ingredient. Mental preparation is the most difficult. The competent pilot of a small airplane plays a very serious game as he flies. He is frequently scanning the terrain, anticipating where he might be able to land the plane should it become unexpectedly necessary. Normally neither the same immediacy nor seriousness of consequence applies to a sailboat, but we can still learn from the pilot's discipline.

As we sail along, spending a bit of time thinking "what if" can go a long way toward enhancing our self confidence.

The imagination requires a long range.

Such thinking becomes even more critical in tight spots or adverse weather. If you have already mentally imagined the failure of a windward shroud and selected your course of action, should it actually occur you will react automatically. It may mean the difference between no damage done and losing the entire rig over the side.

Actually, the "what if" game should start long before you set sail. It should start with the preparation of your boat for cruising. Every imaginable situation should be considered and a course of action decided upon. If you have modest sailing experience, draw on the experience of others through reading (see "Former Inhabitants; and Winter Visitors"). Both the potential problem and a (not necessarily *the*) workable solution will normally be included in a cruising narrative. Much can be learned from those who have been there before you.

First of all a man must see, before he can say.

We see mental and physical preparation as inextricably linked. Good mental preparation will lead to competent physical preparation. Being physically prepared reinforces the sense of well being and improves the mental preparation.

What exactly do we mean by physical preparation? Are we talking about lifting weights or doing aerobics? Not a bad idea, but no. We are talking about preparing the boat to be handled by one person. We have already demonstrated in this chapter that even though there may be two or more aboard, many situations may arise requiring an immediate and solitary response.

SINGLE-HANDING

Of course, the ultimate in self-dependency is single-handing. One of the appeals of cruising is that it places the participant more in charge of his or her own life than most other lifestyles. Here, single-handing excels.

> . . . *the man who goes alone can start today; but he who travels with another must wait till that other is ready, and it may be a long time before they get off.*

There is never a need to consult with anyone about preferred destination, to run from a gale when you would prefer to face it (or vice versa), or to take aboard corned beef if you hate it.

Do we advocate single-handed cruising? No. There are, in our opinion, a number of serious risks in cruising single-handed. The most obvious is the inability to keep a proper watch. A sailboat is a very large machine with inherent risks of personal injury to the operator. Any kind of debilitating health problem for the solo sailor can quickly escalate into tragedy. Simply falling overboard underway is almost certain to be fatal.

We also feel that the pleasures of cruising are immeasurably improved by sharing them. That is our reason for writing this book. The last lines of a Haiku poem by Taigi best expresses our feeling: "'Look!' I almost said,—But I was alone."

Nevertheless, we recognize that everyone is not of the same temperament. We are also aware of a number of single-handers out there crossing the world's oceans. They are aware of the risks, and since the risks are primarily to themselves, we are not nay-sayers about single-handing either.

What we do advocate is single-handed *sailing*. Semantics? Not at all. We think that even on a boat cruised by a couple, both should be able to handle the boat competently. Aside from being prepared to deal with an emergency, the ability of both to single-hand the boat will allow the person off watch to be completely off, and it will yield a tremendous sense of satisfaction to the person handling the boat. The best way to assure oneself of that ability is to single-hand, even with others aboard. That means handling everything yourself from anchor up to anchor down and everything in between. Such an exercise is a great confidence builder, for all members of the crew.

Sailing a large boat (as compared to a dinghy) competently in varying conditions is at the very least a satisfying experience. It may be exhilarating to go one-on-one with nature. A feeling better experienced than described, it is one of the reasons some choose to cruise alone.

There are a number of other reasons. Richard Henderson in his excellent book *Singlehanded Sailing* cites ten reasons why some choose to sail alone: practical reasons (money, for example), self-significance, curiosity, recognition, independence, escapism, adventurousness, competitiveness, solitude, and a factor he calls the "mother sea" (an affinity with the ocean). There is little doubt that those who choose to cruise alone do so for more than one of these reasons.

> *My interest in the sun and the moon, in the morning and the evening, compels me to solitude.*

Even those of us not so compelled can profit from examining the preparation of a boat for single-handed cruising. It seems obvious that enhancements to a boat that facilitate its management in all conditions by one person will likewise simplify the handling of the boat by two or more.

SELF-STEERING

We have already selected a boat of a size that lends itself to being sailed alone. There are considerations other than size. For most of the history of small-boat cruising, the single most important characteristic of a single-hander's boat has been *balance*. Old Joshua Slocum sang the praises of *Spray* based upon her ability to hold a course for extended periods without attention to the helm. Others copied her lines in hopes of having a vessel with that ability.

Later single-handers discovered that self-steering could be vastly improved by connecting the headsail sheet with the tiller. When the vessel paid off, the sail would harden, pulling the tiller to leeward and bringing the boat back up to its course. If the sail luffed, the sheet would lose tension allowing the shock cord tied to the tiller from the windward side to put the helm down. By today's standards, sheet-to-tiller self-steering seems rather crude, but it works. With practice, a reasonably well-balanced boat can be made to self-steer on every point of sail. Surgical tubing (spear gun rubber) works better than shock cord.

Those boats easiest to balance usually had a split rig (schooner, ketch, or yawl) and a long straight keel, neither frequently found among today's pocket cruisers. The small cruisers of today are most often sloop rigged. A look at the underbodies soon reveals that the long keel with an attached rudder has fallen from favor with most naval architects. You are much more likely to encounter a short keel and a separate rudder. Directional stability has given way to minimizing wetted area. This is not necessarily a change for the worse. All other things being equal, the short-keeled boat will be faster, probably handier too, but it will be difficult to coax into self-steering.

Those involved in the elite sport of racing across oceans single-handedly found themselves facing a problem. They needed directional stability to be able to sail the boat effectively. They also needed the speed promised by the modern designs. Their solution to this problem was the development of *windvane steering systems*. In a short period of time, systems were developed with ample strength to overcome poor balance. Solo cruisers were quick to see the advantage of such a mechanical crew member, one that would do long tricks at the helm without requiring sustenance or infringing upon the single-hander's "space."

I never found the companion that was so companionable as solitude.

Nor did they, Mr. Thoreau—until now.

It did not take cruising couples and families long to recognize the vane's potential either. Windvanes were, for a time, epidemic among the cruising community. A framework of tubing hanging off the stern with a vane on top rocking back and forth soon became the badge of the long distance cruising boat.

Despite the endurance and vigilance of this new crew member, it is not very bright. There have been cases of the vane sailing the boat right up on the beach in broad daylight. The vane's charter called for maintaining the boat on a constant heading, *relative to the direction of the wind,* and that is exactly what it did—right up until the instant the boat struck. It is a rude way for the skipper to become aware of a wind shift.

Many coastal cruisers also opted to install windvane steering. However, since the direction of the wind along a coast is rarely constant, and coastal navigation is more often concerned with *compass* headings, the vane was not extremely useful.

Coastal sailors envied the directional *autopilots* already in broad use on large power yachts, but the electrical demand of a typical autopilot was beyond the capacity of most small sailboats. Advances in the field of electronics led to the development of autopilots designed specifically for sail. Compact and energy efficient, there are now a number of autopilots on the market at affordable prices, with exceptional records of dependability.

We are convinced that self-steering is the most satisfying enhancement the single-handed (or short-handed) cruiser can make. If you simply cannot afford anything beyond a length of surgical tubing, then put that aboard and learn to use it to make the vessel self-steer.

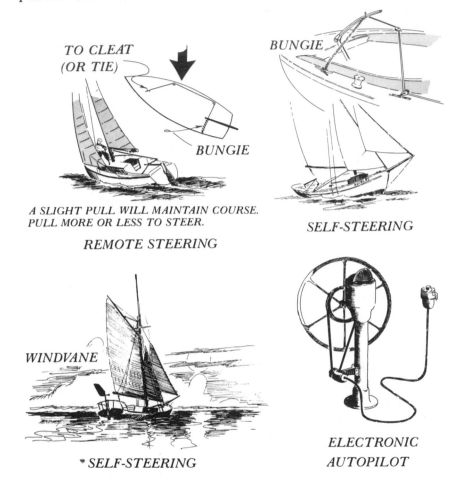

TO CLEAT (OR TIE)

BUNGIE

BUNGIE

A SLIGHT PULL WILL MAINTAIN COURSE. PULL MORE OR LESS TO STEER.

REMOTE STEERING

SELF-STEERING

WINDVANE

SELF-STEERING

ELECTRONIC AUTOPILOT

Self-steering and remote steering can be accomplished a number of ways.

The windvane may appeal to those trying to hold power consumption to a minimum, but for coastal cruising with no long offshore passages, the vane gear is not a good choice. If you can afford it, we recommend without hesitation the electronic autopilot. The reason we select it over the vane gear is that it is more versatile, as we have already indicated in the previous chapter, and being less expensive, it is a better value. We think the autopilot is the sensible selection.

COCKPIT CONTROLS

After self-steering, the single-hander looks at enhancements that will minimize his exposure to the risk of going overboard.

For an impenetrable shield, stand inside yourself.

And stand yourself inside the cockpit, sailing the boat as much as possible from that security.

In a previous chapter we mentioned roller furling which allows hoisting and furling the sail without going forward. Hank-on headsails may also be handled from the cockpit. The key is to lead the jib halyard aft. Once the sail is hanked on and ready to hoist, the single-hander can return to the security of the cockpit for the actual hoisting. When it is time to drop the sail, a trip forward is unnecessary; the halyard is simply released. A downhaul rigged and also led aft will assure that the sail will come down.

A further enhancement to this system is lifeline netting on either side of the foredeck. This will keep the dropped sail from slithering over the side, and it might do the same for the sailor.

Handling the main can likewise be simplified by leading the main halyard into the cockpit. Hoisting away, then dashing for the helm is as risky as it looks. Aside from providing the single-hander with the safety of the cockpit during the hoisting process, an aft-led halyard also places him in a convenient position for handling the helm and the sheet. Dropping the main is also simplified, and if the slides are kept lubricated and the boat headed up, the sail should come down without assistance.

JIFFY FURLING

Once down, both sails must be controlled. This is one of the advantages of a roller-furling headsail: when rolled, it requires no further attention. The best way to store the hanked-on headsail is with a "teardrop" headsail cover. The sail remains attached to the stay and is stuffed clew first into the cover. The cover closes around the stay, either with lacing or a synthetic zipper.

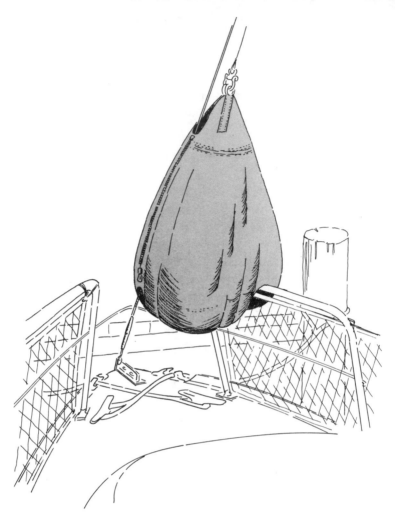

"Teardrop" headsail cover stows the jib off the deck, provides a shield from the sun, and the jib is hanked on ready for use.

The quickest and easiest method we have encountered for controlling the mainsail is with a permanently rigged shock cord on one side of the boom. Attached to eyes forward and aft and passing through three or four guides, the cord is grasped between guides and stretched over the furled sail to hooks attached to the other side of the boom. This system is not appropriate for a boat with roller reefing, but then roller reefing is not likely to be a single-hander's choice.

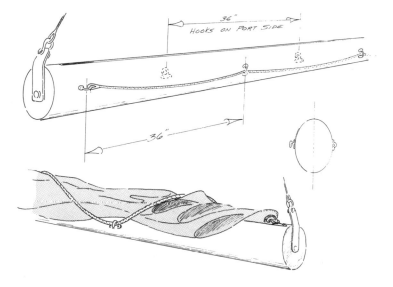

Mainsail jiffy furling uses shock cord mounted to one side of boom with hooks on the other side.

STERN ANCHOR

Many single-handers anticipate a time when the ability to get an anchor over the side instantly may be of paramount importance. The easiest way to resolve this concern is with a stern anchor. Mounted at the stern rail, it must be ready for immediate use. That means the rode is attached and ready to run at all times and the anchor is secured in such a way that it can be instantly released.

The usual stern anchor is the lightweight, either the Danforth or the similar but much lighter aluminum Viking anchor. Besides being light, both stow flat (on the lazarette or against the stern rail) and have exceptional holding power. Good for kedging or anchoring by the stern, they are not the choice for an emergency anchor. The situation requiring such immediate action may mean the boat still has way on. Even at less than two knots, the lightweight anchor may plane, never even reaching the bottom. The CQR or the Bruce, mounted on a stern roller, is a better choice for an emergency anchor.

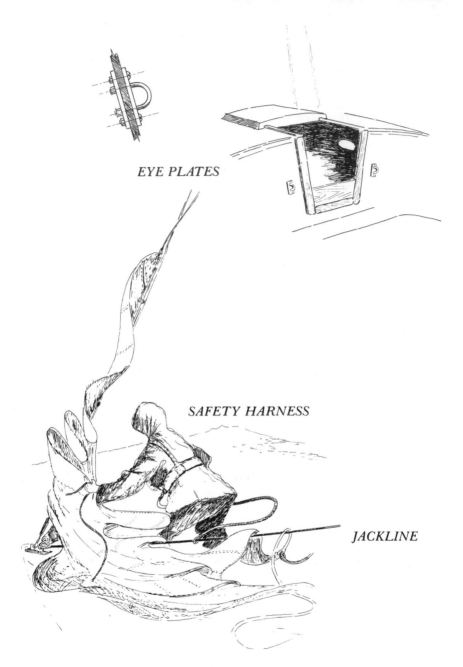

EYE PLATES

SAFETY HARNESS

JACKLINE

Eye plates provide exceptionally good connection points and permit hookup of the safety harness from the cabin before going on deck. Jacklines provide an effective attachment for going forward on deck.

SAFETY HARNESS

The greatest and most constant risk to the lone sailor is becoming separated from the boat. The surest way of avoiding that risk is to attach oneself to the boat. The single-handing sailor should wear a safety harness at all times, certainly at night and in boisterous conditions. It is your life, so you will have to make the decision. We like eye plates securely mounted (through-bolted to a back-up plate) near the companionway so we can hook up before even coming on deck.

You should select the strongest harness available and the lead should have two spring-loaded carbine hooks spliced in, one at about four feet, a second at about seven feet. You should try to stay attached with the short lead so that you cannot go over the side. Even attached, getting back aboard could be nearly impossible. The reason for two hooks is so that you are never unattached even when you are changing attachment points. We select carbine hooks like those used in mountain climbing because failure or unexpected release can have similar consequences in both activities. You would not hang from a 3,000-foot cliff with a brass snap hook. Do not trust one with your life on board either.

JACKLINES

Obviously situations will occur that will require the single-hander to leave the relative safety of the cockpit. We discuss lifelines in a later chapter, but the single-hander requires greater security than lifelines provide. For going forward, a jackline should be rigged. Nothing more than a strong cable stretched tightly between the cockpit and the foredeck, it allows the single-hander the freedom to go forward and at all times remain attached to the boat. Plastic-coated wire makes the best jackline, shackled in place so that it may be removed in port. Rigging dual jacklines, one on either side of the mast, allows going forward on the weather deck on either tack.

LINE ORDER

Order is imperative aboard the short-handed boat. Special equipment is of little value unless it can be located when required. There is also a safety hazard with anything lying on deck or in the cockpit sole. Sheets are especially troublesome. If you do not want to end up like Captain Ahab, consider a couple of canvas bags screwed in place in the cockpit. Excess sheet is stuffed into the bag, safely out of the way. Do not forget to put drain holes in the bags.

Halyards could be similarly stored, particularly those which lead to the cockpit. However, a tangled halyard can be a real problem when

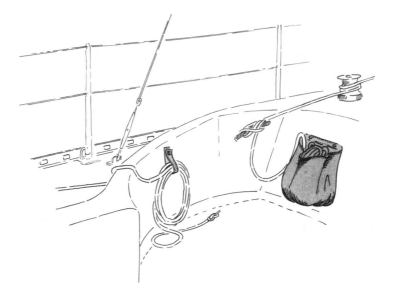

Line order in the cockpit will be improved with canvas bags and hang straps.

trying to get a sail down in a hurry. Halyards are better coiled, and a hanging strap with a snap will keep them in place and in order.

GOING ALOFT

If going aloft can wait, it is always safer at the dock (or at anchor) where help may be enlisted. If the situation arises when you must go aloft alone, you will appreciate mast steps. Be sure you are also attached with a safety line. You may also hoist *yourself* with the aid of a four-part vang reeved with a very long line (four times the height of the mast). One fiddle block is connected to the halyard and hoisted to the masthead, the other block (with the cam cleat) attached to the boatswain's chair. A pull of about one-fourth of your weight will hoist you. Do not trust your safety to the cam cleat and be sure that you have a safety line attached at all times.

Mast steps, or alternatively ratlines, are also useful for extending the visible horizon and for improving the visibility into the water when navigating through shoals or reefs.

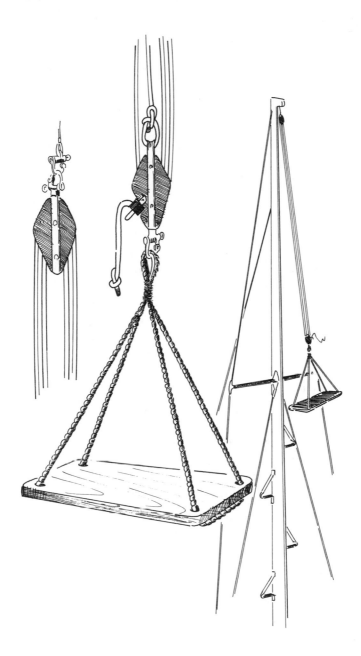

A multi-part vang with long line can be rigged to hoist yourself aloft. Mast steps to the spreader shorten the hoisting distance.

121

BILGE ALARM

Silence is audible to all men, at all times, and in all places. She is when we hear inwardly, sound when we hear outwardly.

Even while listening to that inner self, there are some sounds that we want to be able to hear. One of them is the bilge pump running. It is not that we want the bilge pump to run; it is that we definitely want to *know* it if it does. For one thing, the pump may be trying to drain the battery. Even more importantly, the boat may be trying to drain the ocean. A failed through-hull, a burst hose, even a hole in the exhaust system will be quickly detected if we are aware that the pump is running.

Even if you cannot miss the pump, a high water *bilge alarm* is good insurance. At the very least, it is disheartening to step below to a cabin sole awash in bilge water because the pump clogged, the battery died, or the float switch stuck. This likelihood is increased on a single-handed (or short-handed) boat because no one may go below for many hours. The bilge alarm is a simple device and should have its own battery for obvious reasons.

KEEPING WATCH

On the single-handed cruiser, there is also a dangerous shortage of time spent on deck, keeping watch. The international regulations, COLREGS, require (Rule 6) that "every vessel shall at all times maintain a proper lookout, by sight and hearing as well as by all means appropriate in the prevailing circumstances and conditions so as to make a full appraisal of the situation and of the risk of collision."

It would not be difficult to conclude that on a boat with only one person aboard, sleep is illegal. However, the greatest risk for such civil disobedience is to the offending single-hander, so we stated at the outset that we would not take exception. It is well documented that much commercial shipping ranges the oceans without a vigilant lookout, sometimes without radar or even running lights. We are not sure of the point, except to show the difference in consequence of breaking Rule 6.

Single-handers take different approaches to the sleep problem. Some sleep in the daytime, putting trust in being visible to other shipping. Others sleep for only short periods, using a timer or an alarm to awaken themselves every hour—more often where shipping is likely to be encountered. Some turn on a masthead strobe (also illegal for this purpose) and sleep through the night. No matter how they break it down, there are periods of time every day when no watch is being kept. This situation is avoided when two or more are aboard.

Recently, some single-handers have been made aware of shipping in the area through the use of a radar detector. Described in the previous chapter, this unit can keep watch around the clock, but only "sees" vessels with operating radar.

A VHF scanner might also be used similarly to detect nearby VHF transmissions, but its usefulness in collision avoidance seems minimal. Away from the coast, any VHF transmission you might pick up would likely be directed at you, meaning that the calling vessel is already aware of your existence. It will also come in on channel 16, so leaving a standard VHF on stand-by is probably just as effective.

CABIN BULKHEAD

Another way to improve watch keeping is to minimize the number of trips that need to be made below. This will also improve dispositions. Anything that you use frequently should be close at hand. The cabin bulkhead on either side of the companionway should have an array of racks. Binoculars should always be within easy reach, as should the hand-bearing compass. For daylight sailing, you should be able to grab your polarized sunglasses without leaving the cockpit. At night, a flashlight or two should be reachable automatically.

How many times have we said, "While you are below, hand me a paper towel"? If you wear glasses, you know what we mean. When you are the only one who goes below, there is no one to ask. A sensible solution is to also have the paper towel rack near the companionway where it can be reached without going below. Another tip for glasses wearers: keep a spray bottle filled with fresh water in the cockpit to periodically remove the dried salt.

THERMOS

During a chilly night sail, we look forward to the change of watch and a few minutes of subdued conversation before going below to a warm bunk.

The man I meet with is not often so instructive as the silence he breaks.

Spoken like a true single-hander. For the cruising couple, the change

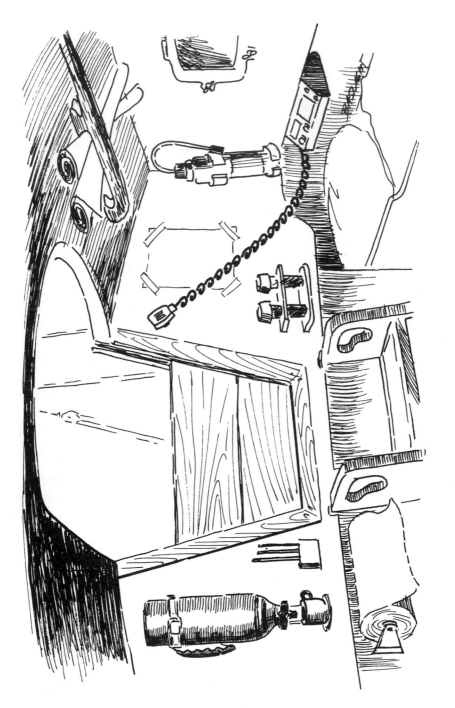

Reduce the need for going below while sailing by mounting often-used items within reach from the cockpit.

in watch marks the passage of the night. For the single-hander, punctuation may be an occasional warm cup of coffee or tea. A securely mounted thermos belongs on the bulkhead. The one pictured is all stainless and was obtained with a spigot and cup holder for mounting as shown. The pump-type is even more efficient, yielding water too hot to touch more than 24 hours after it was put in the thermos.

GIMBALED BURNER

Meal preparation is also a bit of a challenge. For the long distance solo sailor, a double-gimbaled burner may make the difference between cold meals and hot ones. While it will handle only one pot, it requires no attention. A can of soup or stew can be heated and watch maintained at the same time.

Gimbaled burner permits one-dish meals, soups, coffee, etc. while underway.

SOLITUDE

There are undoubtedly hundreds of small enhancements that can make a boat easier, safer, and more comfortable for sailing by one person. Many will apply as well to any short-handed cruiser. Careful preparation can relieve much of the apprehension of being in charge of your own destiny—you alone. Solitude should not represent a threat. It is a relative term anyway.

> *How far apart, think you, dwell the two most distant inhabitants of yonder star, the breadth of whose disk cannot be appreciated by our instruments? . . . What sort of space is that which separates a man from his fellows and makes him solitary? I have found that no exertion of the legs can bring two minds much nearer to one another.*

Those who do not dream of cruising cannot appreciate your dream. If you feel a greater kinship with those cruising than with your co-workers, you already know about solitude, at least its negative side.

In contrast, the solitude that we encounter while cruising is almost always a positive thing. There are the revelations of introspection, the salve of deep silence, and the satisfaction of self-dependency. Just the opportunity to be alone is something we all need occasionally. In an increasingly crowded world, solitude is becoming more difficult to find.

> *I would rather sit on a pumpkin and have it all to myself than be crowded on a velvet cushion.*

We echo Mr. Thoreau's distaste for the crowded velvet cushion, but we are rather inclined to share the pumpkin.

VISITORS

I suspect that the child plucks its first flower with an insight into its beauty and significance which the subsequent botanist never retains.

HE pleasures of cruising are many. Sunsets seen from the dock are never quite as vivid, meals eaten ashore never quite as tasty, books read in bed never quite as meaning-ful as those experienced aboard. A pod of bottle-nose dolphins diving and weaving and leaping through the bow wave excites even the crustiest old salt. With two aboard, there is twice the excitement. With three, it triples.

Herein lies one of the attractions of having visitors aboard. They invariably bring aboard an excitement, a sense of wonder at aspects of cruising that, though we daily experience, we no longer notice. It makes us notice them again, gives us a renewed appreciation for what we are doing. In the previous chapter, we talked about solitude. This is a chapter on sharing.

WHY?

The special pleasures of cruising are multiplied by the addition of guests. For us, the time spent cruising with visitors aboard is often our highest quality cruising time. Lest we start to sound too goody-goody here, we want to hasten to point out that with three aboard, the bad times are also three times as bad. You will not have to ask far in the cruising community to learn that guests aboard can also be a disaster. On balance, the experience of visitors aboard is a good one.

Inviting visitors to join in your adventure is a unique gift, one you may not always be able to give. Motivations may be altruistic.

> *Again, as so many times, I [am] reminded of the advantage to the poet, and philosopher, and naturalist, and whomsoever, of pursuing from time to time some other business than his chosen one—seeing with the side of the eye.*

Even a glimpse of the cruising life provides a certain change in perspective. Good or bad, it is an experience that your visitors will come to treasure.

SELECTION

There is a misconception among novice cruisers that having visitors aboard is much like having house guests. It is not. If you want to simulate cruising guests, the next time you have house guests have them stay in your bedroom with you. You will quickly realize why cruising sailors do not extend guest invitations indiscriminately.

> *Those whom we can love, we can hate; to others we are indifferent.*

Like every other aspect of a successful cruise, cruising with guests requires careful consideration, planning, and preparation.

When we talk of guests, we do not mean crew. The crew member comes aboard aware that he or she will have certain responsibilities for the safe operation of the boat. The guest is a visitor with no responsibilities other than enjoying himself without endangering the vessel or crew. Clearly, both guest and crew need to know how to operate the head so as not to flood the boat, but the guest need not know a sheet from a halyard. Of course, guests often are either sailors or wish to be, and may want to participate in the operation of the boat. There is no reason why they should not, but the wise skipper will keep in mind that a person invited as a guest is still a guest: cranking in the genoa is a pleasure, not a responsibility.

By visitors, we mean friends and family joining the cruise along the way, usually for at least a week, often longer. The appeal of friends meeting us along the way is universal, both to cruisers and to their fortunate friends. But there is no guarantee that the experience will be a pleasant one. Most friendships can survive a miserable weekend cruise, but on a longer cruise, the implications on friendships are far more serious.

The cruiser may have made numerous compromises to accommodate the guests' availability and the guest may have expended a considerable sum of money for airfare and wasted his annual vacation on an activity that sounded far better than what was actually delivered. Too often, the host is guilty of embellishment, the guest of wearing blinders.

COMPATIBILITY

To many, the term "cruise" evokes a picture of an ocean liner, or at least a 100-foot yacht with uniformed crew. There is no question that most of your friends would find a cruise aboard the QE II enjoyable. That is not to say that the pocket cruiser cannot be accommodating.

> It is surprising how many great men and women a small house will contain.

The key to a successful cruise with visitors is *compatibility*, both with the environment and with the hosts. Imagine yourself in a very confined space for two weeks with your potential guests. Can you take them for that long? Just as important, are they aware of the restrictions and can they take you? Little things that are nothing more than an annoyance when you spend a day with your friends can become insufferable in two weeks.

As an example, we have some very close friends, another couple, with whom we spend a lot of time ashore. One half of the twosome is a non-stop talker and on a day together in the bay would probably hear about it from the other three of us. We can enjoy the day in the bay, we even look forward to it, but we do not extend an invitation to this couple to join us during a cruise. Quiet time, time to contemplate, to reflect, simply to enjoy the beauty of nature is important to us, and we know that the welcome for our friend would soon wear thin. We value the friendship too highly to risk it on a well-intentioned cruise.

> *For my own part, I am thankful that there are those who come so near being my friends that they can be estranged from me.*

The best test of compatibility is an earlier cruise together. Arranging a weekend sail with those you are considering as cruise guests, before or during the preparation stage of your cruise, will provide a better basis for the final decision on extending an invitation. Similarly, the prospective guests have an opportunity to experience the realities of cruising. Maybe the lack of privacy, the absence of air conditioning, and the shortage of water had not occurred to them before. No matter how much we love it, accommodations on a 30-foot sailboat will not compare favorably with a first-class hotel.

MATCH-MAKING

If a prior cruise is not possible, then you will have to trust your own judgement, and a bit of luck. You can improve the odds with your approach. Try to match the rendezvous location with the temperament of your guests. For example, if your friends are sailors, you may invite them to join you when you are in the process of moving the boat from one cruising area to another. Perhaps they will fly to your location and for the next two weeks actively participate in moving the boat. Limiting the distance covered will provide ample opportunity for sailing and visiting numerous new places and for the more sedentary pleasures of cruising.

> *Behind every man's busy-ness there should be a level of undisturbed serenity and industry, as within the reef encircling a coral isle there is always an expanse of still water . . .*

When the guests are non-sailors, you should consider staying in one cruising area. Your guests' arrival and departure will be simplified.

VISITORS

You will be able to sail every day if that is what your guests enjoy, or to never sail at all if you discover early in the visit that they do not find sailing an enjoyable experience. It is not unusual to have friends who will thoroughly enjoy being on or near the water, especially certain aspects of it such as diving or beachcombing, and yet for either biological reasons or personal preference not enjoy sailing. By bringing non-sailing guests into a well-protected sailing area you are able to accommodate such a turn of events.

Do not shy away from non-sailing guests. The people we enjoy sailing with the most and who join us for some time on almost every cruise never set foot on a sailboat otherwise. Yet invariably they provide some of the best times of the cruise.

Try also to consider your potential guests' likes and dislikes. Those with a bent toward tourism and shopping should be scheduled for a visit in an area that can accommodate those preferences. Guests who want to get away from it all, who want to try their luck with a hook or spear, should join the cruise in a more remote area.

ARRANGEMENT MAKING

Making the arrangements can sometimes be so difficult that it may sour you on ever having guests join you again. The degree of difficulty will depend upon where you are trying to make arrangements from. Do as much as you can before you ever leave your home mooring. Besides, your guests likely have shore-side responsibilities and will need to schedule time off well in advance, or at least plan their work schedule around their visit.

Before you leave, be sure your guests recognize that such things as poor weather or equipment failure may delay or cancel the cruise altogether. To avoid any misunderstandings, all parties to the cruise should understand well in advance the potential for the tenuous thread of a cruise to be broken. It is nothing short of foolhardy to say as you are pulling away from the dock, "Meet us in Tahiti on May 15; we will be there." Much more sensible is, "Plan on May 15; we will call you when we arrive." Even more sensible, "Collect."

Also establish the parameters of your invitation. It is usually not a good idea to invite visitors to "stay as long as you wish."

> *Objects of charity are not guests. Men who did not know when their visit had terminated, though I went about my business again, answering them from greater and greater remoteness.*

131

Sounds like leaving them on the beach. It is better to clarify early the stipulations of the invitation.

GUEST PREPARATION

As the host, it is your responsibility to try to insure that your guests enjoy themselves. Just like yours, the success of their cruise begins with preparation. Those without any previous experience will need your guidance. It is an excellent idea to provide future guests with *written* instructions and guidance. A rigid suitcase and a pocket cruiser are simply incompatible, but your guests may not know that unless you tell them. It is also helpful to give the guest a good idea of what ought to be in the bag. For warm weather cruising, most guests' preference, clothing is not a problem. Still, all guests should be encouraged to bring some clothing to protect themselves from the damaging rays of the midday sun. Point out the need for long pants and at least one long-sleeved shirt, a hat, sunglasses, sunscreen, etc. If the nights are cool, or if cool weather may be encountered, guests should be advised to bring sweaters, jackets, or whatever is appropriate.

The Guest Log is an invaluable and interesting reference.

If either you or your guest is anticipating spending time fishing or diving, information regarding the equipment on board will be very helpful. Most cruising boats accumulate an array of fishing equipment. If you have light tackle aboard but are not really set up to do trolling, let your guest know. If his heart is set on trolling, he can bring his own gear.

If you plan to have guests, you should have a couple of extra, inexpensive masks, snorkels, and pairs of fins among your diving equipment. A serious diver will bring his own equipment, but many have never had the opportunity to dive and do not know if they would like it. They may not buy equipment to bring, but if the equipment is aboard most can be coaxed into using it. This is an area where sharing is at its best. In tropical waters there is no better way to spend a day than floating over a living reef. Your keel passes over incredible beauty that you never experience unless you dive.

> *... I am affected as if in a peculiar sense I stood in the laboratory of the Artist who made the world and me ...*

Introducing a guest to the world beneath the surface is one of the great pleasures of cruising. The "child plucks its first flower."

Required adaptations for a cruising vacation should be outlined. Cover the realities of 12-volt power as well as the general absence of 110-volt power. There is little point in bringing an electric razor or hot curlers. If water will be scarce or expensive, brief the guest on how much is aboard and how it is conserved. Ashore, everyone leaves the faucet running while brushing his teeth. Your guests will not know better unless you tell them. If your water delivery system is manual (hand or foot pumps), water wastage by guests will be much less of a problem.

The difficulty of dealing with laundry may merit mention. You should also give your guests instructions regarding towels and linens; are there ample aboard or should they bring their own?

Away from the United States, communications may be a problem. If communications with "home" will be difficult or impossible, be sure your guest knows that well in advance.

> *To speak critically, I never received more than one or two letters in my life ... that were worth the postage.*

Presumably Mr. Thoreau would have felt the same way about the telephone, had it been around. Parents away from their children will not concur.

If the port is foreign, advise your guests of Customs and Immigration requirements. If you have not already arrived at the rendezvous point, how can they contact you if an emergency delays (or aborts) their arrival? Where will the boat be? How do they get there? What happens if they arrive and you are not there?

Your guests will appreciate any information you can provide on expenses. Their largest expense will probably be getting to where you are. Airfare is usually involved and guests can obtain that information for themselves. Ground transportation (or, in some cases, water transportation) may be necessary at your end and if you can forewarn the guest of the approximate cost it will ease some of the anxiety.

As guests, our friends are not expected to buy groceries. We stock the boat sufficiently to accommodate company. Ours is not a universal approach. Many cruisers do ask their guests to defray the additional food expenses. This is perfectly acceptable as long as the guest understands your expectations from the beginning.

Even when you do not ask, guests often want to assist. A two-week cruise with free accommodations and meals furnished may be one of the least expensive vacations that your guests have experienced. They are both able and insistent that they contribute to the operation of the boat. In this case, we have "allowed" our guests to bring as many "goodies" as they would like, things like nuts, packaged meats (salami, pepperoni, etc.), cheeses, chips, dips, pickles, candies, and anything that we crave but find unavailable where we are. When your guest arrives with a small duffel packed with items that you considered too luxurious to put aboard, it will enhance not only your pleasure, but theirs as well.

Make your guests aware of the spending opportunities available to them in the particular area where they will be joining you. In a larger port, they may wish to buy souvenirs or gift items, eat at restaurants, visit tourist attractions, rent a car, or try their luck at the local casino. In more remote areas, the spending opportunities may be very limited indeed. In either case, guests with prior knowledge of what is likely to be available can better plan their actual expenses. They should not be surprised when they total the cost of their vacation.

Finally, cover in advance your anticipated itinerary, how much or little sailing you may do, and where you are likely to visit. Clarify that all is dependent upon weather, the condition of the boat, and the desires of everyone aboard as the cruise progresses.

HOST PREPARATION

Your own preparation is as important as theirs. Clean the boat thoroughly to ensure that everything is neat when your guests arrive. The larger the group aboard, the more important neatness becomes. Set the example. Launder towels and linens so that sufficient are available to accommodate the duration of the cruise. In fact, do all the laundry. The romance of the cruise will be tarnished for your guests if the interior of the boat has an odor reminiscent of the bottom of the clothes hamper. Top up water tanks; fuel tanks also if necessary. It is amazing what an undisciplined dinghy can collect; clean it out. If fresh foods are available, put some aboard.

Do some mental preparation as well. For the duration of the visit, it is your responsibility to ensure that your guests have as good a time as possible. You assumed this responsibility voluntarily and you must resolve not to allow problems or incompatibilities that may arise to spoil their cruise, or yours.

We have found value in greeting the guests with a welcome banner or perhaps a brightly painted shell with something like, "Welcome Ron and Nancy to Green Turtle Cay." This lets the guests know that you have been anticipating, not dreading, their arrival and immediately provides a needed diversion to calm any concerns that they may have. Leave orientation for a few hours, serving snacks or drinks and talking about what is happening back home.

Once everyone seems to be a bit more comfortable, then go through an informal but carefully considered orientation covering those things which guests need to know. Show the guests how to operate the head, how to use the galley pump, and restate any earlier concerns about water usage. Talk about the importance of turning off lights not in use and of minimizing the amount of time the ice chest or refrigerator is open. Show your guests where towels and linens are kept. Non-sailing guests should be told a little about sailing, particularly about keeping their heads below the boom and about the normality of heeling in a sailboat. Keep first day orientation to a minimum. Rather than trying to cover every possible question, concentrate on making visitors feel sufficiently comfortable to ask when faced with anything about which they are unsure.

THE PAYOFF

Then forget about all the preparation and simply enjoy the special times that invariably follow, sharing your dream with someone else. It is a fair trade: they will be sharing their wonder with you. One of the benefits we have not yet mentioned is that friends who wondered about your sanity when you were preparing for your cruise may, as visitors, come to understand your choice.

> *Thus that modest worth which no scrutiny could have detected when it was most industrious, is, by the very tint of its maturity, by its very blushes, revealed at last to the most careless and distant observer.*

Their lingering "Why?" may be satisfied. Be prepared for their next question: "How?"

THE BEAN FIELD

Shall a man go and hang himself because he belongs to the race of pygmies, and not be the biggest pygmy he can.

E have stated repeatedly that we think the ideal cruiser for most people and for most cruises will be between 25 and 35 feet in length. Our reasons have to do with initial cost, maintenance, ease of handling, and handiness, to name a few. They do not have to do with space. Madison Avenue types like to say "a 25-footer with the interior space of a 35-footer." It sounds wonderful, but we have yet to find a boat that can deliver. A 25-footer has the interior space of a 25-footer. Of course, some 25-footers are roomier below than others, but add ten feet to the design and we promise that the cabin will be larger. If you want the space of a 35-footer, you are simply going to have to buy a 35-footer.

Wait! Don't call the broker yet. Why do you want more space? Is it because you are six feet eight inches tall and the bunks are barely six feet two inches? No. Maybe you see an analyst about your claustrophobia? Not that either. It is not really you that you are worried about, is it? It's the stuff. Stuff. You know. Sails and lines and tools and paper towels and life jackets and fenders. And food for goodness sake. Where do you put all that stuff in a pocket cruiser?

TOO MUCH STUFF

There are, the way we see it, three solutions to the "too-much-stuff-for-the-space-available" syndrome. One is to buy a larger boat.

> *What can ye give which I have not?*
> *What can ye take which I have got?*

If it provides more space but you have to postpone the cruise while you pay for it, in the business of life it is a poor investment. Besides, when (if) you finally do go cruising, the larger boat will also be full.

The second solution may be to get rid of some of the equipment aboard. There is an old story told to most prospective grooms that if he will put a bean in a jar every time he and his wife make love during the first year of marriage, and after the first year take a bean out every time, the jar will have enough beans to last his lifetime. An affair with a sailboat is about the same. Our first year we take aboard an endless stream of non-essential items. As space demands, over the years we grudgingly take an item or two at a time off the boat, never emptying the jar. Even though many of the items hold little potential for use, we cannot bring ourselves to remove them.

> *. . . for these are more easily acquired than got rid of.*

Do we take seriously the earlier advice that ten bags of sail aboard are not desirable? No. Even worn-out gear stays aboard, "just in case." When we change a plug in the outboard, do we toss the old one? No. When we re-reeve the main sheet, do we discard the old one? No. We even complicate matters by adding to the jar. When we see a good (might make an anchor float) crab trap buoy on the beach, do we leave it there? No.

It is particularly important on a pocket cruiser that every item aboard earn its right to occupy space. If it does not, get rid of it. If you cannot bring yourself to throw it away or give it away, then store it—ashore. Save the space for those items that must be aboard.

It is the third method of solving a space shortfall that this chapter is about. The farmer with a lot of land can plant his beans and let them lie as they will. When land is more precious, a different approach is indicated. Even the smallest bean field has ample space above it, and the wise farmer makes use of it. Each plant is staked or tied so that it grows up, not out. What the second farmer lacks in space, he makes up for in ingenuity.

The pocket cruiser has an enormous amount of unused space available to anyone with imagination to use it. Our purpose in this chapter is to show you how to add an inch here and an inch there until you have a larger boat. We harbor no delusions that our suggestions are all inclusive or even that original. As with the rest of the book, what we really seek to do is to put you into a certain frame of mind, to plant a few ideas if you will. It is up to you to cultivate the plants.

You must prevail of your own force, as a plant springs and grows by its own vitality.

NEATNESS COUNTS

We recently ordered a new office chair. When we went to pick it up we were concerned about how large the box might be. We need not have worried. It was about the size of a case of beer. We thought there must be another box, but there wasn't; the chair was disassembled and all neatly packed inside.

Almost everyone has had the experience of unpacking some purchase, perhaps a gift, and then trying to get it back into the box it came in. You would swear that a box twice the size was needed, if *you* had not taken it out of the box to begin with. Packing a boat works the same way. On more than one cruise, dock watchers have looked at our pile of food and equipment on the dock and said "no way." Had they come below later, they would not have found a single item in sight. The only evidence that it was all aboard was a sunken waterline.

(Allow us a momentary digression. The sunken waterline is troublesome on a cruise since it soon raises a crop of its own, and not beans. If you have a cruise planned, the next time you do a bottom job, raise the waterline several inches. Then, even loaded, the anti-fouling paint will do its appointed job.)

The cabin may not always look so neat at the beginning of a cruise. On some of our first cruises, a number of cardboard boxes played musical bunks for the first couple of weeks, living in the V-berth by day, the settee by night. It is not the most satisfactory way to carry groceries, but it works. The advantage, of course, is it is self-correcting. As we ate the supplies, the boxes disappeared.

The longer you sail a boat, the more familiar you will become with her storage capabilities. You will learn what items fit into a particular locker with minimum wasted space. You will learn to pack large items first, filling in the cracks with the small items. You will also discover some of that hidden space, although we hope to hasten the process.

Much of the storage space, hidden or otherwise, lies against the hull. Padding is not a bad idea. It will minimize the abrasion of the hull on, say, canned goods, and vice versa. It also quiets the lockers. Rubber-backed carpet is often used for padding. Perhaps a better choice is heavy, clear plastic carpet protector, such as the runners you see in model homes which protect the carpet from wear. It is cheap, easy to clean when canned tomatoes rust through and cover it with gunk (use it bumpy side down), and heavy enough to stay in place without any attachment. Locker padding will not protect glass jars. Slip them into old socks (clean, preferably) before you stow them.

You must learn to deal with the realities of tightly packed lockers. There are the obvious ways: items used often must not be stowed beneath items rarely used. Some adaptations are not so obvious. For example, stowage against the hull means that when you remove a can, everything shifts to fill the open space. Despite scientific evidence to the contrary, the removed can will then no longer fit in the locker. By labeling every can on its top with a felt tip marker, the contents may be determined without having to lift the can.

LABELS

Lockers should also be labeled. There is little point in digging through a locker looking for a can of tuna if the tuna is actually stored elsewhere. For items that permanently reside in a specific location, a semi-permanent label is appropriate. If you have access to a plastic-tape label-maker, it will work well for this purpose (brown is unobtrusive against teak). Aesthetically, we prefer the labels on the inside of the locker door or hatch, but that means opening the door to determine the contents.

For more transitory items, labeling can take two approaches. A piece of paper can be affixed to the inside of the locker and its contents listed on the paper. Some cruisers list every item, crossing items off as they are removed. This method lets you know that the last jar of beluga caviar is gone before you embarrass yourself by offering some to guests. We have never been quite that organized. Our approach has been to label a locker with a category of contents, i.e. meats, canned fruits, canned vegetables, snacks, etc. Soon we find ourselves referring to a particular locker as the meat locker and if we buy a couple of cans of corned beef along the way, there is no question where they will be stored.

> *By simplicity . . . my life is concentrated and so becomes organized . . .*

With numerous small lockers, consider grouping the items by color and labeling the lockers to correspond.

THE STOWAGE PLAN

When you get away from groceries, broad categories are not always so useful. We have already concluded that a well-found boat has a broad array of items aboard. They might as well not be aboard if you cannot find them. For example, if you put a spare bearing aboard for the raw water pump five years ago and the pump bearing fails, you must be able to locate the spare. One way is to tear the boat apart, locker by locker, container by container. You may find the bearing or you may only expand your vocabulary of four letter words.

> *When I see an individual thus beside himself, thus desperate, ready to shoot or be shot, . . . I think he is a candidate for bedlam.*

There is an easy solution. It is the preparation of an equipment stowage plan. One method is to give each locker a number and label a page in a notebook with a corresponding number. Every item in that locker is listed on the corresponding page in the notebook. Need a water pump bearing? Ah, here it is, in locker 23. Now, where is locker 23? Wow, another four letter word!

We like the plan illustrated below better. This equipment stowage plan is taken from *The Complete Sailor's Log*. Lockers are drawn in on the hull outline and the contents of the locker are penciled into the appropriate balloon. A general label will normally be specific enough. As long as all spare bearings are stowed together, the entry "bearings"

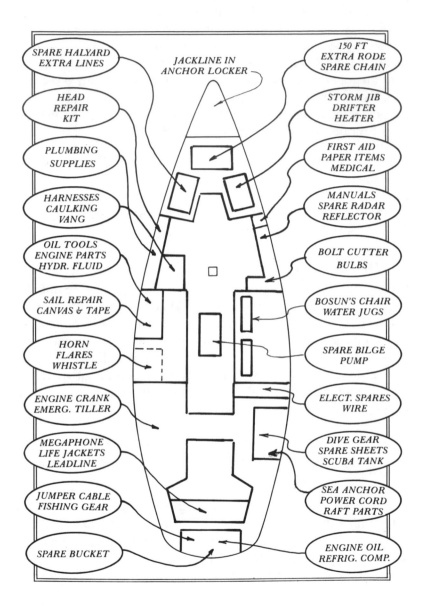

SPARE HALYARD
EXTRA LINES

JACKLINE IN
ANCHOR LOCKER

150 FT
EXTRA RODE
SPARE CHAIN

HEAD
REPAIR
KIT

STORM JIB
DRIFTER
HEATER

PLUMBING
SUPPLIES

FIRST AID
PAPER ITEMS
MEDICAL

HARNESSES
CAULKING
VANG

MANUALS
SPARE RADAR
REFLECTOR

OIL TOOLS
ENGINE PARTS
HYDR. FLUID

BOLT CUTTER
BULBS

SAIL REPAIR
CANVAS & TAPE

BOSUN'S CHAIR
WATER JUGS

HORN
FLARES
WHISTLE

SPARE BILGE
PUMP

ENGINE CRANK
EMERG. TILLER

ELECT. SPARES
WIRE

MEGAPHONE
LIFE JACKETS
LEADLINE

DIVE GEAR
SPARE SHEETS
SCUBA TANK

JUMPER CABLE
FISHING GEAR

SEA ANCHOR
POWER CORD
RAFT PARTS

SPARE BUCKET

ENGINE OIL
REFRIG. COMP.

Equipment Stowage Plan (from *The Complete Sailor's Log*).

is sufficient. Every individual bearing need not be listed.

There are those who recommend the listing of each item aboard in a notebook so that when the item is used, it is crossed out of the notebook—a kind of cruising inventory control. Forget it. Who wants to review the inventory notebook every time you go ashore? Just label a sheet "Replace," and every time you use an item, write it on the sheet. You will have an automatic shopping list when you arrive in a port where parts are available.

Again, we are tempted into a small digression. Most of the spare parts put aboard a cruising boat are what would be termed long shelf-life items. If five years pass before you need them, they should still be as good as the day they came aboard. Unfortunately, that is not always the case. The damp environment of a boat can quickly deplete your spare parts inventory. It is discouraging (and expensive) to locate the needed bearing only to find it corroded beyond usefulness. We suggest protecting the part before it goes aboard with the help of a device usually known by the copyrighted name of Seal-A-Meal.

The Seal-A-Meal does no more than to allow you to custom make heavy, heat-sealed plastic pouches. The pouch stock may be purchased in a roll. New parts are individually bagged and sealed, lightly oiled if appropriate. Prepared this way, the spare part is never exposed to salt air or an accidental dollop. If the part is boxed, box and all may be bagged, or the part may be removed, bagged, and re-boxed. On larger items we prefer the latter approach because the bagged boxes do not stack well. If you have a freezer aboard, the Seal-A-Meal is also outstanding for its intended use, packaging food items.

HIDDEN SPACE

We do not often think about it, but one of the bathrooms in a modern home is likely to have more space than the entire living quarters of a small cruiser. Even those living in the lap of luxury aboard a 40-footer have no more space than a good sized bedroom. How can this be? Because naval architects and yacht manufacturers take the time to stake the bean plants. Every bit of space aboard a cruising sailboat is utilized; well, most of it anyway. What we are looking for is those areas that were too inaccessible, too much trouble, or too expensive to use; or ideas that the architect or the builder just never thought of.

Each make and model of boat will be different. Some already have ingenious stowage space incorporated into the design. Others have a vast amount of seemingly inaccessible "dead space."

The universe is wider than our views of it.

That is always the problem, the limitation of our own views. In the next few paragraphs, we will try to get you to look at your own boat critically. Some of the ideas we suggest may apply. If not, perhaps they will lead you to ideas of your own.

We will be looking for ways to improve the utilization of the space contained by the hull. In a few cases, using the space will require nothing more than being aware of its existence. In others, minor additions or modifications will be required. In some cases, major modifications may offer significant benefits.

ALONGSIDE THE HULL

If your boat has drawers (some do not) that are located near the cabin sole, commonly underneath a settee or bunk, they are probably concealing a significant amount of wasted space. This occurs because the drawer bottom is flat but the hull is curved. Pull out each drawer and see how much extra space is available. The space beneath the drawer can be used without any modification and is ideal for stowage of infrequently needed items; spare parts, for example. Look behind the drawer also. If there is no partition, if the curvature of the hull continues right up to the top of the bunk, there is wasted space behind the drawer as well. Utilizing this space requires glassing in a partition behind the drawer and cutting an access hole, probably through the top of the bunk.

HIDDEN SPACE

Additional stowage space may be under, or behind built-ins.

When we use the word "cutting," we want to remind the reader of the old carpenter's adage, "Measure twice, cut once." Always keep that in mind when cutting or drilling aboard. Aside from the very real danger of electrocution, drilling a hole in what you have identified as dead space only to have the ocean suddenly rush in can ruin your whole day. Problems are not limited to drilling through the hull. An attempt to use space beneath the cabin sole can go sour when you learn that you have just cut the top off of the main water tank. Some apparently unused space may actually be tankage for water, fuel, or waste. Before cutting or drilling, be sure that you know what is behind the surface you are attacking. The best way is to ask the builder. Design drawings may be available for a modest fee, but subsequent boats in a series are often altered from the original design. With or without drawings, proceed very carefully.

We have seen other wasted space which results from the curvature of the hull. Every straight fore and aft cabinet or bulkhead should be inspected to establish what is behind. Often the backs of settees hide a large amount of space with no access. The simplest solution is an access hole allowing for some use of the space between the back and the hull. Another approach is a hatch, hinged at the bottom, providing better access.

Beneath the settee *cushion* is the traditional place for chart stowage. Either flat or folded, the charts should be slipped into a vinyl envelope to protect them from the moisture the cushion will retain. If you prefer rolled charts, consider installing chart-width lengths of large diameter (three or four inch) PVC pipe in otherwise unusable space; above a quarterberth or against the bottom of the counter top, for example. Access is required at only one end.

There are ways to utilize some of the space that sometimes exists alongside the hull in the engine compartment. Small bulkheads can be glassed to the hull a foot or two apart. On the hull side, they would match the contour of the hull, coming to a point at the bottom where the straight, vertical side intersects. Slats (or a piece of clear acrylic) run fore and aft across the straight sides of the bulkheads, creating one or more wedge-shaped bins in the engine room. This space is ideal for the storage of engine oil, a funnel, the oil-change pump, and anything else related to engine maintenance.

Built-in cabinets may harbor wasted space. Especially wasteful are the cabinet in the head or the hanging locker. At first there may appear not to be a way to effectively use the space against the hull, particularly high in these areas. One answer is a canvas pouch, similar to a shoe bag for a closet door. The size will depend upon the space available and the anticipated contents. With a couple of grommets in the upper corners, the bag may be easily hung along the hull. (Where hooks may not be screwed into the bottom of the cabinet top, a couple of small blocks of wood may have to be glassed or epoxied to the hull to accept the hooks.)

Custom constructed, such bags can provide storage for anything from tools to clothes. Be certain that the pouch is insulated from the hull if you plan to use it for clothes.

THE HANGING LOCKER

There is a better course of action than the canvas pouch for the hanging locker. A traditional feature in almost every cruising boat, the hanging locker is usually a ludicrous waste of space. Few, if any, cruising clothes require hanging. In fact, it is undesirable. Hang a jacket in the hanging locker and start off for Tahiti and you might as well put the jacket in a dryer and leave it running for a week or two. The constant motion will soon wear out the hanging clothes. The best way to store clothes aboard is either folded or rolled. Rolling will reduce the wrinkles.

So if you do not hang anything in the hanging locker, what do you do with it? Is this where you carry those extra ten bags of sail? If you still have those aboard, you have not been paying attention. The best thing to do with a hanging locker is to convert it into a bureau. Few things could be more useful and convenient than an extra half dozen roomy drawers. Unfortunately, there is another tradition that prevents such a conversion on most pocket cruisers: the location of the hanging locker.

Usually located opposite the head compartment, there is barely room to pass between the two on the way to the forecabin. There is certainly no room to open drawers, at least not drawers as long as the hanging locker is deep. In this case, shelves are the next best alternative. A hanging locker is thus converted to a pantry, a much better use of the space. This is a fairly easy conversion, requiring little more than screwing cleats to either side of the hanging locker and cutting plywood shelves to fit. The shelves may need to be cut to the contour of the hull on their outboard edges.

If the locker is to be used for the storage of soft (and relatively light) items like towels, linens, clothes, or paper products, canvas shelves may be satisfactory. A heavy piece of canvas is hemmed to roughly the size of the equivalent plywood shelf, with two or three grommets installed on either side. Heavy cup hooks are screwed into the sides of the hanging locker to facilitate easy installation, and removal if desired. A more permanent installation would call for screws and finishing washers. Possibly an improvement on the canvas shelf is the use of heavy netting, bordered all around with about two inches of canvas and installed the same way. The netting provides for better

A "bean field" of ideas to help utilize available space.

ventilation, an important consideration for any locker containing clothes, linens, or soft goods. Cane inserts or nautical motif cut-outs in doors both provide good locker ventilation.

NETTING

Heavy netting has other possibilities for increasing the storage capacity of a cruising boat. Used in conjunction with elastic shock cord (bungee), netting provides the opportunity to use overhead space that might otherwise be wasted. For example, a piece of netting held by shock cord against the underside of the deck in the forepeak locker might provide convenient storage in an otherwise unused area for the seldom (never?) used storm jib.

Similarly, the space above a quarter berth might become a repository for charts, sail covers, or at least the bedding for the berth. We particularly like netting on the underside of cockpit locker hatches. It provides the perfect place to stow life jackets; they are easily accessible, never under anything, and not likely to get soiled. The next time the Coast Guard boards you, they will be impressed. The next time you sink, you will be impressed.

Many boats have small, open shelves running along the hull above bunks and settees. Provided with a two- or three-inch fiddle rail, these shelves are ideal for paperback books, flashlights, cassette tapes, and 101 personal items—until you start sailing. Then everything comes crashing off the shelves. A length of netting attached to the inside of the rail at the bottom and to a piece of line with an eye in either end at the top broadens the shelves usefulness. A cup hook at the top of the shelf on either end completes the installation. At anchor, the netting lies unnoticed behind the fiddle rail. When sailing, the line is strung between the two hooks capturing even large items that may be stored on the shelves.

If the head has a counter with a sink on one end, there may be room to install a laundry hamper on the opposite end. A net bag is a good choice for storing dirty laundry in this otherwise wasted space. An opening hatch, either in the top of the counter or the front of it, with a net bag suspended inside the cabinet below the opening is all that is necessary. The bag provides a good receptacle for the clothes, keeping them from piling up against the hull and providing for good air circulation. If you find that the head sink gets little use (we did), you might remove it, using both the opening and space for the more useful hamper.

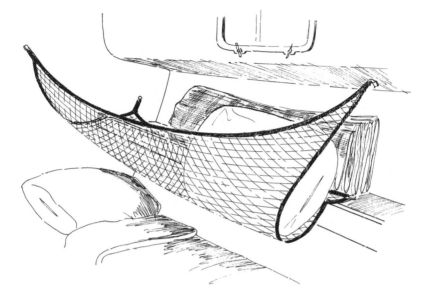

A length of netting attached to the inside of shelving and suspended by hangers can greatly expand shelf stowage space.

PREFABRICATED ADDITIONS

Almost every marine supplier carries a line of prefabricated, often preassembled, teak products to satisfy specific stowage needs. These items range from bookshelves and dish racks to a toothbrush holder or a box just for that hockey puck compass you are hoping someone will buy for you. Look around the boat for empty bulkhead space and see if one of these additions would be practical and pleasing. Almost every boat can accommodate a teak bookshelf somewhere and it will help solve a stowage problem that is bound to arise.

One nice feature of these assemblies is their material of construction. Not only is teak usually a pleasing addition to cabin decor, but the unit can be readily modified if it is not exactly right for your use as supplied. If you are handy with woodworking tools, you may elect to use the catalog offerings only for ideas, preferring to do your own construction. Considering the price of rough teak in small quantities, duplicating a prefabricated item is not likely to represent a significant cost savings and will take a lot more time to accomplish the same objective.

> *But labor of the hands, even when pursued to the verge of drudgery, is perhaps never the worst form of idleness.*

We knew that. Anyway, a shelf for a particular corner of your boat may be unavailable any other way than custom construction. Here, the

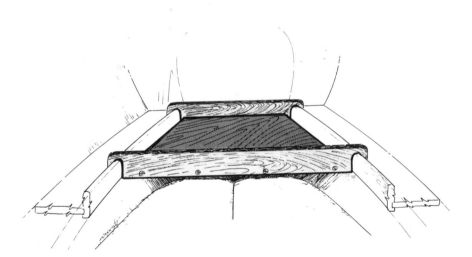

Added shelf across the V-berth. This simple installation is easily removed for access to forepeak locker.

do-it-yourselfer will save considerably over the price that a cabinet maker will charge. If you will be doing some of your own shelf building, look closely at the forecabin. If shelves run along either side of the hull above the V-berth, it is a simple matter to construct a shelf that sits across these two shelves at the forward end of the V-berth, providing more usable space. Such a shelf blocks the hatch for the forepeak locker, so it should be constructed so that it can be simply lifted out of place.

GARBÁGE

We never cease to be amazed at the amount of trash that accumulates on a cruiser in a short time. Somewhere in the cabin, you will need a garbage receptacle. The key in making this decision is to keep in mind what you are dealing with. You do not want the garbage occupying prime storage space.

Over the years, we have dealt with garbage and observed it handled in a number of different ways. When we go to the boat show, we sometimes see a tilt-out bin in the galley cabinet. It is a nice feature, but a terrible waste of precious cabinet space, not to mention the fact that everything else in the cabinet may soon smell like old potato peelings.

Alternatively, on a boat with a side galley, we have seen a hatch in the counter top behind the sink. Beneath the hatch, a rigid plastic pail is suspended by a lip around its top, somewhat like a second sink. As opposed to the tilt-out in the front of a cabinet, this lift-out design in the rear uses space that would be difficult to use effectively for any other purpose.

If you have a companionway ladder, the space behind it, probably otherwise not useful, may be a good location for a regular kitchen garbage can (with a lid). We once had a 27-footer with an aft galley. The top companionway step hinged up as the first in a sequence of steps to gain access to the engine compartment. Beneath the step, we installed a small plastic can (lined with a plastic bag) for the garbage. It worked well.

With no other alternative, a Piper system might be used. Available at most supermarkets, this is a metal hoop that is affixed to the inside of a cabinet door. A plastic bag stretches open over the hoop (just like the lip of a garbage can) and a lid closes the assembly. When the cabinet is opened, the bag swings out with the door. This has some of the same drawbacks as the tilt-out, but its small size means that it occupies less space and the bag must be changed often, minimizing odor problems. Whatever solution you select or devise, a supply of large bags will be necessary to contain the garbage between stops with garbage facilities. Please do not toss your garbage overboard or bury it on the beach.

COCKPIT

I did not wish to take a cabin passage, but rather to go before the mast and on the deck of the world, for there I could best see the moonlight amid the mountains. I do not wish to go below now.

Well, alright. We're through below anyway. Out in the cockpit, we can also help our stowage capacity. Most boats have at least one deep cockpit locker. In a small cruiser, the other one is sometimes sacrificed to a quarter berth. A particular boat may have other lockers in the cockpit as well, a lazarette for example. Just like below, simply learning how to pack a specific locker can increase its capacity. And similarly, there are some stowage tricks.

The canvas bags or the slatted bins we mentioned earlier can also improve the versatility of the deep cockpit locker. The objective is to avoid just piling everything in; instead, we are trying to get smaller items secured yet available without emptying the locker. A very simple approach that we have always found useful is to attach a small container or two to the cockpit side of the locker at the very top. A plastic wastebasket will work well. Often used items such as snatch blocks or deck filler keys can be thus stored, out of the way yet instantly available.

The capacity of a locker can be improved if line stowage is addressed. Lines should be coiled and *hung* in the locker, not dropped in a pile. Commercially available hanging straps may be affixed to the inside of the locker; or you can make your own, using strips of leather (old belts work nicely), each with a hole near one end, the other end screwed to the bulkhead by a cup hook. The leather strap passes through the coil and the hole slips over the hook. Thus hung, the bottom of the locker is open for sails or fenders or other large items and the lines look very shipshape indeed.

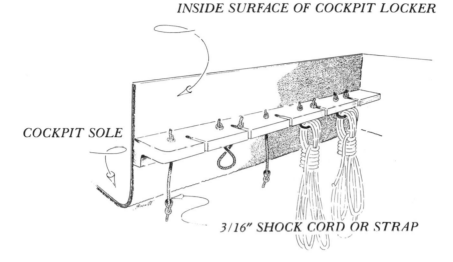

INSIDE SURFACE OF COCKPIT LOCKER

COCKPIT SOLE

3/16" SHOCK CORD OR STRAP

Hanging lines inside the cockpit locker can improve accessibility
and increase locker capacity.

CUTOUTS

Many newer boats have gotten away from the traditional wooden
cockpit coaming and gone to a molded coaming, which is usually
both high and wide. This design provides a good winch base and is
easier to sit on than the one-inch-wide edge of a wooden coaming. It
also encloses space that would be useful if we had access to it. A few
boats have coaming lockers or boxes in this space. If yours does not,
consider adding them.

The coaming box is the simplest; it is nothing more than a box
relieved into the hollow coaming, open into the cockpit. Kits are

available, complete with template, trim ring, and a teak fiddle to contain the box's contents; or you can build your own. In either case, be sure that the box is tilted so it will drain or it will become a source of constant irritation. The coaming locker is simply a coaming box with a hatch to provide some protection from the weather.

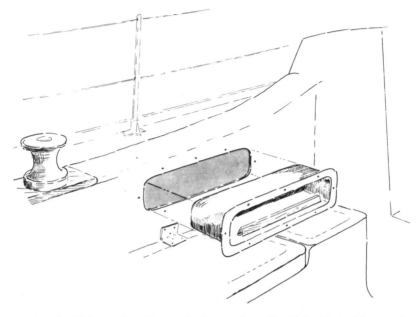

Prefabricated additions such as this coaming box can be easily added with careful measuring.

Among other things, coaming boxes are traditionally used for winch handle stowage but we prefer a vertical winch handle holder mounted in the cockpit. It holds the handle more securely and at the same time provides the functional advantage of ready availability, not tangled under a pile of jib sheet tail. You can purchase the soft, white PVC type holder or save a few bucks and buy a short length of clear hose big enough for the handle to slide into. Cut the top of the hose at an angle (to coax the handle into an accessible position) and screw the tubing in place using finishing washers. Put your savings in the bank. You may have to buy that hockey puck yourself.

COCKPIT BOX

Sometimes the cockpit sole is more than ample. In a large cockpit, if additional stowage space is absolutely essential, it may be obtained through the construction of a stowage box mounted in the sole. The most unobtrusive location is likely to be at the aft end of the cockpit, beneath the tiller or perhaps behind the rudder post.

The box need not be large to be useful. On the other hand, the layout of the cockpit may allow for a narrow box across the full width of the cockpit. This type of project is strictly custom work. Even if you chose not to go to this extreme, a small, open box mounted in the aft end of the cockpit will prove useful for temporary stowage of items in use. We have for years used a teak binocular rack mounted aft in the cockpit, sometimes for binoculars but more often for innumerable other small items. It would be one of our first additions to a new boat.

LONG ITEM STOWAGE

Clever stowage ideas notwithstanding, some items aboard simply cannot be stowed neatly in a locker. These are the long items: boat hook, awning poles, whisker pole, dinghy oars, fishing rods, and pole spears to name a few possibilities. Sometimes these items end up lying along the side deck, tied to shrouds and stanchions. Besides being hard to get to, being underfoot on the side deck makes them a safety hazard.

More often they are stowed on the cabin top, lashed to the hand rail. No doubt being out from underfoot is an improvement, but now they seriously inhibit the necessary function of the cabin top hand rail.

A better solution is a long canvas bag, opening at one end. A flap on either side of the bag secures it (using several turn-button fasteners) to the cabin top inboard of the hand rail. All items are accessible from the cockpit yet out of the way. A heavy item, like a spinnaker pole or a giant whisker pole, would better be stored along the deck in special mounts.

INGENUITY

It is undoubtedly possible to do an entire book on this aspect of cruising preparation; in fact, it has been done. For our purpose, we have spent enough time in the bean field. As we indicated at its start, it was not our intention in this chapter to provide step-by-step instructions for expanding the space on your boat. We just hoped to get you looking at your boat with a more sensitive eye toward better space utilization.

A grain of gold will gild a great surface, but not so much as a grain of wisdom.

Perhaps you have the dollars to buy a larger boat. Greater stowage space thus obtained is at the expense of the other advantages of the pocket cruiser. A bit of ingenuity is a better solution.

THE VILLAGE

*If one would reflect, let him embark on some placid stream,
and float with the current.*

LMOST all first cruises are coastal cruises. Along the east coast of the United States, that may mean sailing for weeks in protected waters. On the west coast, it may mean hugging the coast between harbors. This scenario can as well be reversed. East coast sailors may opt for a passage "outside," to shorten distance, to avoid bridges, or just for the sheer pleasure of an ocean sail. And, in the Pacific northwest, a great deal of protected water is available for cruising.

Inside or outside, coastal cruising means nothing more than cruising with land nearby. It can be the most relaxing kind of cruising, but in some ways it is the most demanding. It is certainly the most interesting and often the most satisfying. In this chapter, we will be looking at some of the practical aspects of coastal cruising.

SAILING VS. CRUISING

The essential difference in daysailing and cruising has to do with destination. Out for a sail, the destination is not as important as the pleasure of the sail.

So am I blown by God's breath, so flutter and flap, and fill gently out with the breeze.

We can sail upwind, downwind, or put the boat on a reach, whatever we prefer. When cruising, the choices become limited by our selection of destination. If the village we plan to call at for the evening is dead to windward, we can count on a day of beating.

Idealistically, we could suggest selecting an alternate destination, one reachable with freed sheets. In some instances, this is an appropriate course of action and where it is, we wholeheartedly endorse it. Realistically, the general direction of a planned cruise is set before we leave the dock. We can only wait so long at each stop for a favorable slant of wind for the next run. The cruising sailor learns to expect to occasionally punch the boat hard to windward. To like it? Not necessarily. To accept it? Definitely.

The second difference in sailing and cruising is that cruising takes us out of our home waters. Daysailing, we rarely get more than 20 miles from our home dock. The waters are familiar; we know them well because we have observed them near at hand for a long time. Cruising takes us some distance afar to unfamiliar waters.

Many a man, when I tell him that I have been on to a mountain, asks if I took a glass with me. . . . It was not to see a few particular objects, as if they were near at hand, as I had been accustomed to see them, that I ascended the mountain, but to see an infinite variety far and near in their relation to each other, thus reduced to a single picture.

It provides a broader view, a more varied experience. And it takes more skill to get there and back.

PILOTING

A familiarity with the principles of coastal navigation is essential to successful coastal cruising. Sailing around the bay on sunny afternoons, you can get away indefinitely with indifferent navigation. Cruising to (relatively) unknown ports requires a higher degree of expertise and attention.

It is beyond the scope of this book to delve deeply into the intricacies of navigation. Volumes have been written on the subject. *Dutton's* is over 900 pages, *Bowditch* more than 1,500. It is a fascinating subject, one sailors often become enamored with, a hobby really. To safely cruise, you need only understand a fraction of the body of knowledge available. Of course a broader knowledge may be very beneficial in some circumstances and we encourage it, but awe at *Bowditch* should not prevent you from going cruising.

It is surprising how many venture into unfamiliar waters, attempting a coastal passage, without having first learned coastal piloting. They feel confident because land is close at hand despite the fact that, with few exceptions, navigational deficiencies subject the boat to greater risk in close proximity to land. Particularly when weather is not a factor, problems are almost always the result of poor piloting. In popular cruising areas, most hazards are well charted, yet if a sailor is unable to determine whether he is a mile offshore or two miles off, a reef plotted a mile offshore is very dangerous to him. The rudiments of competent coastal piloting should be learned and learned well by anyone planning a cruise. This knowledge is at least as important as the boat you select to sail.

Just as knowledge of only a few knots will get you by (despite the fact that Ashley lists 3,900 different knots), knowledge of a half dozen piloting tricks will allow you to deal safely and effectively with most situations. Even if you already know those, we still recommend that you put aboard a good book on navigation and give yourself a much broader education in this important area when you can. Better yet, enroll in a navigation course before you leave.

To my astonishment I was informed on leaving college that I had studied navigation!—why if I had taken one turn down the harbor, I should have known more about it.

The courses are better today, Mr. Thoreau, much better.

CHARTS

Every cruise begins with charts. They are valuable in the planning stage and essential during the actual cruise. A good selection of charts and a high degree of comfort with them should be aboard every cruising boat.

Familiarity with road maps leads novice navigators to expect little more from a chart than the course from point A to point B. Charts are vastly more informative than that, providing data on the depth of the water, the type of bottom, the location and characteristics of aids to navigation, the location of sunken vessels and other underwater obstructions, the contour of the shoreline, and the topography of the land near it.

The detail of a chart varies according to its scale. The smaller the scale, the larger the area covered by the chart, with correspondingly less detail. That is not as confusing as it sounds. Small scale refers to the divisions on the chart. If each mile is small compared to a mile measured on a large-scale chart, one can see that a piece of paper of a specified physical size will accommodate a much larger area in small scale. It is also easy to see that detail will be more difficult to include.

The point of all this is to suggest that you purchase the largest-scale charts available for the areas you intend to cruise. Often a single, small-scale chart will cover a long stretch of coastline. To cover the same area, several larger-scale charts may be required. Charts have increased in price over the years, and more increases loom on the horizon. There may be a temptation to save on chart expense by purchasing only the small-scale chart. Save somewhere else. Small-scale charts often omit many details, including secondary aids to navigation. Harbor charts, the largest scale and most detailed, may not be absolutely necessary, but a coastal cruise should be made with large-scale coastal charts.

We want to stay true to our premise of sensible cruising. The expense of charts can be substantial. Voyagers often trade charts with other voyagers going in the opposite direction. If you can trade for or borrow the charts needed, fine. Most of us cannot. One solution for east coast and southern California sailors is the readily available, spiral-bound Chart Kits. We prefer the individual chart, but the savings represented by purchase of the Kit cannot be overlooked. For the cost of a dozen charts, you get 50. If they cover your cruise area, they are a great value.

THE VILLAGE

Virtually every text on cruising encourages the use of "current" charts. Ours is no exception. Obviously, the more recent the chart, the more its accuracy can be relied upon. But there is a sensible side to this. Most significant chart updates are a result of some man-made change. However, in areas where man is not making changes, the contours of the land and the ocean floor change very slowly.

The works of man are everywhere swallowed up in the immensity of nature.

A specific cruising area may reflect no significant changes for decades. Many charts are based on surveys done in previous centuries. Go aboard any long-term cruising boat and you will be shocked at the age of the charts. Some are religiously updated; most are not. Either way, charts a few years old may still be used. Just do not trust them implicitly. For that matter, brand new charts do not merit total trust.

GUIDE BOOKS

We are predisposed to think of cruising guides as usually a worthwhile investment. A good cruising guide is packed with valuable information. It not only tells where the best anchorage is and what the holding is like, but often gives directions to the nearest bank or laundromat. In some areas, the cruising guide is ubiquitous. In the Bahamas, for example, you are not likely to encounter a cruiser without a copy of *The Yachtsman's Guide to the Bahamas* aboard. It is the very best source of information on cruising the area.

Not all guide books are as valuable. Before you purchase a cruising guide, you should look through it carefully. If you are purchasing it in the area it covers, ask around first to see if other cruisers have it aboard and how useful they have found it to be. Few things can simplify a cruise more than a good guide book. Nothing is more worthless than a bad one.

TOOLS

The tools of the coastal navigator are relatively simple. Those with more to spend will have a depth sounder, a radio direction finder, and perhaps Loran C aboard. These electronic tools have been discussed in an earlier chapter. They are useful though not essential.

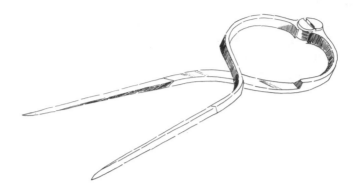

One-hand dividers.

Essential tools for coastal piloting, aside from detailed charts, are little more than dividers, parallel rules, and a means of taking bearings, preferably a hand-bearing compass. *Our* preference is for one-hand dividers, and for parallel rules rather than for plotters or protractors.

A means of measuring the boat's speed is needed. A log is the preferred alternative, but estimating the vessel's speed may be sufficiently accurate. Depth can be gauged with a lead line. Timing may be done effectively with a wrist watch.

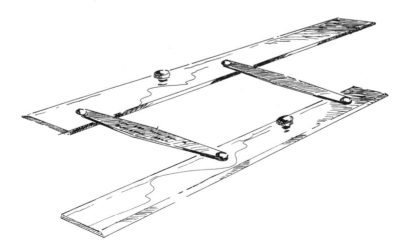

Transparent parallel rules are preferred.

A horn is required in fog and for opening bridges. Freon horns are the most popular but a *good,* marine-grade (non-corrosive and non-magnetic), lung-powered one can be a more sensible selection. It does not require the periodic expense of pressure canister replacement, and it never fails when you need it.

Binoculars are also a useful tool to the coastal navigator. There are differences in binoculars and the expensive ones have far superior optics and light-gathering characteristics. They are vastly better at night and in general a joy to own, but do not fare well in a tight cruising budget. Inexpensive binoculars will do the job and, if given reasonable care, will last for many years. Without a long explanation, binoculars for marine use should be 7 X 50.

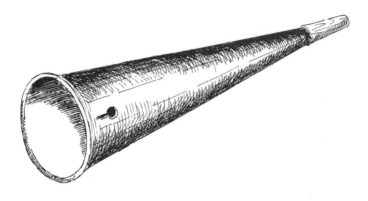

A horn that never fails.

AIDS TO NAVIGATION

The coastal waters of the United States are blessed with the most extensive system of aids to navigation in the world. We have lights and buoys and daymarks marking all major channels and obstructions, and most of the less important ones as well. The navigator knowledgeable of the buoyage system can sail the coastal waters with relative safety. In some areas, aids are so numerous that the chart is rarely consulted.

If your cruise is domestic, learn to identify and understand the array of aids. If your cruise will take you away from the U.S. coast, learn to do without aids. In many foreign cruising areas, aids to navigation simply do not exist. Even if an aid is charted, do not count on it being there. Of those aids really on station, major lighthouses are likely to be the only lighted ones actually lighted.

Of course, our warning does not apply to every foreign cruising area, but few countries are as vigilant at aid maintenance as the United States. The sensible approach is not to entrust the safety of the vessel to a charted aid. If it shows up as promised, great. What if you count on it and it doesn't show up . . . ? Be sure you have an alternative.

TIDE

We find tides and currents to be among the most confusing aspects of cruising. Along the east coast, tides are typically semidiurnal (two roughly equal high tides, two similar low tides per day). On the west coast, we may encounter mixed tides (two highs and two lows, but varying in height). Tides along the Gulf coast are diurnal based (one high and one low per day) but sometimes exhibit only one change, sometimes three changes.

Tide refers to the rise and fall of the ocean level, and tide tables are the easiest way to deal with these fluctuations. Knowledge of the time of high or low water can be very helpful in navigating a shallow area or determining the seriousness of a grounding. Tables give both the time and the predicted height of each high and low tide. Weather can materially affect tides; a strong onshore wind, for example, might hold the water against the land causing unusually high tides.

Other than while under the influence of unusual weather, tides are easy to predict with the aid of a tide table. The rise or fall *per hour* may even be calculated for semidiurnal and mixed tides with the *twelfths rule*. In the first hour after low tide, the level will rise 1/12th of the total rise, 2/12ths in the second hour, 3/12ths in the third hour. This, with 3/12ths for the fourth hour also, is the period of maximum rise, dropping to 2/12ths in the fifth hour and to only 1/12th in the sixth and final hour. Falling tide follows a similar pattern. This calculation is very useful for shallow water navigation.

It is the resulting currents that are confusing. At a given location, ebb may continue to run hours after low water at that location. The tide flooding onto a bank, or into a bay, may come from all directions. You may find the current easterly on one side of the bank, while at the same time the current on the other side of the bank is westerly. In the middle, the direction and strength of the current will be unpredictable. The coastal navigator must learn to recognize current by its influence on the boat and take it into account in plotting a position.

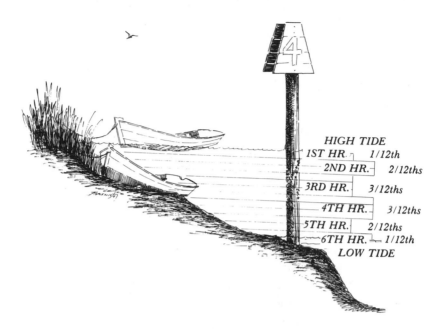

HIGH TIDE
1ST HR. — 1/12th
2ND HR. — 2/12ths
3RD HR. — 3/12ths
4TH HR. — 3/12ths
5TH HR. — 2/12ths
6TH HR. — 1/12th
LOW TIDE

Rule of 12. Used to determine rise and fall *per hour* of tides.

NIGHT SAILING

For many, a cruise will be the first experience with sailing in the dark. Most cruisers view night sailing with a certain amount of apprehension.

> *I believe that men are generally still a little afraid of the dark, though the witches are all hung, and Christianity and candles have been introduced.*

Do I detect a note of sarcasm? Sure, it's no big deal to follow a dark path back to Walden Pond. Finding your way around on a dark ocean is not so easy.

It is not that difficult, either. In well-marked areas, candles have indeed been introduced. With a chart and a watch, you can easily identify lighted aids at a great distance. A powerful spotlight will be very useful in locating unlighted aids. If you *know* where you are on the chart, darkness represents very little threat.

In exchange for the apprehension, night sailing can be truly spectacular. The other senses are heightened. There is a sensation of speed and power that cannot be described. Even under reduced sail, a prudent tactic for nighttime cruising, the boat feels as though it is rushing across the sea. A luminescent wake adds to the sensation.

The heavens contribute to this sensual feast. On a dark night, they are incredibly crowded with stars. The moon may treat you to a spectacular rise or, in concert with scattered clouds, the proverbial silver lining. If the sail lasts all night, a certain and welcome sunrise awaits you at the other end.

> *Late in the afternoon, for we had lingered long on the island, we raised our sail for the first time, and for a short hour, the southwest wind was our ally; but it did not please heaven to abet us long.*

Thoreau describes the typical evening calm, usually soon replaced by a breeze flowing off the nearby land. Cruising down a coastline at night, you may take advantage of the land breeze. The land mass loses its heat more quickly than the adjoining water. The air above the land thus cools also, sinking and flowing toward the warmer, lighter air over the water. This phenomena results in a land breeze. It provides particularly pleasant sailing: a beam wind and flat sea conditions.

There are times when night sailing simply is not prudent. It is never a good idea to attempt to transit reefy waters at night. Approaching an unknown harbor at night should also be avoided. Even if the harbor is well lit, lights on shore may be confusing. If there is any doubt at all, it is invariably better to wait until daylight to make the entry. But when the circumstances are right, night sailing is one of the special pleasures of cruising.

WEATHER

The coastal cruise is not the same slave to weather that the offshore passage is. With safe anchorages close at hand, coastal cruising is possible in any season, taking advantage of good weather and waiting out poor. Obviously, ice is a deterrent. For most of us, so is cold. Scheduling your cruise for the best season for the cruising ground selected will improve your odds for good weather.

> *The weather is very clear and the sky bright. . . . Methinks this is a travellers month.*

Even cold is more bearable if the weather is clear and bright. If you elect to cruise in a cold climate, a warm cabin will be a welcome refuge. Numerous types of cabin heaters are available, each with its own advantages. We do not especially care for cold water cruising, so we will leave heater selection to you. Our only comment is to be sure that the heater is properly vented. Particularly in the small volume of a pocket cruiser's cabin, a poorly vented heater can deplete the air of oxygen resulting in a tragic end to any cruise.

Maybe the sensible thing is to forget the cold stuff. If you want to cruise up north (down east?), do it in the summer or early fall. When winter arrives, join the southerly migration. The eccentricity of cruising should not prevent you from at least showing as much good judgement as the wild geese.

PACE

We started this chapter with a comparison of sailing and cruising. Cruising, we said, is going somewhere. There seems to be an almost universal tendency to rate the success of a cruise by how far away that somewhere is, on the number of miles registered on the log. That is too bad, because cruising is also *being* somewhere. Planning too long a cruise for the time available will almost certainly detract from your enjoyment and can easily ruin the cruise altogether. If the time available will not allow a leisurely pace to your chosen destination, select a closer one. If circumstances conspire to keep you from going where you planned, enjoy where you are.

> *With the utmost industry we cannot expect to know well an area more than six miles square, and yet we pretend to be travellers, to be acquainted with Siberia and Africa.*

To drive boat and crew to hold to some ambitious itinerary without regard to changing circumstances and preferences is to miss altogether the essence of cruising.

THE PONDS

I suspect that, if you should go to the end of the world, you would find somebody there going farther . . .

HIS is not a book about blue-water sailing. It is not about circumnavigating. It is not about dragging anchor in Patagonia or weathering a gale in the Aleutians. It is a book about ordinary people leading ordinary lives that include ordinary sailing. It is about taking an ordinary boat and at least sampling an extraordinary lifestyle. It is both about why to do it and how to do it.

BLUE WATER

In many areas, cruising need not involve any blue water at all. A three-month cruise of the Chesapeake, for example, can be a very satisfying experience without the bow once lifting to an ocean swell. Even in cruising areas where sailing in the ocean is required, ocean sailing is usually in close proximity to land. Nearby harbors and anchorages offer refuge from threatening weather and add variety to the cruising experience.

Why, then, travel so far when the same pleasures may be found near home?

There are at least two reasons why many cruisers will elect to include blue-water sailing in their cruise plans. The first reason is that at least some of the cruising area the sailor wishes to visit lies beyond a blue horizon. The only way to get there is by crossing a piece of ocean. Perhaps it is only a short run, 50 miles from Florida to the Bahamas for instance. Perhaps a thousand-mile run to the Caribbean. Perhaps 3,000 to Polynesia. Whatever the distance, it is blue-water sailing nonetheless.

The second reason is entwined with reasons for cruising in the first place. A sailing cruise offers the promise of adventure. Somehow, the contemplation of an ocean passage enhances that promise for many. To those, pottering around in a bay or among the islands of an archipelago cannot be satisfying unless juxtaposed against a blue-water voyage. It is a matter of pride, status perhaps; a matter of personal satisfaction.

With the first reason, the blue-water passage is a means to an end; with the second reason it is an end itself. Regardless of the reason, most cruisers eventually find themselves out of sight of land. It is an interesting and rewarding experience. The symmetry of a world of which you are the center is a sensation not soon forgotten.

Let us wander where we will, the universe is built round about us, and we are central still. If we look into the heavens they are concave, and if we were to look into a gulf as bottomless, it would be concave also.

There is little reason to conclude that a blue-water passage is beyond the capabilities of the pocket cruiser. For those choosing to include blue water in the cruising plan, the requirements are a seaworthy design, meticulous preparation, and adequate seamanship.

DESIGN

The number of very small cruisers specifically designed for ocean cruising has shown a significant increase in recent years. Many have made very respectable voyages safely and in relative comfort, their seaworthiness never in question. Each design differs from every other design in numerous ways. There are no common specifications that we can sight as the mark of a seaworthy passage-maker.

Traditional blue-water cruisers have been of moderate to heavy displacement with a long keel and powerful rudder. These characteristics still offer advantages. The heavier displacement boat may not be inherently more seaworthy, but will have a greater load-carrying capacity. The long keel provides directional stability, easing the work of the helmsman or the autopilot. It also allows the boat to take the ground with less risk, and in many places will be much easier to haul for maintenance or repair.

Light displacement has its own advantages, not the least of which usually is speed. Overloading the boat for a long cruise will negate this advantage. By reducing the wetted area a fin keel and spade rudder may give a design lively performance as well, but the fin keeled boat can be hard to manage in strong winds. Except with a radical underbody, the fin keel should take the ground without damage. The disadvantage of difficult hauling is overrated, particularly for a cruise of a year or less. You will be home for the bottom job.

Underbody design is a matter of preference (or of what you already have) and not as important as the integrity of the boat. If your pocket cruiser was designed and constructed for sailing in protected waters, stay in protected waters. If you are fortunate enough to own a sturdily built and well-designed little cruiser, a blue-water passage is surely among your options.

Every sunset which I witness inspires me with the desire to go to a West as distant and as fair as that into which the sun goes down.

If you are uncertain about the seaworthiness of your particular boat, seek professional help: a qualified surveyor or a naval architect, not a psychiatrist.

Underwater design is important, but is not nearly as important as the integrity of the boat.

PREPARATION

Assuming a seaworthy vessel—and do not go to sea in anything less—careful preparation will result in a safe and satisfying voyage. There are, of course, the basic preparations like laying in supplies and filling water and fuel tanks. However, these are preparations for any cruise. An offshore passage requires some special preparations. It is not that the risks offshore are any greater; they are not. It is that help is much more distant. Offshore, self-reliance is thrust upon you. You must be prepared to handle any situation that might arise.

The best cure is prevention. That is the purpose of offshore preparations. Since we are already confident that the hull will handle any punishment, the next thing is to establish the same trust in the rig. That means going aloft and carefully, very carefully, checking every fitting, every tang, every bolt, every rivet, every cotter pin, every spreader, and every inch of wire.

> *Associate reverently and as much as you can with your loftiest thoughts.*

While aloft, inspect the running rigging carefully, particularly masthead sheaves and blocks, and the halyards that pass over them.

172

Worn running rigging should be renewed; it will be much easier to do this sitting at anchor than while swooping down the faces of eight-foot seas. With questionable standing rigging, there are no options. Fix it.

As you inspect the rig, keep in mind that on an ocean passage you are going to have to face whatever is encountered. On a coastal cruise, you can usually wait out bad weather in some snug (or at least tenable) anchorage. That option is unavailable to a boat at sea. You may find yourself:

. . . flying against the stiff gale with reefed wings. . . .

You want to be darn sure that in such conditions the rig will stay up.

Confidence in those "wings" is almost as important. Before going offshore, go over every sail seam by seam. Now is the time to repair a broken stitch or to notice a cracked clew ring or a torn batten pocket. We would hesitate to go offshore with very old sails. We just recently encountered a couple attempting a cruise of more than 6,000 miles, a significant portion offshore, in a 20-year-old boat with the original sails. To their faces we wished them luck; to ourselves we wished them better judgement.

Once you are satisfied that the hull, rig, and sails are capable of handling whatever conditions you are likely to encounter, the only remaining potential weakness is the crew. Barring illness, injury, or falling overboard, the competent crew should encounter no difficulty.

Illness, other than seasickness, is providentially rare. It can be made even more unlikely by staying warm and dry. Proper clothing and good foul weather gear should be aboard. Seasickness can be debilitating and consequently cannot be dismissed lightly, particularly on a short-handed boat venturing offshore. Fortunately, seasickness seldom lasts more than a day or two. If you or your crew are subject to seasickness, preventative medication should be taken aboard. Most of the oral preventatives such as Dramamine or Bonine (dimenhydrinate and meclizine, respectively) cause drowsiness. Users of the ear patches, like Transderm-Scop (scopolamine), sometime experience severe side effects. It is a very good idea to try whatever medication you anticipate using well before your offshore passage to evaluate its other effects. Hallucinating during a gale at sea is not the kind of adventure you are seeking.

Injuries are usually caused by your falling against something or something falling against you. In the first instance, the best defense is sea legs which no amount of preparation will provide. Until they arrive (by boat), move around cautiously and with a firm handhold.

Early preparation could take the form of being certain that handholds are available and that, to the extent possible, no sharp corners exist to fall against. A safety bar in front of the galley stove is an excellent addition to an offshore boat.

Keeping things from hitting you means nothing more than ensuring that everything aboard is secured in place. We hate this implication, but it is where offshore preparation should start: what happens to everything aboard if the boat is turned upside down? Lockers should have positive latches (hooks or barrel bolts), not friction catches. Drawers should be similarly secured. Heavy items, the ship's batteries, for example, should be strapped in place. Items stored on open shelves should be confined with strong netting or stored in a closed locker.

If you prefer not to sink like a stone, it is advisable to put barrel bolts on the top companionway washboard to keep the boards from falling out. Cockpit lockers should have sturdy, positive-locking latches. Anchor wells should also be securely latched closed. Oversized portholes are not normally a problem with a pocket cruiser, but if you do have them and plan a long passage, plywood shutters are imperative.

The third risk to crew is falling overboard. The first defense is not falling—period. Failing this, we can minimize the consequences. Examine the lifelines and their fittings before going offshore, paying particular attention to swages. Be sure stanchions are secured and firmly backed. Rig the jackline between the cockpit and the bow and establish a rule that at night and during boisterous weather, harnesses must be worn and attached before coming on deck. Develop a strategy for keeping the boom under control, either with a permanent preventer or using the vang attached to the toerail.

Exhibit appropriate vigilance, and neither the ship nor her crew need be at risk during an offshore passage.

Furrowed by care, but yet all over spread
With the ripe bloom of self-wrought content

An apt description of most cruisers, somewhere in the middle of an ocean passage.

WEATHER

The one factor which you cannot control through caution and vigilance is the weather. The likelihood of encountering poor weather depends to a great extent upon the length of your exposure—the length of the passage. If your plan calls for an overnight ocean sail, you can normally avoid poor weather. If you will be offshore for several days, the weather encountered will be less predictable. On a longer passage, the best that you can do is plan the trip during a time when the recorded weather has historically been the most beneficial, or at least the most benign.

There is, no doubt, a particular season of the year when each place may be visited with most profit and pleasure, and it may be worth the while to consider what that season is in each case.

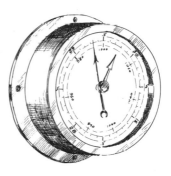

Barometer.

If you are visiting a popular cruising area, weather information will be easily obtainable in sailing books or magazines or through word of mouth. If you have an unusual passage planned, you will need to invest in Pilot Charts of the area. Pilot Charts graphically depict prevailing winds and calms, percentage of gales, tracks of cyclones, wave heights, currents, surface air and water temperatures, fog, and among others, recommended routes for sailing vessels. A chart is printed for each month of the year. The charts provide no guarantee of good weather or fair winds, only a higher probability in specific months.

The ability to forecast the weather is a valuable one to a cruiser, particularly offshore. If you are near the coast and have a VHF aboard, you may be able to receive an excellent local forecast on one of the weather channels (WX-1, WX-2, etc.). Further offshore, the two best tools for weather forecasting are the barometer and your eyes. It is not the barometric pressure that heralds weather activity, but the *change* in pressure. The more rapid the pressure change, the more severe the weather change will be. The forecast chart below may be helpful with barometric predictions. Looking at the sky can be just as informative. There are several books available that can aid you in learning to read weather signs in the sky.

Our concern is not so much with weather prediction as with recognizing that whatever happens (predicted or not), you must be prepared for it. Except in very severe cases (fortunately very rare), heavy weather management at sea involves little more than reducing sail and ensuring the watertight integrity of the hull. The latter we have already mentioned.

In coastal and sheltered waters, a reefing jib provides a quick and easy way to reduce the headsail area in strengthening wind. We do not like

BAROMETRIC READING	RISING NEEDLE	FALLING NEEDLE
29.8 OR BELOW	CLEAR AND COLDER	STORM AND HEAVY PRECIPITATION
30.0 OR BELOW	CLEARING WITHIN A FEW HOURS. FAIR FOR SEVERAL DAYS.	RAIN CONTINUING
30.10 AND ABOVE	FAIR, FOLLOWED BY RAIN WITHIN 2 DAYS.	RAIN, PROBABLY IN 12 TO 24 HRS.
30.20 AND ABOVE	FAIR FOR SEVERAL DAYS FOLLOWED BY RAIN.	SLOWLY RISING TEMPERATURE, & FAIR FOR 2 DAYS.
	IF STATIONARY: CONTINUED FAIR, WITH NO DECIDED TEMPERATURE CHANGES.	

Weather Forecast Chart (from *The Complete Sailor's Log*).

the reefing jib for storm use because it will not be as heavily built as a storm jib and because in rough conditions the reef may tear out if a wave comes aboard. Similarly, we do not think that a roller-reefing headsail is appropriate for storm conditions. It will not set well, will not be heavily constructed, and we find the specter of a broken furling line allowing the sail to unroll a frightening prospect.

In contrast, a deep-reefing main is an adequate storm sail for the common man. Not very vulnerable to boarding seas, the main is normally of a cloth weight that, because of the drastic reduction in sail area of the reefed sail, is sufficiently strong even in storm conditions. The reefing system should be quick and easy. We find that well-thought-out jiffy reefing is invariably the best system.

NAVIGATION

An ocean passage requires navigational skills unnecessary for coastal cruising. There are no aids to navigation offshore—except those overhead.

Naught was familiar but the heavens, from under whose

176

roof the voyager never passes . . .

Celestial navigation is the surest way of finding your way across an otherwise featureless ocean. The intimidation this term effects is unwarranted; celestial navigation is not difficult.

Think momentarily of standing in a big parking lot (the ocean) with a street light (stars) at either end. With some instrument (the sextant) we measure the angle (altitude) between the base of the light pole (horizon) and the light (star). If we know how high the light (star) is, and we do, simple mathematics allows us to determine how far from the base we are by the angle we measured. We are standing on a circle (line of position) so many feet from the base. The same process on the second light (star) yields a second circle (LOP). Where the two circles (LOPs) intersect is our location (fix). They intersect in two places, but we already have a good idea of where we are to begin with, so confusion is unlikely.

With tables and a formula, the math required for celestial navigation is very simple. The most difficult aspect is accurately measuring the necessary angle using a sextant on the pitching deck of a small sailboat. There is no substitute for practice. Time used to be a problem (our street lights are moving), but today even cheap digital watches are incredibly accurate, and to check them, Coordinated Universal Time (replacing Greenwich Mean Time some years back) is broadcast around the world on numerous frequencies. With a sextant, watch, and appropriate tables, you can find your way to anywhere in the watery world.

Sextant.

Under the same catholic sun glances his white ship over Pacific waves into their smooth bays, and the poor savage's paddle gleams in the air.

If you are still apprehensive, you can buy a calculator that handles all the math, or even a computer that requires input of only the time, the sextant reading, and the heavenly body. Or you can depend on man-made heavenly bodies by putting aboard SatNav. If your destination is not too distant, Loran C can point the way. Regardless of the electronic aids, the sensible cruiser is able to find his way without them. Imagine failure of the SatNav at mid-voyage. If you are going offshore, put the necessary tables and a sextant aboard and learn to use them, even if the sextant never leaves its case during the actual passage. The $20 plastic variety will be adequate.

For an offshore run of a couple of hundred miles or less, in good weather, a well-compensated compass may be the only navigational instrument required. Maintaining a periodic and accurate dead reckoning (DR) position will be adequate. If there is a radio beacon at your destination, with the aid of an RDF even a small target can thus be attempted with confidence.

SEAMANSHIP

There is no substitute for seamanship. Good seamanship is a sense of knowing what action is required in every situation. It is good judgement. It (or the lack of it) is exhibited in every aspect of cruising. We can judge a person's seamanship by the way he enters a harbor, approaches a dock, or drops anchor.

Offshore, seamanship is most often manifested in two ways: how well the vessel is prepared for the voyage and how the skipper and crew respond to the unexpected. Good preparation, by definition, minimizes the unexpected, either by preventing it or by expecting it. The importance of preparation to the safety of boat and crew cannot be over emphasized and we will later devote an entire chapter to this subject ("Higher Laws").

Response to the unexpected is neither easy to write about nor easy to plan for. There are a few things that the cruiser can do. The first is to *learn the boat*. How long can it carry sail safely? Will the stern lift to a following sea? Will the boat heave-to? Can it be controlled at speed? Where is the emergency equipment located?

Learn about the crew. The prevalent cruising couple usually already know each other very well. If either member cannot be counted on to respond appropriately to a stressful situation, the other must compensate. Evaluate strengths and weaknesses and be prepared to draw on that information.

Learn from others. Few experiences are unique, even in cruising. Listening to or reading about the experiences of others can prepare you for a similar experience.

THE PONDS

Learn about yourself. Can you stay calm or do you panic easily? Can you think quickly, or does your mind freeze up under stress? Do you lie to yourself, or do you face the truth? Is your judgement normally sound or could it sometimes be better? Do you trust yourself? Are you sure that when the chips are down, your seamanship will be up to the challenge? Positive? Then you are probably right. Bon voyage.

THE PASSAGE

Cruising and voyaging are distinctly different activities. This is a book about cruising, but the necessity of an occasional blue-water passage cannot be overlooked. Nor should we fail to convey a sense of the offshore alternative, not just the satisfaction of a voyage completed, but the experience of the voyage itself.

> *The wind came blowing blithely from the southwest . . . , and stepped into the folds of our sail like a winged horse, pulling with a strong and steady impulse. The sail bends gently to the breeze, as swells some generous impulse of the heart, and anon flutters and flaps with a kind of human suspense. I could watch the motions of a sail forever, they are so rich and full of meaning. I watch the play of its pulse, as if it were my own blood beating there.*

The offshore passage provides a oneness with wind and sail that is otherwise unavailable. There may be things more sensible than crossing the pond but few are more rewarding.

BAKER FARM

There should always be some flowering and maturing of the fruits of nature in the cooking process. Some simple dishes recommend themselves to our imaginations as well as palates.

AFETY considerations aside, there is little doubt that food is the most important ingredient in a satisfying cruise. A good meal can salvage the worst cruising day. Even though it is raining and blowing outside, it is hard to feel deprived when secure in a cozy cabin enjoying a small feast.

Food is necessary to fuel our bodies for the rigors that sailing can sometimes impose. Just as important, it is the punctuation of the day, breaking an endless string of time into manageable segments. It also serves a valuable social function. At meal times, the crew gathers together, sharing the group experience and providing the opportunity to share individual experiences as well. Social interaction with other cruisers is also typically centered around food: a shared meal or mid-afternoon snacks.

Our journal as often reflects a memorable meal as a memorable sunset. We look forward to eating aboard. Our pre-cruise grocery list enjoys the same reverence as the charts of the cruising area. We have given a proper galley as much attention as proper ground tackle. The weekend cruiser may be content with sandwiches or a reheated casserole from home, but the long-term cruiser certainly will not. A well-found cruiser will carry aboard a broad array of foods as well as the facility for their preparation, a workable galley.

LOCATION

We could talk at length about the appropriate location for the galley of a pocket cruiser. On modern designs, the galley is almost always located aft near the companionway, sometimes running beneath the companionway steps. Some older designs have what is called a linear galley. That is a galley running down one side of the hull, port or starboard, usually directly across from a dinette arrangement.

Either location has advantages and disadvantages. With the aft galley, the cook is always in the path of cabin traffic, and anyone coming below risks stepping on the cook or the food in preparation. The linear galley is hard to fault in port, providing vast counter space with cavernous lockers. Its big disadvantage is that under sail on the tack that places the galley on the high side, cooking becomes quite difficult.

In the upper range of pocket cruisers, the boats become large enough and deep enough to accommodate a U-shaped galley, normally located aft and well clear of companionway traffic. Where the choice is available, we believe this to be the best galley, both in design and location.

The fact is, for most of us, the question of location is one of only idle interest. Whatever boat we have (or select), the galley will already have been located by the designer and that is where it will undoubtedly remain. There is little value in lamenting that location.

Cease to gnaw that crust. There is ripe fruit over your head.

It is better to spend the time improving the workability of the galley, regardless of location.

STOVE SELECTION

In prehistoric times, some Neanderthal hunter accidentally dropped his share of the day's kill into the fire. When he realized that none of the other members of the clan were jumping to offer him a piece of their share, he fished out the blackened meat with a stick and ate it anyway. Wow! Mammoth never tasted like this before. We have never looked back.

The single most important appliance in the cruising boat galley is the stove. With the choice of a half dozen different fuels and dozens of different styles, stove selection requires careful consideration. Stoves come in fixed or gimbaled varieties, with two or three burners, with or without an oven, and porcelain coated or made of stainless steel. In some cases, the selection is a matter of preference, in some a matter of cost, and in others a matter of anticipated use.

If you have the choice, stainless steel is the best material for a cruising stove, particularly in a salt water environment. Cruisers on a very tight budget may choose a porcelain-coated stove intended for use in a recreational vehicle (RV). The RV stove is comparatively inexpensive, but in the marine environment will soon rust and will be unsightly for most of its brief life.

The question of an oven can only be answered by your cooking habits. Folding ovens that sit on top of the stove, covering one or both burners, are available. Such units are fairly expensive and only mildly successful. It is difficult to maintain an even heat and impossible to achieve high oven temperatures. Most of the heat goes instead into raising the temperature of the cabin. We have cruised extensively both with an oven and without. There is no doubt that a good oven broadens the menu possibilities. There is also no doubt that an oven is not essential equipment and many boats cruise without this item aboard.

It is the rare cruising cook indeed who has three dishes going at once. The two-burner stove is more than adequate for preparation of the usual cruising fare, which includes some fabulous meals. The three-burner variety is bulkier, occupying space that could be put to better use. Unless you have a specific need for three burners, stick with the two-burner type.

GIMBALS

The issue of gimbals should be easy enough. A gimbaled stove is better on a cruising boat. However, a lot of pocket cruisers are fitted with a fixed stove, often recessed into the counter top. This installation is neat and requires minimum space. For many cruises, there is little reason why it would not be satisfactory. Gimbals are only of value if cooking while underway. Most cruisers (as distinct from voyagers) avoid cooking underway like the plague. If your cruise never involves a single passage of more than two or three hundred miles, the gimbaled stove will likely never be used, or at least could be done without.

Beware of gimbaled stoves that are not functional. A small, light stove gimbaled at the stove top is worse than a fixed stove. When you set a heavy pot on it, it is going to be overbalanced. Someone likened this action to two heavy adults standing up in a small dinghy, a good analogy. Proper gimbaling requires that the whole pot sit below the pivot (which is still a bit of a problem because it swings the pot as the boat varies its angle of heel), or that the stove has sufficient weight low to counter the upsetting influences of a couple of heavy pots on top. Some installations look okay until you try to swing them. To be useful, they should be capable of swinging about 30° either side of horizontal. If they hit the cabinet at 15°, you may as well have a fixed stove.

Considering the space required and the necessary weight of a gimbaled stove, if your galley already has a fixed stove installation, you may want to stay with it. A very satisfactory alternative to a major conversion is the addition of a double-gimbaled single burner (either the Sea-Swing or the Mini-Galley) mentioned in a previous chapter. One of these units is not just invaluable to the solo sailor, but can brew coffee, heat soup, even handle the rare preparation of a hot meal underway.

GALLEY STRAP

To facilitate cooking underway, cruising boats are sometimes fitted with a strap to hold the cook in place. Nothing more than a wide belt against which the cook leans, it is usually attached to the counter on either side of the stove. The concept of the strap is good, but its location in front of the stove is a dangerous one; in a sudden lurch, the cook thus restrained may be unable to get out of the way of an errant pot or its scalding contents.

One partial solution we have seen used is a commercial rubber apron, but this has to be hot in the tropics. We prefer to attach the strap to the counter beside the stove so that the cook stands in front of the counter, not the stove, but can still reach the stove. The attachment points should be spaced far enough apart to allow the cook some additional lateral movement in case dodging sloshing stew is necessary.

STOVE FUEL

The legitimate choices of stove fuel for a cruising boat are: coal, diesel, alcohol, kerosene, liquified petroleum gas (propane or butane), and liquefied natural gas. We have also seen sterno, gasoline (Coleman), and electricity, all bad choices. The Sterno generates little heat; a gasoline stove is extremely dangerous on a boat; the electric stove requires shore power or a running auxiliary generator.

Coal and diesel stoves look very similar and have similar applications. They are both popular on commercial fishing boats working northern waters and have been adapted to use aboard yachts cruising in cold climates. They generate a great deal of heat and can keep a boat warm and dry inside in even severe weather conditions. Out of their element, they have little to recommend them. They continue to give off great amounts of heat in a warm climate, making the cabin uninhabitable when they are being used. If you are going south, leave the coal or diesel stove behind.

Despite the fact that we have never met a satisfied owner, the pressurized alcohol stove continues to dominate small boat galley stoves. Its popularity is with boat builders who fear lawsuits and insurance underwriters who fear claims. Alcohol is touted as a safe fuel because an alcohol fire (not nearly uncommon enough to be called safe) can be doused with water. It also burns relatively clean.

The reasons owners dislike the alcohol stove are that it does not burn very hot (just boiling water takes f-o-r-e-v-e-r), it has a sickly sweet smell likely to make you seasick, the burners have to be primed before lighting, it is prone to flare ups (so long, eyebrows), and the fuel is expensive and often unavailable. There are now non-pressurized alcohol stoves on the market which operate on a wick principle. We have had no experience with the non-pressurized type.

The Primus or pressure kerosene stove operates exactly like the pressure alcohol stove except that it uses kerosene for fuel. In fact, by simply changing to kerosene burners, most pressure alcohol stoves can be converted. The results are far more satisfactory. Kerosene burns with a very hot flame. A well-maintained stove is odorless. The fuel is inexpensive and readily available.

Detractors of the Primus point out that it must be primed also, and with alcohol. If the burners are dirty, the stove can smoke and smell. And the flame is not easily adjusted; some kind of "flame tamer" is required between burner and pot for low heat cooking. Even the detractors admit that the Primus is a vast improvement over the alcohol stove. If your boat is fitted with a pressure alcohol stove, it is a worthwhile investment to buy Primus burners and make the conversion.

Liquified petroleum gas (LPG) is without question the most convenient fuel. It burns hot, clean, and odor free; it is easily ignited, easily regulated, readily available, and cheap. If it sounds like the only choice, wait a minute. It is also capable of turning the boat into fiberglass confetti, with a similar effect on the crew.

The explosive nature of LPG is not to be trifled with. It is used safely on a great many cruising boats, but a moment of inattention can have tragic consequences. The problem is that LPG is heavier than air. Should the system develop a leak, the gas will accumulate in the bottom of the boat. LPG has a distinctive odor, but if the level of the gas is below the level of your nose, you may not smell it even though the boat may be explosively full of gas. Strike a match or flip an electrical switch and you wake up looking at all white: a nurse's uniform or Gabriel's robe.

> *In heaven I hope to bake my own bread and clean my own linen.*

You probably won't get the baking detail.

With LPG, *proper installation is essential*. The tank must be installed on deck or in a vapor-proof locker with an overboard drain. It must *never* be installed inside the hull. Two small tanks are preferable to a single large one; one may be left for refill without inhibiting the ability to cook. It is also easier to find an appropriate location for the smaller tanks. In the installation shown, two small horizontal tanks were easily accommodated in the bow anchor locker, utilizing the pre-existing drain.

An electrical solenoid control valve is the single most important safety feature of a proper installation. Required by the U.S. Coast Guard on all inspected vessels, the solenoid shuts off the gas supply at the tanks with a simple flip of a switch in the cabin. When the gas supply is on, the control panel exhibits a red light. When the stove is not in use, the gas supply is shut off, minimizing the risks of a leak in the line or of a burner left on accidentally.

The pressure-reducing valve must also be located at the tank. Reducing the pressure from as high as 250 pounds per square inch to

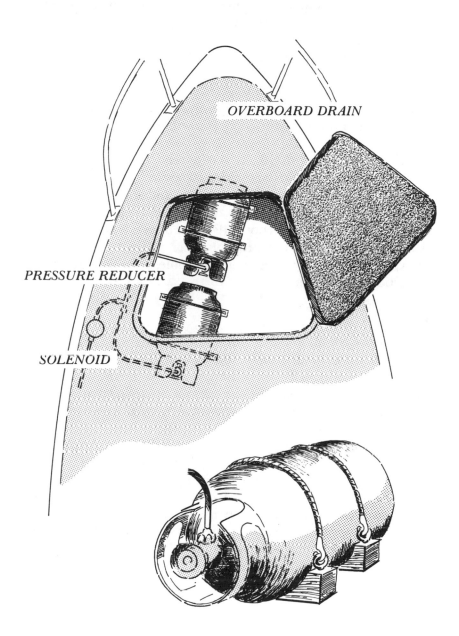

OVERBOARD DRAIN

PRESSURE REDUCER

SOLENOID

Two small horizontal LP tanks, an electric solenoid, and a pressure reducer were installed in this bow anchor locker. The locker has an overboard drain. Tanks were aligned fore-and-aft so boat heel angle would not present a problem.

187

about 0.4 pounds per square inch minimizes the consequences of a leak in the supply line to the stove. Only low pressure line should pass through the boat to the stove.

The bottles and their fittings must be checked for leaks every time they are refilled. Line fittings to the stove should also be checked periodically. Gas lines must be protected from chafe. A gas detector, a "sniffer," located low in the boat is a worthwhile precaution. If you can satisfy your own concerns about safety, you will find an LPG stove a joy to use.

Liquified natural gas (LNG) is a relatively new entrant into the marine stove fuel arena. It has a number of advantages. It is similar to LPG in that it burns hot, clean, and odor free and is easily ignited and regulated. It has a major safety advantage over LPG because it is lighter than air and consequently will not settle in the bilges. Unfortunately, its availability is very limited and, probably as a result, LNG is somewhat more expensive. If it becomes more available, it will merit strong consideration in the future.

THE SINK

There are two common shortcomings in the usual sink installation. First, the sink is too small, usually too shallow. This can be remedied without major modification by exchanging the standard sink for one the same size but deeper. Depth is more important than circumference. A double sink is a nice feature if you have the room, but do not give up all your counter space for one.

The second problem is location. If located off center, the sink will not drain on one tack. In fact, well heeled, the sink may fill, perhaps sloshing sea water into the boat. Centering the sink is probably not practical. Offshore sailors often have a valve in the drain line to keep the sink from filling and a pump in the line to empty the sink underway. Our approach has always been less complex. We plug the sink with a rubber stopper. (In severe conditions, we can close the seacock.) To drain the sink, we pull the plug and head up momentarily, standing the boat up and allowing the sink to drain. Sensible, huh?

WATER

A man may acquire a taste for wine or brandy, and so lose his love for water, but should we not pity him.

In many cruising areas, full water tanks give the cruiser a delightful sense of wealth. We will assume ample tankage for fresh water. What constitutes ample tankage depends upon the number aboard, usage habits, and availability of fresh water. Along the U.S. coast, water is available everywhere for free. Away from the states, it can be very expensive or completely unavailable. If you do not have ample water capacity, you will have to add tankage or augment your supply with portable jugs.

Pressure water systems are very popular on American yachts, even very small yachts. A small electric pump senses the drop in pressure and pumps water to the open faucet. When the faucet is closed, the pump stops. Most systems are simple and very dependable. Since the pump runs only intermittently, the power requirements are not overwhelming. The problem with pressure water is its inherent wastefulness.

The average American uses 65 gallons of water *per day*. We leave the water running while we shave, bathe, remove make-up, brush our teeth, or wash dishes. It is far too easy to bring such habits aboard when you have pressure water. Unless you are both able and willing to fill the boat's tanks often, disconnect the pressure system and install hand or foot pumps. We have used foot pumps for a dozen years and cannot recommend them highly enough. The foot pump allows you to deliver exactly the amount of water that you need and not a wasted drop more, and it allows you to have both hands free in the process.

Just the elimination of a pressure water system will cut fresh water consumption in half. If you are cruising in clean water, you should be able to stretch your fresh water supply even further by using the water the boat is floating in, especially for washing dishes. The simplest way to obtain sea water is to dip a bucket over the side; the most convenient way is to install a sea water pump in the galley. This easy addition allows for an unlimited supply of water for washing and rinsing dishes. The liquid detergents Joy and Dawn work just as well in salt water. An additional through-hull might be avoided by teeing off the raw water intake.

Many boats are fitted with a small (six gallon) hot water heater that operates on either shore power or a heat exchanger when the engine is running. If you are thinking about installing one, forget it; if you have one, remove it. You can make better use of the space. In the first place, the major need for hot water is doing dishes and you are going to do them in sea water. Hot water for a shave or washing your face might be nice, but since the heater is usually located near the engine, you are going to have to empty the lines to get to the hot water. That means pumping as much as a quart of fresh water down the drain before heated water arrives. Where fresh water is a precious commodity, this is not sensible activity.

The most sensible alternative we have found for having available hot water is the pump thermos.

> *I felt even as Diogenes when he saw the boy drinking out of his hand, and threw away his cup.*

We have the thermos mounted in the galley. Each morning during the preparation of breakfast, we heat a kettle of water to boiling and pour

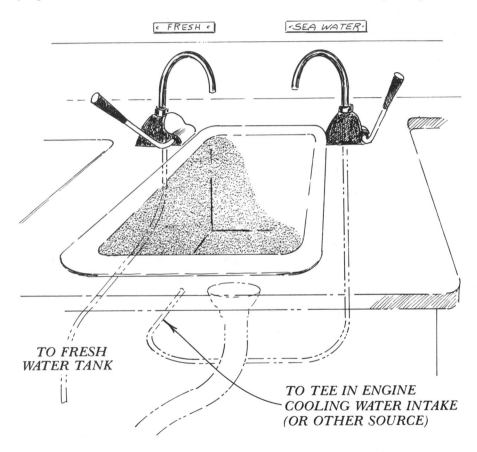

Manually operated pumps for both fresh water and sea water will reduce water consumption.

it into the thermos. What is not used during the day, although still hot the following morning, is returned to the kettle for reheating. Not a drop is wasted.

COUNTER SPACE

What worthwhile comments can we make about counter space? If you have plenty, you do not need our thoughts. If you do not have enough, that is the reality of your boat; you are not changing boats just for more counter space. True, but perhaps you can add to what you have. One way is with a cutting board that fits over the sink. Ferenc Mate' recommends obtaining a plastic box of approximately the same width and length as the sink and gluing it to the underside of the board. It holds the board in place on the sink and, when turned over, makes an ideal dish drainer.

Temporary counter space is often a possibility. A hinged shelf at the end of the existing counter can add needed space during meal

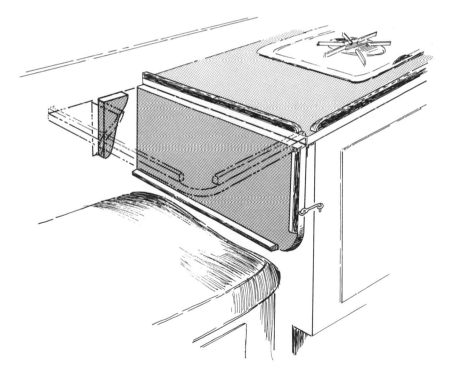

Counter space was extended by installing a drop leaf.

191

preparation and be folded when not in use. A slide-out, like an old-fashioned kitchen breadboard, is also a possibility. Aboard our boat the stove opening is fitted with a cover, giving more counter space when the stove is not in use. When the stove is in use, and additional counter space is needed, the cover is attached to brackets and a swing-out support over the quarter berth.

One shortcoming of many galley counters is a lack of effective fiddle rails. A functional fiddle rail is at least two inches high. With temporary counter space, minimum profile is often essential. Removable fiddles, with pegs that fit into drilled holes in the counter, are a very satisfactory solution.

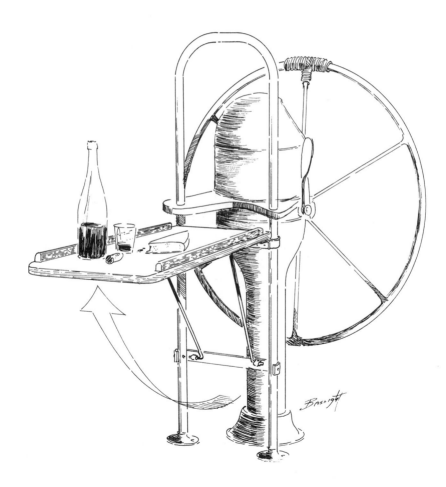

A cockpit table is a worthwhile addition.

TABLES

Like the counter, you will likely live with whatever dining arrangements your boat has. A small dinette or a table that folds against the bulkhead is the most common arrangement. On larger cruisers, the table may be permanently mounted in the middle of the cabin, leaves on either side folding out to opposing settees. Each of these arrangements has advantages; all are functional.

On very small cruisers, a table may not be included in the cabin design. A removable table will enhance the boats cruisability and, with a little thought and duplicate brackets, might also be used in the cockpit for dining outdoors.

Cruising is essentially an outdoor activity. The ability to dine *al fresco* comfortably is an advantage, the cockpit table a worthwhile addition.

I take some satisfaction in eating my food, as well as in being nourished by it.

Pedestal steering manufacturers usually offer a beautifully crafted unit as an option for the pedestal—at a price. A cockpit table need not be expensive. A small folding table available commercially may be satisfactory. With a bit of plywood and a little ingenuity, most cruisers can construct their own. Keep it simple and light.

ICEBOX

Some type of icebox is generally included in the boat's design. On some of the smaller cruisers, we have seen designed space for a portable ice chest, but most designs have the box built in. There may not be a lot that you can do to improve your box. It is probably top loading, the most efficient type, but a bear to find a jar of pimentos in. It is also probably too small (remember, you may have 100 pounds of ice in there before the food goes in) and poorly insulated (four inches needed, two inches normal). You cannot make it any larger and you probably cannot improve the insulation on all sides.

Access is improved by storing the food in baskets or on shelves above the ice. The only thing you can do about capacity is to be sure that only items that require refrigeration are stored in the icebox. Improving insulation depends upon the location and accessibility of the box. If there is space around the box, bringing the insulation up to four inch thickness will make the ice last much longer. Poured urethane foam can be used, but you will have to first build new outer walls around the box.

In many cruising areas, ice is either unavailable or prohibitively expensive. Many cruisers use the icebox for nothing more than dry storage, the most elemental course of action. If you simply cannot cruise without "cold," you may have to consider refrigeration.

REFRIGERATION

There are two basic types of refrigerators commonly seen on cruising boats. One type is electrically powered. This is a tiny unit working just like your refrigerator at home. It is powered by the ship's battery (and sometimes shore power when dockside) and cycles off and on based on the temperature of the box. Installation is simple, and the units are quiet and normally very dependable. They have two major drawbacks. First, they probably cost more than your refrigerator at home.

> . . . and the cost of a thing is the amount of what I will call life which is required to be exchanged for it, immediately or in the long run.

The "long run" is the second drawback. They typically demand about five amps per hour when running and run about half the time. The heavy electrical demand will require running the engine daily, probably for a couple of hours or more. A good wind generator (in a windy area, not Long Island Sound) can sometimes satisfy most of the current demand, but the combined cost of the two units will likely exceed $1,500.

The other type of marine refrigerator is the holding plate system. Still expensive, it is substantially more efficient than the electrical variety. A large compressor, usually belt-driven off the engine, freezes a solution inside a metal box (the holding plate) in the refrigerator. The solution for a system with freezer capacity freezes at 0° F, in effect loading the box with super-cold ice. The ice absorbs the heat in the box, keeping it cold as long as the plate remains frozen. As the plate warms, the compressor must be run again. The length of time between each running, the holdover time, depends upon the size of the plate or plates, the size and insulation of the box, the amount of food inside (full is better), and the ambient temperature. In the temperate zones, a good installation may require as little as 30 minutes per day running time. The same installation in the tropics will probably require at least an hour-and-a-half running time, maybe more.

There is a high price to pay for any type of refrigeration. Not only is the installation expensive, but there is considerable wear and tear on either the batteries or the engine, or both. You will need to spend the time to learn how to maintain or repair the system and the money to put the necessary tools aboard. And running the engine an hour or two a day becomes a chore; no, a torture. It daily disturbs the tranquility of the cruise, and you chafe at how the time drags before you can shut it off.

The silence rings; it is musical and thrills me.

Yeah, right, but the sound of ice cubes in a glass is pretty thrilling music, too. It is not an easy choice. If you are considering refrigeration, consider every aspect before you commit.

UTENSILS

Cookware aboard your cruiser is a matter of preference. For space reasons, take only what you need. The one item we specifically recommend is a pressure cooker. If you do not have one, buy one and learn to use it. The pressure cooker will cut your cooking time in half on many dishes with a corresponding fuel savings, but the real advantage is that in a warm climate you minimize heating the already-plenty-warm-thank-you cabin. The locking lid of the pressure cooker also makes it valuable as the safest pot for use underway, even as a regular saucepan. Four quarts is a good size and a stainless steel cooker will handle the environment better. Other cookware should be stainless steel as well; aluminum soon corrodes from salt water washing and should be avoided.

Dishes are likewise a matter of preference. We have tried every type and have settled on stoneware. It is robust; it does not cut or scratch; it keeps food warm; and, with a custom dish rack, breakage has never been a problem. Stainless flatware is also a good choice, accepting salt water washing with little complaint. A smooth design minimizes inevitable rust stains.

Wilkinson-Sword self-sharpening kitchen knives deserve special mention. Available in most department and drug stores, they come in a variety of styles, each with a sharpening holder. They are ideal for the galley. The holder is permanently mounted (we chose the inside of a cabinet door) and the knives are secure, always available, and always sharp.

We used to spend a small fortune on Tupperware or similar containers until another cruiser pointed us in the right direction. A visit to your friendly restaurateur or the local school cafeteria will yield an unlimited supply of large, plastic screw-top jars. Originally containing institutional quantities of mayonnaise, salad dressing, or pickles, they make perfect cruising canisters. We use them to store flour, sugar, rice, potato flakes, and numerous other bulk items. And they are free.

Rx

The possibilities for improving the average galley are almost endless. The time put into making your galley a joy to use will be time well spent. In adverse circumstances a good meal is often the best prescription, yet if meal preparation is difficult, you will avoid this simple remedy. When food preparation is simplified, you can take advantage of the extraordinary power of a good meal.

> *It always intoxicates me, makes me sane, reverses my views of things.*

The boat may sail on its bottom, but the sailor sails on his stomach.

HIGHER LAWS

I think that . . . we are inclined to spend more on luxury than on safety and convenience . . .

O cruising book can be complete without a chapter on safety. It probably should be the first chapter in the book, but if it was, few would read the book at all. Safety preparation is too often cursory, safety equipment too often a budget casualty. Despite paying lip service to safety considerations, too many cruising sailors subscribe to the Ostrich School of Boating Safety: "It can't happen to me. I'm careful." Not good enough. In cruising, both the boat and the activity need to be looked at with a critical eye toward safety. Closing your eyes to shortcomings is a nautical form of Russian roulette with the potential for consequences just as serious.

No matter how sedentary, life is always fraught with danger.

> *. . . if a man is alive, there is always danger that he may die, though the danger must be allowed to be less in proportion as he is dead-and-alive to begin with. A man sits as many risks as he runs.*

Life at sea in a sailboat is undoubtedly safer than tooling down the freeway on a Kawasaki, or in a Buick for that matter. Even though sailing is a vastly safer activity than living and working in the city, there are steps we can take, attitudes we can adopt, situations we can avoid that will make it safer still.

Most of us survive the dangers of our society because we have learned to cope with or eliminate many of them. We do not walk in the middle of a busy street; we avoid certain areas of the city after dark; we do not plug in the hair dryer while standing in the bath. All of these precautions have been learned though we hardly think about them now. They have become automatic.

As one becomes more familiar with sailing, cruising safety becomes just as automatic. Until it *is* automatic, a conscious effort must be made to consider every aspect of this activity from a safety standpoint. In previous chapters we have mentioned some safety concerns. In this chapter we will try to establish a mind-set that considers safety first in virtually every situation. As a child, we were taught to look both ways before crossing the street; today it is automatic. Safety in cruising is no more difficult to achieve.

STAYING ABOARD

> *On land only the grass and trees wave, but the water itself is rippled by the wind.*

When the boat heels for the first time to a strong breeze, or when a choppy sea begins to pitch and roll the boat erratically, or, as is usually the case, when both happen simultaneously, falling overboard comes to mind. There is a survival instinct that tells us to hold on. That instinct is correct. Unless we stay aboard the boat, other safety considerations may not matter.

Of course falling overboard is not necessarily disastrous. Recovery is possible, even likely in most cases. One fine day, sailing down Biscayne Bay, we encountered a girl treading water in the middle of the Bay. Our puzzlement was relieved when she waved us off, telling us that her father's hat had blown in the water and she had jumped in to retrieve it. The incident had taken place just as they approached a narrow channel through a sand spit. Her father was obliged to carry on through the channel before coming about and sailing back to pick up hat and loving daughter.

On the Great Bahama Bank, with a bit more wind and a crew of four, we, too, lost a hat overboard. In deference to its distressed owner, we decided to go around and pick it up. A spotter stood at the stern rail while the rest of the crew dealt with sails and lines. A tangled sheet delayed our tack momentarily and, in the three-foot seas, our spotter lost sight of the hat. At the encouragement of sailing magazines, we had occasionally tossed a cushion overboard, then sailed a reciprocal course to retrieve it, always with good results. That had been the extent of our preparation for a man-overboard emergency. As we picked up a reciprocal course, we felt certain that we would momentarily sight the brightly colored hat. We never saw the hat again.

Perhaps the hat sank. Consider then our loss of a white dinghy at night in a strong wind. A two-hour search was fruitless. Another night incident involved the accidental loss of an automatic man-overboard strobe. Despite the fact that the strobe was the best quality available and functioned perfectly, by the time we got the boat stopped and turned, we could hardly find the light. Each of these incidents was a shock but unexpectedly profitable in making us realize what a false sense of security we had gotten from retrieving a floating cushion in calm waters.

There is always some accident in the best things . . . The thought came to us because we were in a fit mood; also we were unconscious and did not know that we had said or done a good thing.

We are not suggesting that practice with a cushion is not a good exercise. It is, and returning to the spot where the cushion went over should be practiced on every point of sail in varying conditions until it becomes automatic. But what happens if the person overboard goes under, like the hat apparently did? What happens in high wind and sea conditions? What happens if it is night? What happens if you are alone on deck, or worse still, alone on board? There is only one acceptable solution—prevention.

The risk of failure in a recovery effort is far too great to allow the development of a situation requiring recovery. After our failure to recover the hat, we looked through new eyes at our own boat and at every other boat we sailed. Before leaving the dock in any cruising sailboat, you should be certain that its design and construction, and your seamanship, facilitate staying aboard.

THE BOOM

Crew members are more often lost overboard as a result of a runaway boom, due either to an accidental jibe or to an accidentally released (or parted) main sheet, than any other reason. Aside from knocking the crew member overboard, the impact of the boom may result in a serious and perhaps incapacitating injury, hurting the odds for a successful retrieval. The main boom should be treated with great respect.

Out of habit, the head of the experienced sailor is almost always below the level of the main boom—

Wisdom does not inspect, but behold.

—even when there is no risk of a jibe. When sailing free, particularly dead downwind or by the lee, a preventer on the main boom may prevent more than just a rig-stressing jibe. A preventer may be rigged by running a line from the boom end well forward, through a firmly attached block, and back to the cockpit where it is cleated off. The boom vang may be pressed into service as a preventer by shackling it to the toerail or other side deck attachment. Remember that a vang attached to the base of the mast does not act as a preventer.

HAND RAILS

The best defense against going overboard is always maintaining a secure hold on the ship. For this reason, a safe boat has strategically placed handholds from stem to stern. Hand rails that run the full length of the cabin top on either side are excellent insurance against going overboard. Keep in mind that they are handholds and not fiddle rails for boat hooks, dinghy oars, and the like.

We can show you a very well-known cruising book that demands hand rails in one chapter, then subsequently shows, complete with photo, how to stow long items on deck secured to the hand rail. The

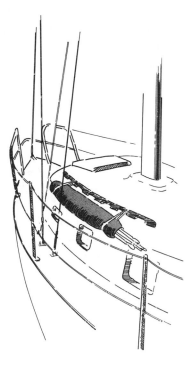

Bags for stowing long items may be suspended from hand rails but must not interfere with the intended purpose of the hand rail.

caption should be, "What is wrong in this picture?" If you want to store items on the cabin top, make the long canvas bag described in an earlier chapter and attach it with twist buttons, or install some pad-eyes for tying down the lot. The point is, when the boat gives an unexpected lurch and you make a desperate grab for the rail, you do not want to jam your fingers into an oar blade. Keep hand rails clear.

PULPITS

Bow and stern rails are essential stay-aboard gear. A sturdy pulpit allows for a high level of safety when foredeck activity is required. For most boats, the stern rail is not quite as essential. However, those with a yawl rig or a ketch rig with an overhanging boom may find worthwhile additional security in the stern rail. Also any boat with a stern-mounted windvane should be fitted with a stern rail. Aside from the obvious protection afforded at the bow and stern of the boat by rails, they provide a strong attachment point for the ends of the lifelines.

LIFELINES

Stout lifelines are a vital part of any safe cruising boat. Some sailors view lifelines with suspicion, feeling that they offer a false sense of security. Surely the best way to stay aboard a pitching sailboat is to always maintain a firm handhold on something solidly attached to the boat, but the lifeline represents an excellent secondary measure, a safety net should your handhold fail. To be effective in this capacity, lifelines should be mounted at least 30 inches above the deck; 36 inches is better. They should be firmly attached to both the bow and stern rails and supported in the middle by stanchions through-bolted to the deck. The stanchions should be of heavy-wall construction and braced well above the deck if possible. A body hurled five or six feet into the lifelines can generate tremendous force and the lifeline system must be capable of absorbing that impact and remaining intact. Weak lifelines are indeed a liability.

Lifelines can be successfully made from either wire or rope. Solid rails are also seen, but rarely on the pocket cruiser. If rope is used, it should be of polyester and a large enough size to minimize stretch. Wire is more common because it can be of a much smaller diameter and is thus less obtrusive. We prefer lifelines attached with friction end fittings (i.e., Sta-Lok or Norseman) or with Nicopress sleeves. (The friction fittings are less likely to snag sails or lines.) Factory-installed lifelines are often swaged. If you own a boat with swaged lifeline fittings, check them as carefully and as often as you check the rigging fittings. They are subject to the same hairline cracking as rigging swages with consequences of failure equally as serious.

Double lifelines are preferable to single, both for the added security they provide should a crew member slip underneath the top lifeline and for the additional support they provide for the stanchions. If children are aboard, netting laced to the lifelines provides a high level of safety. Ditto for Fido.

NON-SKID

Keeping your feet is just as important as maintaining a good grip. Deck surfaces must be non-skid. Teak decks are the traditional non-skid surface and are very effective. However, when teak decks are oiled to enhance their beauty, they lose some of their non-skid characteristics. Great care must be taken with a teak deck to ensure that it remains non-skid.

Many production sailboats have molded-in, non-skid surfaces which provide adequate traction. As the boat ages and the deck requires painting, too often the paint acts as a filler on molded-in non-skid and significantly reduces its effectiveness. Non-skid decks may be made from sand, walnut shell, or some other aggregate mixed with deck paint. During refitting, a more effective non-skid may be achieved using a glue-on sheet product such as Treadmaster.

All surfaces upon which you walk should have some type of non-skid treatment. Strips of non-skid tape should be applied even on Lexan hatches, particularly those located where sail handling may take place. Do not overlook the non-skid characteristics of good boat shoes.

TOERAIL

A good toerail is also indispensable for good footing. Heeled well down with the necessity to attend to some matter on the leeward side of the boat, a substantial and firmly attached toerail will provide invaluable assistance in staying aboard. Bulwarks at least four to six inches high are much better for this purpose. The aluminum toerail/ genoa track found on many newer production sailboats serves well also, but most such tracks are only about two inches high, supporting only about half of the foot. A higher rail or a bulwark increases the margin of safety.

THE FOREDECK

There are a number of other things that can be done to reduce the risk of anyone going overboard. On a cruising sailboat, as much sail handling as possible should be done from the relative safety of the cockpit. All sheets and topping lifts should be led into the cockpit. Primarily for the purpose of avoiding foredeck work, a cruising boat may use a roller-furling headsail to advantage, with the furling line leading into the cockpit. With such an arrangement, the only sail handling that would require leaving the cockpit would be raising and lowering the mainsail. Fortunately, going to the mast does not represent nearly the same level of exposure to risk that going to the foredeck does.

Despite all lines leading aft, the occasion will arise when you will have to go to the foredeck, perhaps in the worst conditions. Even in an apparent emergency, resist the tendency to rush forward. Take a moment to think through the problem and decide on the best and *safest* course of action. Then go forward *deliberately*—if conditions merit, with your harness attached.

In bygone years, the jib boom enjoyed some popularity for making the headsail self-tending. Unlike the main boom, you cannot duck under the jib boom and it can sweep the foredeck with lethal force. Perhaps for this reason, the jib boom is no longer very popular. If you sail with a jib boom, you should show it great respect.

Another source of trouble on the foredeck is the clew shackle. Too many sailors attach the jib or genoa sheets to the headsail with a heavy shackle. With a stuck jib hank or a jammed furling drum, the flailing headsail alone becomes extremely dangerous to the person trying to sort things out. It is three times as dangerous with a heavy shackle attached to the clew. A pair of bowlines is much safer.

ON DECK STOWAGE

When conditions are rough, or the potential for rough conditions exists, the hard dinghy must come aboard. On smaller cruisers there is a tendency to carry the dinghy on the foredeck. Such an arrangement seriously inhibits foredeck work and increases the risk of going overboard. A dinghy on deck should be stowed in such a manner that it does not in any way interfere with mobility and sail handling. Generally, that means the dinghy must be carried on the cabin top beneath the main boom. Even there it inhibits the helmsman's view forward and it may be a risk in reefing conditions, but a far smaller one than a dinghy on the foredeck. If your dinghy will only fit on the foredeck of your boat, you need a different dinghy. There are creative solutions, such as a nesting dinghy or one with a removable transom. There is also the standard solution to this problem, the inflatable.

The bowline is a safer means of attaching jib sheets to the clew.

In addition to the dinghy, there is a tendency for cruisers to store other items on deck. If jerry jugs must be stored on deck, they should be stored well aft, not blocking the side decks or access to the foredeck. Whisker poles, awning poles and what-not should similarly be stowed in such a manner that they do not represent a hazard to the crew member going forward. When underway, the anchor line should not be left coiled down on the foredeck. If it must be left out to dry, it should be securely stopped and attached to the boat well clear of the area normally used for sail handling.

STAYING AFLOAT

Keeping the water on the outside of the hull where it belongs is the only secret to staying afloat. This is done by either preventing the entry of any water into the hull or by pumping water out at a faster rate than it enters. The first method is the best one but the occasion may arise when the second method comes into play.

The watertight integrity of the boat is the first consideration. The ability to close and securely latch all openings into the boat was covered in an earlier chapter. This includes not only the forward hatch and the companionway, but also the cockpit hatches, the lazarette, and all portholes and ventilators. Having the ability to secure hatches is of little value if you do not secure them; keep them closed and latched if there is any threat.

COCKPIT DRAINS

Many pocket cruisers have proportionally large cockpits. An eight-foot cockpit is only 20% of a 40-foot boat, but it is a third of a 25-footer. The difference in relation to displacement (or buoyancy) is even more marked. A small boat with a large cockpit is vulnerable to a boarding sea, the weight of the water in the cockpit pinning the boat for the next punch. It is imperative that the cockpit drain quickly; most standard cockpit drains are woefully inadequate. They must either be enlarged or augmented. If the cockpit sole is well above the waterline, a single two- or three-inch drain passing straight out the stern is a much easier solution than changing through-hulls and seacocks.

SEACOCK

Functional seacocks are a safety imperative and dependent upon adequate maintenance. At a minimum, seacocks should be opened and closed periodically to ensure their operation. Bronze seacocks should be dismantled and greased annually. All intake and discharge hoses should be double clamped (all-stainless clamps, please), with the clamps also inspected periodically. Use your fingers to feel all the way around the clamp. A corrosion fracture is as likely to be on the side you cannot see.

Even with periodic maintenance, a hose can split or a through-hull fitting fail. A one-and-a-half-inch through-hull six inches below the waterline will admit water into the hull at the amazing rate of 1,900 gallons per hour. It can sink your boat fairly quickly, but it need not happen. The solution for that danger is a soft, wooden, tapered plug for each through-hull fitting. The plugs are shaped ahead of time and then attached to their respective seacock with a piece of light line. In the event of a failure, it is a simple matter to cut the plug loose and drive the tapered end into the seacock. Similar plugs should be cut to fit the

A tapered wooden plug should be attached to all seacocks.

stuffing glands for both the prop shaft and the rudder tube if your vessel has either. Using such a plug, we were able to replace a prop shaft without having the boat hauled.

GROUNDING

A serious grounding can hole the boat, leading to flooding. Hitting a rock, a coral head, or going on the beach in a surf can be costly errors. The first line of defense against such an eventuality is competent piloting.

> . . . using new passages and all improvements to navigation;—charts to be studied, the position of reefs and new lights and buoys to be ascertained . . .

The second is vigilance. To relax vigilance is to invite disaster.

An increasing number of sailors are going offshore depending solely upon their electronics, specifically Loran or SatNav. This is a dangerous trend. There is not a thing in the world wrong with navigating across the wide Atlantic based on SatNav fixes *if* someone aboard can get you on across in case of an electronic or electrical failure. Otherwise the safety of the vessel hangs by a tenuous thread.

> . . . *lying on my back across the seats, in a summer forenoon, dreaming awake, until I was aroused by the boat touching the sand, and I arose to see what shore my fates had impelled me to . . .*

This is fine for drifting down the Concord, but no way to cross an ocean.

FLOAT PLAN

Regardless of your ultimate destination, a float plan is a good precaution. It should contain your destination, your planned route, and when you would consider yourself overdue. It should also contain a description of the vessel, including name, size, color, rig, and registration or documentation number. This information would facilitate a search, should one become necessary.

The most important considerations are that the float plan is left with a responsible person, that you do not fail in your responsibility to notify that person of your safe arrival, and that you are realistic in your estimate of time required to reach your destination. To be responsible for an unnecessary search is unforgivable.

Sometimes people file a float plan for a trip down the Intracoastal Waterway or across the bay. That is overkill. We file a general float plan for a six-month cruise and call home periodically to update it. Take whatever approach you find both secure and sensible.

WEATHER

Weather is a major cause of difficulty aboard a cruising boat. The *voyager* faces whatever Mother Nature throws at him, hoping that he and the vessel are prepared. It is true that you cannot get bad weather experience without experiencing bad weather. If your cruise could expose you to bad weather, it is a good idea to spend a few windy, rainy days sailing in home waters to learn the rudiments of heavy weather sailing and to allay fears and build confidence.

> *I find it good to be out this still, dark, mizzling afternoon; my . . . voyage is more suggestive and profitable than in bright weather.*

Even prepared, the sensible voyager tries to select the season with the least risk of bad weather when crossing a particular body of water.

The *coastal cruiser* can be more selective about weather. It is foolish to challenge the elements beyond the limits of good judgement. While a competent skipper can successfully sail through dense fog or gale conditions, it is far more sensible to avoid such conditions if possible. For a few, such conditions represent a challenge, but for most they represent discomfort and increased risk. The romance of an ocean storm endured in a small boat is highly overrated.

> *The horizon has one kind of beauty and attraction to him who has never explored the hills and mountains in it, and another, I fear a less ethereal and glorious one, to him who has.*

The sensible cruiser stays aware of impending weather and chooses his sailing days to minimize the risk.

COLLISION AVOIDANCE

Collision with another vessel is another cause of sinkings and is to be avoided, regardless of right-of-way. We recall an old Department of Public Safety ad on television showing a state trooper walking through torn metal and broken glass, the aftermath of a major accident. Picking up a fragment of the debris, the trooper said something like, "Yes, he was right—dead right." The same warning applies to sailors. Simply do not get into a position where pressing a claim for right-of-way may risk a collision. It is not a matter of principle; it is a matter of good sense.

There are of course rules, the *International Regulations for the Prevention of Collisions at Sea* (COLREGS), to determine right-of-way, but even these rules recognize the need for good sense, for seamanship. The rules themselves require " . . . due regard . . . to any special circumstances . . . which may make a departure from these Rules necessary to avoid immediate danger." There is a lot of open space in the world's oceans, bays, and lakes and very little reason for two boats to ever insist on occupying the same bit of it at the same time.

When dealing with other sailboats, there are rules (summarized in the illustration below) to be followed. In encounters with power boats, the power boat is supposed to keep clear. Don't count on it. Too often the skipper does not know of his obligation, or he just does not care. Commercial fishing vessels, on the other hand, have the right-of-way

HIGHER LAWS

(THE DARKER BOAT
GENERALLY HAS
RIGHT OF WAY)

TO PREVENT COLLISION:

When two sailboats are on different tacks:
- sailboat on starboard tack holds course and speed; sailboat on port tack gives way.

When on the same tack:
- sailboat to windward gives way; sailboat to leeward holds her course and speed.

When a sailboat and a powerboat are converging:
- sailboat holds her course and speed; the powerboat gives way.

A sailboat under both power and sail must exhibit a black cone shape (point down) in her rigging:
- if over 12 meters (about 40 feet) long in inland waters, and
- if over 7 meters (about 23 feet) long in international waters.

Meeting head-on: KEEP RIGHT.
Crossing: Give right of way to boats ahead and to the right of you (in DANGER ZONE).
Passing: Give right of way. KEEP CLEAR.

HORN SIGNALS:

In conditions of restricted visibility:
- sailboat sounds one long and 2 short blasts on her horn every minutes.

If collision is imminent:
- give danger signal of 5 short blasts.

To open a bridge:
- give one long and one short blast.

RIGHT OF WAY: Generally the higher category has priority:
- *unable to steer*
- *limited in turning ability*
- *restricted to channel water depth*
- *commercial fishing*
- *sailing*
- *power driven*

These are only the most important rules of the road that apply to the cruising sailor. The prudent sailor will become familiar with the complete body of rules.

Simplified Rules of the Road for sailing vessels.

over sail, as do large vessels in restricted areas due to their inability to maneuver. For a sailor in a 30-foot sailboat, the most sensible and least confusing procedure to adopt is simply to stay well clear of all other vessels.

It is surprising how much room there is in nature—if a man will follow his proper path.

It is also surprising how little room there can appear to be in a channel or restricted harbor. Here a familiarity with the rules is required. If it appears that the approaching vessel is not going to proceed according to the dictates of the COLREGS, then you should take early and clear evasive action. Afterwards, if you want to tell the skipper what you think of his seamanship, either vocally or through sign language, fine. But do not collide with him.

When approaching a commercial vessel, you should consider yourself to be the burdened vessel in all cases, regardless of whether you are in restricted waters. Any vessel that requires three miles to come to a full stop, or a half mile to answer the helm, is "unable to maneuver" in our book, even in the middle of the ocean. Fishing boats with trawls and tug boats with tows should be given a wide berth. If you sail at night, you should familiarize yourself with the lighting characteristics of these vessels.

Those venturing offshore will eventually encounter ships. In some areas shipping traffic is very heavy, particularly in coastal shipping lanes. It is not a place to go to be at one with nature. Shipping lanes are best avoided. When encountered, lanes should be crossed at right angles to minimize the time that the yacht is in the lane. The surest way to avoid being run down by a ship is to stay away from ships.

When an encounter is inevitable, be absolutely certain you know what the situation is at all times. If you are converging with the track of an oncoming ship and its bearing from you remains constant, you are on a collision course. Do not trust this judgement to casual navigation. Take a compass bearing on the ship, then compare it to a second bearing in a few minutes. If you are on a collision course, take early action to pass well clear of the ship, behind him, not across his bow.

Do not depend upon the ship to see you. You will be better off if you always assume that he is *not* aware of you. In good weather you are probably visible and may be detected. In inclement weather your chances of being seen are not as good. In bad weather merchant ships rely heavily on radar. Without a radar reflector, you probably will not even appear on the screen. With a good reflector mounted up high, you will show up, if someone is watching the screen; but if the seas are heavy, you are going to be lost in the wave echoes, or "enhanced" right off the screen by the unit's anti-clutter control.

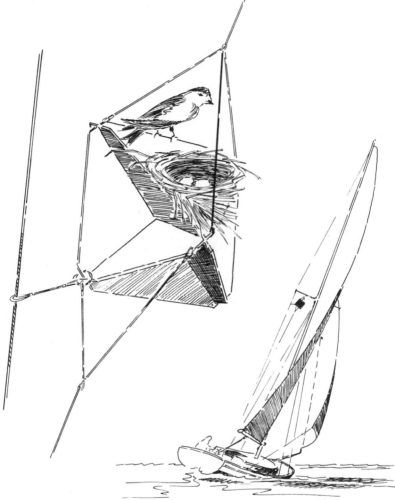

To be most effective a radar reflector should be mounted high and cocked in such a way as if to catch and hold water.

As a consequence, it is imperative that *you* see all approaching vessels. This imperative presupposes maintaining a constant watch.

> . . . *having made all tight without and withdrawn under hatches with a merry crew of thoughts, leaving only my outer man at the helm, or even tying up the helm when it was plain sailing.*

Self-steering is good, but does not relieve watch-keeping requirements. The view of a large area to one side of the bow is often restricted by the headsail (and perhaps the dinghy). You must either have a lookout with an unrestricted view, easy to do with an autopilot handling the helm, or get in the habit of heading up periodically to check the area behind the sail, like looking in the rear-view mirror when driving.

EXPLOSION

Those vessels with an LPG stove or a gasoline engine are exposed to the risk of explosion. We have already outlined the proper safety precautions for both installations. Those not so equipped should nevertheless be cognizant of this risk. We have seen cruisers store gasoline for the dinghy inside cockpit lockers. This is a very risky practice. If it can be avoided, no explosive chemicals should be stored inside the hull.

FIRE

The chemicals mentioned above are also a fire hazard and should be stored with that risk in mind. A lesser-known fire hazard is charcoal. Many cruisers carry a stern-mounted grill and a supply of charcoal. When charcoal is damp, it is subject to spontaneous combustion. Clipper ships carrying coal were regularly lost to spontaneous combustion and more than one yacht has been lost this way. If charcoal is aboard, great care must be taken to keep it dry.

SNEAKY LEAKS

Any leak below the waterline, if not detected, will result in the sinking of the boat. Insurers claim that the number one cause of sinkings is a faulty head installation. It is unlikely that your boat will sink from an overflowing head while you are aboard cruising. Such a problem would soon be apparent and is relatively easy to deal with. However, if left unattended for a few days, a stuck valve in the head may very well take the boat to the bottom. If your head has a direct overboard discharge, a loop above the waterline with an anti-siphon valve at the top is recommended. Even with this installation, seacocks for the head should be closed anytime the vessel is left unattended.

There are other installations that may result in flooding. We have previously mentioned the off-center sink. When the boat is heeled well down the sink may be below the waterline, resulting in an inward flow of water. It is not likely to go unnoticed long enough to endanger the vessel but may result in serious damage to equipment and supplies.

Some electric bilge pump installations, on the other hand, may result in sinking. Under sail, heeling submerges the discharge. The bilge pump runs. When it stops, water in the discharge line runs back into the boat, setting up a suction and siphoning in sea water. The pump may handle the flow as long as the battery holds out. Once the boat begins to fill, the problem is compounded by the discharge line moving below the waterline regardless of heel. Such an underwater leak may be very difficult to locate, particularly in a boat underway. A check valve is one solution but often restricts the capacity of the bilge pump. We prefer to locate the discharge in the stern well above the waterline.

Deck leaks, leaks around portholes, or poorly bedded chainplates and stanchions may allow water into the hull. More than just an annoyance on a wooden boat or a fiberglass one with a wooden core, a chronic fresh water leak will lead to rot, costly repair, and possibly to a serious safety hazard. Although they will not sink you without warning, deck leaks must be attended to. There are some outstanding bedding products available, but they must be properly applied to be effective.

MAINTENANCE

Poor maintenance is a blatant display of poor seamanship. The potential for disaster is no less significant than inadequate ground tackle or incompetent navigation.

> *The vessel, though her masts be firm,*
> *Beneath her copper bears a worm;*
> *Around the cape, across the line,*
> *Till fields of ice her course confine;*
> *It matters not how smooth the breeze,*
> *How shallow or how deep the seas,*
> *Whether she bears Manila twine,*
> *Or in her hold Madeira wine,*
> *Or China teas, or Spanish hides,*
> *In port or quarantine she rides;*
> *Far from New England's blustering shore,*
> *New England's worm her hulk shall bore,*
> *And sink her in the Indian seas,*
> *Twine, wine, and hides, and China teas.*

Wooden vessels still require thorough precautions against worms. Modern fiberglass boats do not risk teredo attack, but they are not maintenance free. Electrolysis will attack underwater fittings unless sacrificial zincs are renewed regularly. The dependability of such equipment as sheet winches or an anchor windlass can be enhanced with regularly scheduled maintenance. The engine and rigging require regular attention.

A sailboat does not need an engine. However, few of us choose to cruise without one. We come to depend upon it. It is that dependence that places us at risk. When we entrust the safety of the vessel to an engine, we must be certain that the engine will not fail. Periodic maintenance is our best assurance of that. The sensible cruiser will learn to maintain his engine and carry with him the necessary tools and supplies.

Standing and running rigging should be examined regularly. We keep records of the last oil change; the rig deserves at least as much care. A schedule of rigging inspection religiously followed will greatly reduce any risk of rigging failure.

HANDLING THE UNAVOIDABLE

No matter how far-sighted you are, situations may occur that you had not specifically planned for.

> *Who can doubt that men are by a certain fate what they are, contending with unseen and unimagined difficulties, or encouraged and aided by equally mysterious auspicious circumstances?*

If you do have an emergency, the severity of the consequences may depend upon how well you handle it. Like preparations for emergency avoidance, providing yourself in advance with the tools for dealing with the unimagined will undoubtedly improve the outcome.

MEDICAL KIT

> *The old and infirm and the timid, of whatever age or sex, thought most of sickness, and sudden accident and death; to them life seemed full of danger,—what danger is there if you don't think of any—and they thought that a prudent man would carefully select the safest position, where Dr. B. might be on hand at a moment's warning.*

When Doctor B. is not around, you will have to handle medical emergencies. A pre-packaged first aid kit is fine for weekend cruising, but is inadequate for long-term cruising. At the other end of the spectrum, many long distance vessels carry a comprehensive kit which includes a dental kit, suturing supplies, and a wide array of prescription drugs. There is not likely to be a need for such a well-equipped medical kit on most cruises. On a coastal cruise, trained medical assistance is never very distant. If your destination is more remote, your medical supplies should handle a broader array of eventualities. A comprehensive first aid manual is a necessary companion to any medical kit.

BILGE PUMP

There is a tendency in pocket cruisers, particularly those at the smaller end of the range, to be satisfied with a single electric bilge pump, usually a submersible with an automatic switch. This is a serious omission of essential safety gear. In addition to the electric pump, every cruising boat, no matter how small, should have a high-capacity *manual* bilge pump on board, either permanently mounted or board mounted. Only the diaphragm type should be considered.

A failed seacock on a 25-footer will let in exactly the same amount of water as the same fitting on a 60-footer. And the 60-footer can accommodate a lot more water before being in danger of sinking. This makes a case that the smaller the boat, the larger the bilge pump required. If a large pump takes up valuable stowage space, so be it. The time may come when no other piece of gear is more important.

HULL REPAIR

The ability to stop a leak may mean the difference between a scare and a disaster. For holes already in the hull, we have recommended tapered plugs. Unplanned holes in the hull are likely to be of an irregular shape, requiring a more flexible solution. For damage above the waterline, silver duct tape can be very effective. When the hull damage is below the waterline, stuffing the hole with rags or cushions can reduce the leak. In some circumstances, underwater epoxy can effect a more permanent repair.

FIRE CONTROL

Fire control depends almost exclusively on properly placed and well-maintained fire extinguishers. Federal regulations require the pocket cruiser to have two small (B-I) portable extinguishers or one large (B-II) one. An approved fixed system can be substituted for one of the small portable units.

The safety of the boat is much more important than the regulations. We prefer to have an extinguisher located both forward and aft of the galley stove so that fire-fighting equipment is available immediately regardless of your location when a fire starts. An extinguisher near the stove (not behind it, please!) will allow the cook to gain quick control of a galley fire. Against the possibility of an engine room fire, one should be located near the engine access. An extinguisher located in a cockpit locker could be the only one accessible in the event of a cabin fire. It sounds as if five extinguishers are recommended, but some can do double duty. Three should be adequate: one forward, one in a cockpit locker, and one close to both the galley and the engine hatch.

LIFE RAFT

For a long offshore passage, the life raft may offer some additional margin of safety. For the pocket cruiser, the life raft seems to be of dubious value. Foundering offshore is unlikely and an emergency close to shore is better addressed by a maneuverable vessel, the dinghy for example. Some thought should go into storing the dinghy, rigid or inflatable, so that it is quickly accessible in an emergency.

MAN OVERBOARD

If you still have a nonchalant attitude about the risk of going overboard, we encourage you to read Hank Searle's gripping novel, *Overboard*. Man-overboard equipment is something that you hope never to use, but it is essential cruising gear. At a minimum, the boat should have an orange or bright yellow horseshoe buoy ready for immediate deployment, *not* clipped to its rack. The buoy should have a drogue to keep it from being blown quickly out of reach. An attached dye marker and whistle may prove invaluable in facilitating recovery.

If night sailing is contemplated, a strobe should be attached to the horseshoe. A more satisfactory alternative (because the person overboard may be unable to connect with the buoy) is a personal strobe worn by each crew member. For offshore work, where a person in the water may soon be lost from sight because of the sea running, a man-overboard pole raises the height of the target ten feet. One equipped with a strobe will be valuable at night.

As important as the equipment are the procedures. Everyone aboard should know what to do in case of a man-overboard emergency. Much has been written on the subject, but practice is the only acceptable way of learning. It is imperative that the correct response be automatic. The

Fast response in deploying man-overboard equipment will improve the chances of success.

basic steps are as follows, but may require alteration to account for crew availability and wind and sea conditions:

1. • Instantly deploy the horseshoe buoy and any other overboard equipment (the pole or strobe).
   • If others are aboard, shout "Man Overboard!"
   • If others are available, assign someone the sole responsibility of continually pointing at the person in the water.
   • Begin counting (as a means of determining how long you have sailed away before getting the boat turned).
   • Observe the compass course and the boat speed.

2. • Turn the boat as quickly as possible and sail a reciprocal course, under power if necessary (and possible).
   • Count again as before, maintaining a reciprocal course and similar speed.
3. • Make the final approach upwind, to keep from being blown down on the person.
4. • Get a line to him immediately. Unless the man overboard is injured, no other person should enter the water.
5. • Get a boarding ladder over the side; this is when the permanently mounted transom boarding ladder really shines.
6. • In the event of injury, hoist him aboard with a rope sling beneath the arms attached to the main halyard, or in the belly of the mainsail lowered into the water as a sling.

If the overboard occurred unobserved, the problems are more complex. Assuming a constant course, the boat is placed on a reciprocal course and several buoyant items (cockpit cushions, life jackets, anything) are tossed overboard to mark the limit of the search area. Determine how long prior to discovery the person may have gone overboard and calculate the distance covered. The reciprocal course is maintained until the same distance has been sailed. If on the return trip, the crew member is not located, more buoyant items are jettisoned to mark the second limit. Continue to sail back and forth between the floating objects. If other crew are aboard, placing a spotter on the spreaders will widen the area of visibility. Get help in the search as rapidly as possible.

CALLING FOR ASSISTANCE

In some circumstances, such as the one just described, obtaining assistance quickly may avert disaster. For coastal cruising, the VHF radio has the best track record for quickly summoning help. Long distance radios such as SSB or Ham are less likely to be effective, not because of a failure to reach someone, but because the great distances involved will delay or even prevent help from arriving. The farther offshore you venture, the more enforced is self-reliance.

In a dismasting, the VHF may become inoperative due to the loss of the antenna. We keep an emergency antenna near the radio at all times as a hedge against this possibility. It is very inexpensive insurance.

For an offshore passage, we find few items offer the sense of security of the emergency position indicating radio beacon (EPIRB). The EPIRB is a floating transmitter capable of sending out an emergency signal for days. Originally designed for locating downed aircraft, the marine version still broadcasts on an aircraft frequency and the signal may be picked up by any commercial or military aircraft passing overhead as far as 300 miles away. The most exciting part of this technology is that EPIRB signals are beginning to be monitored by satellite, linking the unfortunate sailor with potential assistance from almost anywhere in the world. A coastal EPIRB (for use inside the 20-mile limit) has recently been approved that transmits on VHF Channel 16.

Visual distress signals are now Coast Guard-required equipment on every pocket cruiser. This requirement may be satisfied without flares by selecting smoke signals (three) or a distress flag, and an automatic, electric S.O.S. light. Most skippers choose to put flares aboard. A minimum of three are required; they may be handheld, meteor, or parachute. There is little question that of all choices, the relatively expensive parachute flare has the greatest opportunity of being observed. Flares have an expiration date and require replacement every three years. When we freshen our supply, we keep the old flares. If they are kept dry, even expired flares should perform if called upon.

WEAPONS

There seems recently to be a great deal written about pirates or sinister drug smugglers. That is too bad because the risk of a life-threatening encounter with pirates or criminals is so small that it does not appropriately merit mention among the risks of cruising. Weapons are *not* cruising gear and their mention in a cruising book should be as out of place as their mention in a home furnishing book, despite the fact that many homeowners have weapons. Still, because this issue is on the mind of so many would-be cruisers, we cannot avoid a brief comment.

Ample ground tackle and a large capacity bilge pump are essential cruising equipment. A revolver is not. Yet sailors are susceptible to an insidious fear of pirates.

The unlimited anxiety, strain, and care of some persons is one very incurable form of disease.

It is the fear of facing whatever occurs completely alone. Forget it. Cruising is far safer in this aspect than living ashore. Besides, in the hands of most cruisers, a gun aboard does not reduce the risk, but increases it. The likelihood of a normal cruiser encountering a situation meriting deadly force continues to be remote. With a firearm aboard, the likelihood of inappropriate use of deadly force is far greater. Should the unimaginable actually occur, a show of weapons will undoubtedly force the issue, perhaps making murderers out of mere thieves—at your expense.

And what of the risk from the native population of foreign lands?

> . . . so similar are the lives of men in all countries, and fraught with the same homely experiences. One half the world knows how the other half lives.

There is a great deal of wisdom compressed into that last sentence.

There are places in the world where self-reliance may very well indicate a need to "protect" yourself, but they are rarely visited by cruisers. Unless your planned cruise takes you through such an area, the most sensible course of action is to leave the weapons at home. It is not the right to arm we dispute; it is the imperative to arm. The greatest robbery risk you face is that of letting third-hand stories and sensationalized press rob you of the tranquility of cruising. Such anxiety is simply not merited.

VIGILANCE

Of all the safety items aboard, none is more important than sound judgement. Recognizing how quickly an emergency can develop and the gravity of such an occurrence is the first step. Sound judgement is exhibited in innumerable ways. It means relieving motion sickness in a bucket in boisterous conditions rather than hanging weakly over the lee rail. For the male sailor in the same sea conditions, it means answering the call of nature in the head rather than at the rail. It means wearing a harness. It means giving a wide berth to underwater danger, and to other vessels regardless of right of way. it means waiting on improved conditions before setting off on a cruise. It means a diligent approach to maintenance. It means imagining all manner of emergencies and making certain vessel and crew are prepared for them all. It means unceasing vigilance.

Every cruiser can significantly reduce his or her likelihood of encountering an emergency by recognizing the constancy of the risk.

> . . . to stand on the meeting of two eternities, the past and future, which is precisely the present moment . . .

And by never relaxing vigilance.

BRUTE NEIGHBORS

We are made to exaggerate the importance of what work we do; and yet how much is not done by us! Or, what if we had been taken sick?

NLESS you are single-handing, you will be sharing the handling of the boat with at least one crew member. We have already pointed out that the dominant crew composition is the couple. This is not by chance. In the following, we will examine all types of crew. Our examination will lead us back to the cruising couple, but with a better understanding of why this is the most successful combination aboard.

THE PERFECT CREW

We can begin by imagining the "perfect" crew. On a pocket cruiser with some offshore work planned, the ideal crew consists of three perfectly compatible members: one is an expert navigator, neat and precise, with gyroscopic balance for handling the sextant on a pitching deck and a cast-iron stomach for handling the calculations below; one is a gourmet cook, thriving on the challenge of the galley underway, asking no more than a satisfied smile and a clean plate; and one is a fearless, macho deck-ape, happiest changing sail on a diving foredeck, finding humor in green water to the armpits.

Even if we could assemble such a crew, we would need the "perfect" cruise to keep the crew happy. Sail changes must be necessary only while the deck-ape is on watch. We simply cannot allow a wind increase while the cook is on watch. Otherwise, specialties and actual duties do not match.

In light of the realities of any cruise, let's rethink our perfect crew. It should consist of three perfectly compatible members, *each* an expert navigator, a gourmet cook, and a fearless deck-ape. It is starting to sound like three single-handers sharing the same boat. That is close. On a short-handed boat, every crew member should be able to handle the boat alone. Perhaps you have already picked up on the paradox here. What do you think the chances are of combining three qualified single-handers aboard one boat and having them remain *perfectly compatible?*

COMPATIBILITY

Single-handers have recognized this problem with compatibility and resolved it by sailing alone. Some are indeed "loners," placing great value on their solitude and eschewing companionship.

> *I have, as it were, my own sun and moon and stars, and a little world all to myself.*

Many are more gregarious than that, in fact share our penchant for sharing the cruising experience, but simply have not yet found the right crew.

How do you identify the right crew? The most important characteristic is compatibility. It eclipses all others. Perhaps that is not the appropriate word. Compatibility *encompasses* all other characteristics. If you have a high degree of compatibility with a prospective crew member, the crew combination has a good chance for success despite a lack of imagination in the galley. Conversely, incompatibility, even though the prospect may be fantastic in the galley, almost certainly dooms the combination.

OTHER TRAITS

A specific skill or talent is often the least important consideration, particularly aboard a pocket cruiser where there is little room for specialization. This is not to say that there is little value to being able to navigate or to cook. It is just that everyone can learn to navigate or cook; compatibility, on the other hand, either exists or it does not.

More important than bringing a specific skill aboard is bringing the desire and willingness to learn. The operation of every boat is different. The crew member who comes aboard with an open mind and an enthusiastic attitude will invariably be a better shipmate than the sullen or aloof old salt.

No matter how idyllic, some adversity accompanies almost every cruise. A good crew member meets adversity with a smile, or at least without grousing or finding fault with other members. If you are looking for crew among friends or family, you should already know about this trait.

The fault-finder will find faults even in paradise.

Crabs are great in a salad, but a disaster in a crew.

A good crew member has a sense of duty. He can be counted upon to do every task completely and to the best of his ability. He fully comprehends the interdependence of a crew on a small vessel and carries his load. He is selfless, sharing in both the benefits and the costs of the cruise—and in the responsibility. You are comfortable with him on watch.

A good crew member also has a good sense of space. He gives other crew members room, does not infringe on their space. On a small boat, this invariably means neatness. Few things cause crew discord quicker than slovenliness.

It also means silence.

Silence is the universal refuge, the sequel to all dull discourses and all foolish acts, a balm to our every chagrin, as welcome after satiety as after disappointment . . .

On every cruise, there are times to talk, to sing, to shout even. There are also times to remain silent. The good crew member can discriminate between the two.

IMPROVING THE ODDS

Even selecting the most wonderful, easy-going, responsible person or persons that you know is no assurance of a happy crew. A great deal depends upon how you as the skipper fulfill your responsibilities. Your crew's success or failure will be based more upon their attitude, conduct, and participation than upon their knowledge. While their knowledge may not seem important to you, it is important to them, often the difference between anxiety and confidence. It is your responsibility to ensure that your crew knows well in advance what is expected of them.

In part, this means spelling out assigned duties at the very beginning of the cruise. If at all possible, it means instructions even farther in advance. If the crew member is not immediate family, an advance letter can do much to avoid uncertainty. The letter should contain as much information as possible about planned itinerary, expected weather, possible activities, what to bring, anything that you can think of that might help to put your crew member more at ease. Family crew members need the same information, but do not expect your spouse to react well to a letter from you. Try talking at dinner. If you cannot, the cruise is already in trouble.

Despite excellent pre-cruise preparation, some kind of orientation is indicated when the crew member first comes aboard. The detail of the orientation will depend upon the experience of the member and his familiarity with your boat. In preparation for an extended cruise, you might discuss, among others, all of the following:

- Sail handling.
- Anchoring techniques.
- Man-overboard procedures.
- Operation of the engine.
- Operation of the head.
- Operation of the stove.
- Water capacity and conservation.
- Location of electrical switches.

BRUTE NEIGHBORS

- Radio and other electronics usage.
- Operation of the battery selector.
- Stowage.
- Sleeping arrangements.
- Safety harnesses.
- Watch schedules.

WATCH SCHEDULES

Rigid watch schedules on small cruisers are more the exception than the rule, probably because long passages are also the exception. On short passages, the tendency is for everyone to be "on watch" during the day and to divide the night hours into two or three flexible three- or four-hour watches. Beyond a night or two underway, a more structured system will minimize the opportunity for any apparent unfairness and at the same time probably improve the quality of watch being maintained.

The kind of watch schedule put in place will depend upon the conditions, the size of the crew, and perhaps the experience of the skipper or a crew member with a particular watch system. In its simplest form, in daylight and good weather, the watch system may call for four hours on, four hours off. At night, the period may be reduced to three hours, or even two. In rough weather, one hour on watch may be the maximum advisable, even less in severe conditions. Unfortunately, with a crew of two, that also translates into one hour off. The larger the crew, the longer the off watch.

For a lengthy passage, a more elaborate watch system may be beneficial. The one we have chosen to include is known as the *Modified Swedish Watch*. It has been used by numerous yachtsmen through many voyages. With this system, everyone gets an equal share of galley duty, free time, and dogwatches. Watch duration is designed to provide some extended, uninterrupted rest periods. The simplified version, shown below, is simply repeated for as many days as necessary. An excellent watch system, it may not be right for you. Perhaps you are fortunate enough to have a crew member who loves the dogwatch. Do not be reluctant to adapt a schedule to fit your requirements.

EXPENSES

Outside of immediate family, crew on a cruising boat are often expected to share in the operating expenses, but not always. Financial arrangements should be very clear from the outset. Candor is required

MODIFIED SWEDISH WATCH

TIME	DAY 1		DAY 2	
	GROUP A	GROUP B	GROUP A	GROUP B
MIDNIGHT				
1AM	ON WATCH	OFF	OFF	ON WATCH
2AM				
3AM				
4AM				
5AM	OFF	ON WATCH	ON WATCH	OFF
6AM				
7AM	FIX BREAKFAST			FIX BREAKFAST
8AM				
9AM	ON WATCH	OFF	OFF	ON WATCH
10AM				
11AM				
NOON		FIX LUNCH	FIX LUNCH	
1PM				
2PM	OFF	ON WATCH	ON WATCH	OFF
3PM				
4PM				
5PM		FIX SUPPER	FIX SUPPER	
6PM	ON WATCH	OFF	OFF	ON WATCH
7PM				
8PM				
9PM				
10PM				
11PM				

226

about who will pay for such things as fuel, ice, dockage, bait, and reprovisioning. Misunderstandings about fiscal responsibilities are such a common source of crew difficulties that many cruisers recommend getting the exact financial arrangement down on paper before shipping the crew member. That is not bad advice.

RESPONSIBILITY

Especially on a small cruiser, the skipper has a tendency to hoard all the responsibility. If you think it will be better for your crew because they "won't have to worry about anything," you are wrong. A person chooses to crew on a cruising sailboat because he or she wants to participate in the experience, not simply observe it.

All men want, not something to do with, but something to do, or rather something to be.

It is important that every member of the crew have some responsibility for the safety and comfort of the boat. The wise skipper learns to relinquish responsibility to responsible crew members. It enhances the cruise for the crew member and skipper alike.

COMMUNICATIONS

The skipper will often give instructions to or receive information from the other members of the crew. A breakdown in that process can not only put the boat at risk, but cause serious discord among the crew. So that communication does take place, it is important to define terms. If this sounds too basic, consider the following.

When you say:	Do you mean:
Pass it on the right.	The boat will pass to the right of the buoy, or the buoy will pass to the right of the boat?
Maintain a 270° heading.	Keep the bow heading toward 270°, or steer the necessary course to make good 270°?
The bridge is open.	The roadway is open for automobile traffic, or the span is open for boat traffic?
See the marker to the left.	The marker is on your left, or it is on the left (port) side of the boat?

Most of the ambiguity can be eliminated if all references aboard are from the point-of-view of the boat. The marker to the left is on the port side *of the boat*. The bridge is open *for boat passage*. "Pass it on the right," is still ambiguous. Learn to say, "*leave* it on the right," or "*leave* it to starboard," and the meaning is much clearer.

The use of *port* and *starboard* is a matter of preference. Many newcomers to sailing find these nautical terms confusing, particularly in a moment of urgency. If your crew is not comfortable with these references, it is in our opinion a demonstration of good seamanship for the captain to use the more conventional *left* and *right*.

Two of our examples still need clarification. "Maintain a 270° heading" is simply not enough information. It requires further qualification. And all we know about that "marker to the left" is that it is on the port side of the boat. Here we can abandon Thoreau and turn to John Wayne.

This lament for a golden age is only a lament for golden men.

Remember all those old war movies when the Duke would say something like, "Messerschmitts at three o'clock," and everyone immediately looked in the same direction? You also can tell someone where to look for an object using the same system. If you think of the boat as the face of a clock with the bow always pointing a 12 o'clock, when you say, "see the marker at 11 o'clock," the helmsman immediately knows that the marker is off the port bow. Okay, pilgrim?

In some conditions, oral communications are difficult or impossible. For example, in a high wind or with the engine running, a crew member at the bow may have difficulty making himself heard by the helmsman. A pre-arranged system of

Telegraph. Used on large ships to communicate between the bridge and the engine room.

simple hand signals can overcome such interference. Many cruising couples (and crews) utilize hand signals almost exclusively for communication with the bow. Few things look more amateurish than the yelling and shouting that often accompanies anchoring. Competently and *silently* bringing your vessel to anchor will set you apart.

MINIMIZING THE NEED

Conventional opinion is that crew problems are responsible for more aborted cruises than any other single reason. The smaller the crew, the less potential for problems. Choosing a pocket cruiser for your cruise is consistent with minimizing crew requirements. The attending smaller sails and lighter ground tackle allows for a crew that is smaller both in number and in physical strength.

As an alternative to additional crew, the boat may be equipped for short-handed sailing. The most dramatic assistance comes from the autopilot or, alternatively, the windvane steerer. A roller-furling headsail can greatly simplify sail handling. Instead of an extra pair of hands for docking, consider a sturdy rub strake. On the larger pocket cruisers, an anchor windlass will allow anchor handling by even a small crew member. There are numerous ways to reduce the requirements of handling any sailboat; the ultimate is rigging the boat for single-handing. Even on a boat with ample crew, these enhancements will be appreciated.

STRANGERS AS CREW

Crew members will either be strangers, friends, or family. If they are strangers, they might be either paid or voluntary. The likelihood of considering a paid crew member on a pocket cruiser seems remote. In any case, Thoreau would never approve. It is essential that every crew member have an inner desire to participate in the enterprise.

> *It is always essential that we love to do what we are doing, do it with a heart.*

Advertisements placed in sailing magazines or on yacht club bulletin boards are sometimes a source of crew. This approach may be successful in bringing together a short-handed boat and an enthusiastic crew member. Considering the enforced intimacy of a long cruise on a small cruiser, a very careful evaluation of applicants is indicated. We would not consider a long cruise with a recent acquaintance without taking a short cruise first to evaluate the crew chemistry.

Cruising boats often pick up voluntary crew at the dock, usually for assistance in a long passage. Since this is not a book on passage-making, we will limit our comments on this practice to a few words of caution. If you take someone aboard from the dock (or from an ad, for that matter),

> . . . *a stout and hearty man who had lifted an anchor in his day.*

be sure he has references, and check them. Also determine his financial status and his citizenship. Aside from the potential for discord, as the captain you are going to be held legally responsible for your crew in foreign ports.

FRIENDS

The small boat cruiser is much more likely to fill crew vacancies with friends than with strangers. You already know that they are compatible with you (that is why they are friends). You may not know how compatible they are with cruising, but the odds are definitely better than with a stranger.

We met a boat last year whose skipper's main goal was sharing the experience with his friends. For more than a year he had been cruising, with himself as the only permanent crew member. At various ports friends flew in *to crew* for whatever time they had available, assisting with the expenses to the extent they were able. When we met him, he was on his way to the Caribbean, with an Atlantic crossing planned for the following year. He had a broad and scattered network of friends and the logistics were often frustrating, but he never doubted the worth of his efforts.

> *It is not worth the while to go round the world to count the cats in Zanzibar.*

Indeed, it is not. But to provide your friends with the opportunity to experience the cruising life seems like an awfully good reason to go cruising.

FAMILY

Usually the crew aboard a pocket cruiser is some kind of family unit. A couple with small children is common. Children go from being a liability to being an asset as they get older. An infant can be a real hardship, but once a child no longer needs to be held for protection, it need not interfere with the efficient operation of the boat. At about age seven or eight, children reach a point at which they can contribute. At this age, they are almost always enthusiastic about a sailing adventure.

Adolescent children can be outstanding crew members, if it is what they want to do. You may find that your teenaged children have no interest in cruising ("What, and leave my friends!"). It is not a new phenomena.

One generation abandons the enterprises of another like stranded vessels.

A picturesque choice of words, Mr. Thoreau. But all is not lost. You can probably find some aspect to make the cruise more attractive to a teenager, like perfect beaches, skin diving, windsurfing, water skiing, or just racing around in the dinghy. If you promise such an emphasis, plan the itinerary and pace so you can keep your word.

Like close friends, adult family members can be a good selection for crew. Parents, adult children, brothers, sisters, and in-laws merit consideration. We have seen cruises bring families very close together.

SPOUSE

We have already pointed out that the most common cruising crew is the couple. There are very valid reasons for this. To begin with, problems of compatibility have already been worked out. The cruising couple has prior knowledge of each other's strengths and weaknesses and can effect early and judicious divisions of responsibility based upon that knowledge.

Find out as soon as possible what are the best things in your composition, and then shape the rest to fit them.

Specific traits that would otherwise undermine the harmony of a crew, such as complaining, have already been compensated for (Yes, dear; Right, dear). Each half of the couple brings to the cruise a sense of duty toward the other and share equally a sense of duty to the boat and cruise. The inevitable intimacy and limitations on privacy aboard a small boat are not a problem. And there is a prior knowledge of individual needs of space and quiet.

The cruising couple generally share a familiarity with the boat, its equipment and operation. Their relationship as a couple is already based upon mutual trust, which carries over into their relationship as crew. The often touchy question of division of expenses is never raised.

Couples bring to a cruise easier communications based upon close familiarity. This familiarity can also be detrimental to some communication efforts, particularly in stressful circumstances.

> *My companion tempts me to certain licenses of speech, i.e. to reckless and sweeping expressions which I am wont to regret that I have used.*

Far too often, we have heard a husband loudly berate the actions (or lack of action) of his wife. If the same tone and expression were to be used with any other crew member, at best the offending skipper would soon be sailing alone; at worst he would soon be swimming alone. Surely a spouse rates better treatment than other crew members. If that thought does not deter you, consider that other cruisers around you will subsequently refer to you as "that jerk."

Few things add color and texture to a cruise any more than sharing it. The cruising couple has the advantage over any other crew composition in that they genuinely want to share this experience with each other. And last but not least, when the nights are cold, they can keep each other warm.

THE CHOICE

The single-hander runs the least risk of crew difficulties, but there is little doubt that the couple is, for most, the crew of choice. When additional crew is necessary or desired, staying within the family unit will offer the greatest likelihood of accord. Regardless of the actual composition of the crew, like harmony in a marriage, harmony among crew members requires nurturing. It is among the skipper's principal responsibilities.

You should always keep in mind that serious discord can taint or even end a cruise.

> *Here, then, one could no longer accuse institutions and society, but must front the true source of evil.*

If you let that happen, you will have no one to blame but yourself.

HOUSEWARMING

*The necessaries of life for man . . . may, accurately enough,
be distributed under the several heads of Food, Shelter,
Clothing, and Fuel . . .*

HUS far, we have concentrated on the necessities; if not
the bare necessities, certainly not the lap of luxury either.
In this chapter we look at comforts, those which we
have found to be the best value. None of the items in
this chapter are essential to going cruising.

When we speak of comforts, they will be consistent with the premise of "sensible cruising." We will not talk about ice makers. We will not talk about air conditioning. Washers and dryers will not be mentioned. It is not that we do not care for these things. We simply care for cruising more.

There are two problems with many of the so-called comforts. First, if they are inordinately expensive most of us find that we must trade our cruising funds for them. Put another way, the dollars available to finance a cruise are reduced by the purchase of luxury equipment. The irony is that the item we purchase to enhance the cruise either delays it or shortens it. This inevitable exchange deserves more careful consideration than most of us give it.

The second problem is that they add complexity to the boat. People choose to go cruising for any number of reasons. Without exception, the simpler the boat and equipment, the more time available for those chosen pursuits.

What you call bareness and poverty is to me simplicity.

Simplicity is a major criteria in our selection of comforts.

ALL THE COMFORTS OF HOME

We typically spend a great deal of time making our homes "comfortable." Before stereo equipment and over-stuffed furniture, we select wall coverings, floor coverings, and window treatments. We evaluate mirrors, pictures, and shelves. We surround ourselves with colors, textures, and items that make us comfortable. Yet many of us set off on a cruise in a boat whose cabin more closely resembles the inside of a refrigerator than a home.

> *Before we can adorn our houses with beautiful objects the walls must be stripped, and our lives must be stripped, and beautiful housekeeping and beautiful living be laid for a foundation . . .*

Boats come with the walls already stripped. The cold, sterile feel of a molded fiberglass liner is not very comforting. A bit of teak trim can change the look from G.E. to yachty. For more warmth, consider wall covering. Paper is probably not a good choice, but there are many fabric or vinyl coverings that would do wonders for the cabin of a small cruiser. In the quantities required, this is an inexpensive enhancement and installation is quite easy. In such a small area, interior designers would warn against selecting a dark color or a big, bold pattern. You might also elect to cover only one bulkhead, as an accent. Do not overlook the additional benefits of wall decorations such as paintings, mirrors, or photographs.

Carpet on the cabin sole is a matter of preference. In a cruising environment, we have never been very pleased with carpet because it tends to stay damp and accumulate tons of sand. If you have an attractively finished cabin sole, leaving it uncovered is preferred. We like the look and convenience of a throw rug on the main cabin sole. Be sure it is rubber backed so it does not slip.

Curtains are also a matter of preference. They provide additional privacy and can give the cabin a homey feel. Track and hardware are available from marine suppliers or shock cord may be adapted as a less expensive alternative.

BERTHS

Berths that will be used for sleeping should have comfortable cushions. We have seen some cruisers supplied with cushions of three-inch polyurethane foam. About halfway through the night, you will begin to feel the plywood underneath. Mattresses on sleeping berths should be at least four inches thick; five-inch foam is even better. If your cushions require upgrading, select a *firm* foam for better support and longer life. There is no reason why you cannot purchase the foam in a sheet (at a wholesale price) and cut the cushions yourself. A long bread knife cuts the foam amazingly well; an electric carving knife even better.

Upgrading to thicker cushions will require alteration to the covers, or perhaps new covers. If you are handy with a sewing machine, boat cushions are not difficult to cover; if not, any upholsterer can accommodate your needs. Vinyl is not a good fabric choice despite its durability because it is uncomfortable for sitting or sleeping; cold and clammy in cold weather and hot and sticky in hot weather. Choose a stain-resistant woven fabric instead.

SETTEES

Almost as important as a comfortable place to sleep is a comfortable place to sit. How much seating depends upon your needs.

I had three chairs in my house; one for solitude, two for friendship, three for society.

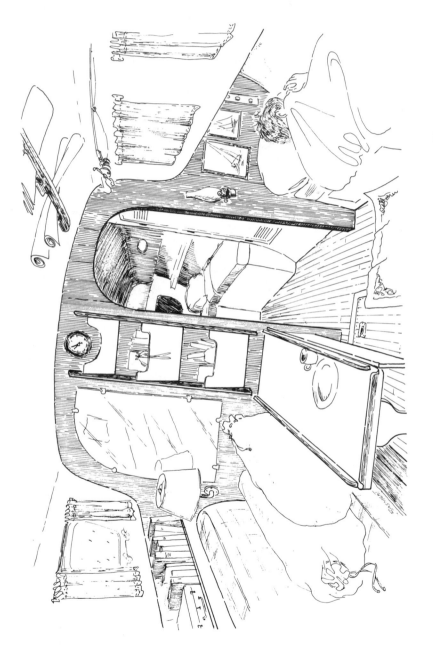

Cabin comforts must be carefully considered in order to prevent adding complexity to cruising.

Reality aboard is that "society" may be dictated by seating rather than the other way around.

Settee cushions need not be as thick as mattresses unless they do regular double duty. For seating only (and occasional bunk use), three-inch foam is adequate. The usual problem with settees is back support. The angle of the back is more often a function of the curvature of the hull than of orthopedic design. Compounding the problem is the fact that settees may be extraordinarily wide to allow their use as bunks also. If you sit against the back, you cannot bend your legs.

Some cruisers solve both of these problems with a wedge shaped back cushion which both narrows the seat and provides a more comfortable angle to the back. In a design requiring the back cushion to also serve as part of the bunk, this alteration will not work. The simplest solution and probably the most comfortable is one that will work on any boat—*pillows*. For effective space utilization, some cruisers make zippered covers and stuff them with blankets or extra bedding. If you are into interior design, put aboard a half dozen color-coordinated throw pillows. If you think that is sissy stuff, a couple of extra bed pillows will be your selection. Whichever way, about halfway through *Bowditch* you will thank us.

OPENING PORTS

Some builders have abandoned opening ports, sometimes because of cost and sometimes because of style. There is nothing stylish about sweat. If your cruise will take you south, you want as many opening ports as practical. Select your cruiser accordingly. If you are already an owner, determine if converting fixed ports to opening ones is feasible.

SHOWER

Whether you consider this item a necessity or a luxury, there is little question of its desirability. Unfortunately, in a pocket cruiser the normal shower installation is not very successful. Typically the entire head is used as a shower stall by installing a drain in the head sole and connecting a telephone shower to the boat's pressure water system. Problem: The typical head compartment is hardly big enough to turn around in. Problem: Wood trim, tissue, toiletries, *everything* in the head gets wet. Problem: The additional moisture below promotes mold and mildew. Problem: The shower sump drains into the bilge, giving the boat a distinctive locker-room odor. Problem: After the third shower, soap and hair clog the drain and the water gets to the bilge by way of the cabin sole. Problem: The pressure pump and the sump pump (if one is fitted) place additional demands on the battery. Problem: Limited tankage can support very few showers between topping. Problem: *Hot* water is unlikely.

Of all these problems, the moisture below and the extravagant use of water are the two most significant. To prevent the moisture below, we recommend showering on deck. We are not suggesting exposing yourself to everyone in the anchorage.

> *What a singular fact for an angel visitant to this earth to carry back in his notebook, that men were forbidden to expose their bodies under the severest penalties!*

There are plenty cruising who agree with you, Mr. Thoreau, but one can shower on deck and still maintain his modesty if he wishes.

Some cruisers connect the handheld shower to a deck fitting and continue to use the ship's pressure water system. Our cruising often takes us to where we cannot countenance such extravagant water usage. We have experimented with several alternatives, including showers that hang in the rigging. The most frugal, durable, and overall satisfactory solution is the plastic garden sprayer. The two- or three-gallon size will provide an amazing number of showers without placing any demand on either the ship's power or water supply. Ours resides permanently at the stern rail, ready with a few quick pumps for a fresh water rinse after a swim or a thorough salt water bath. For bathing in salt water, a small quantity of Joy or Dawn lathers abundantly, as does the shampoo Prell.

STAYING WARM

If you will be cruising in a cold area, some kind of cabin heat is required. The best cabin heaters for a small cruiser are the bulkhead-mounted type, appropriately vented. They may be kerosene or diesel fired, or perhaps burn solid fuel: coal, wood, or charcoal. If you do not have available bulkhead space or your cold weather cruising will be limited, consider a portable kerosene heater. For occasional heating requirements, a couple of clay pots inverted over the lighted burners of the galley stove will heat the cabin admirably.

With either of these last two choices, or with any unvented heater, *never* close the boat tightly and *never* sleep with the heaters lighted. There is an ever-present risk that the heater will burn up all the oxygen in the cabin and asphyxiate the occupants. We know of two such tragedies. We do not want to read about you.

To the sick the doctors wisely recommend a change of air and scenery.

Thank you, Mr. Thoreau; you are absolutely right. This is, after all, a book on sensible cruising. Forget about heaters. When it gets cold, head south.

STAYING COOL

And when you do, you will be faced with the opposite problem: keeping the cabin cool. The universal solution is the wind scoop. Made of very lightweight polyester or nylon (spinnaker cloth), the wind scoop is typically fitted in the forward hatch and funnels even the slightest breeze below.

I did not need to go outdoors to take the air, for the atmosphere within had lost none of its freshness.

Wind scoops may be purchased ready-made, or they may easily be custom constructed. If your cruising will take you to areas where the boat may sit to a current rather than into the wind, consider a wind scoop that will gather in the breeze from any direction.

A typical 12 volt oscillating fan draws less than two amps.

Cowl vents on ships may be six feet in diameter and funnel a tremendous amount of air below deck. The sizes found on pocket cruisers (four inches) are not as effective and unlikely to provide much cooling. Their usefulness is providing ventilation and freshness. The head compartment should always have a vent. The chain locker will also benefit from a cowl vent and it may do double duty as a deck pipe provided it has a sturdy deck plate. Vents into the engine compartment will allow the engine to aspirate better and will allow engine-generated heat to escape rather than to warm the cabin. Vents may be mounted on a dorade box, decreasing their effectiveness but preventing rain and spray from coming below.

On those rare days when the breeze does not blow, fans can be useful. Available for less than $20, the typical six-inch oscillating fan draws less than two amps. If your electrical system will support it, one mounted over the galley will make summertime cooking far more comfortable. On still nights, a small fan over the bunk can make all the difference. With bracket mounting, a single fan can be used in multiple locations.

SCREENS

Depending upon your destination, screens may more appropriately be included with the necessities. We will not soon forget a still night anchored at the mouth of the Snake River, on the Gulf coast of the Florida Everglades. The screens were literally black with mosquitoes, the din they sat up unimaginable, like being in a Hitchcock movie. To imagine anchoring there without screens was a horrifying prospect.

All opening ports should have permanent screens. So should all ventilators. For hatches, removable screens are required. Screens have a significant impact on air flow, so in a warm climate you do not want them on the hatches unless they are necessary.

Hatch screens can be constructed from either fiberglass screening (just like the windows at home) or mosquito netting. The fiberglass is more durable and passes more air, but the mosquito netting is more effective for smaller pests. Neither is very effective against sand flies, descriptively called no-see-ums.

We have seen screens mounted successfully in four different ways. A screened frame may be built that fits into the washboard channels of the companionway hatch and one that fits the forward hatch, held up by twist buttons. Weights are sometimes sewn into the hem of mosquito netting (somewhat like a cast net) and the netting simply draped over the hatch. The screening may be cut to size and edged with a vinyl strip, stitched in place and usually padded for a good seal. Snap fasteners are installed every six or eight inches in the vinyl strip and corresponding studs are screwed to the frame of the hatch.

We prefer attaching the screens with Velcro tape. The screen is bordered with one half of the tape; the other half of the tape is glued to the frame of the hatch. In use, the screen is simply pressed in place, pulled to remove. Unless you enjoy pulling apart a tangled mess, be sure it is the loop tape (the soft half) that you sew to the screen. The hook tape can be made less obtrusive on a wooden hatch frame by dyeing the tape brown before it is installed. It dyes very quickly, so if you want it to match the teak, do not leave it in long.

ENTERTAINMENT

Like food, literature and music seem to take on added importance on a cruise. The library will be out of reach, so take your reading material with you. A selection of paperbacks can serve a dual purpose, reading and bartering. The exchange of paperbacks among cruisers is universal and the only acceptable coin is other paperbacks. Sail with ample wealth aboard.

If you play a small musical instrument, not a piano or a tuba, you should consider taking it. Even the lowly kazoo can be fun. The guitar and the harmonica seem to be especially prevalent among cruisers. The new electronic keyboards are also becoming popular in the cruising community. If you have an instrument and the talent to play it, you will be in demand for every cook-out and beach party.

If all you can play is the radio, take heart. We are many. For a coastal cruise, an AM-FM radio may get a lot of use. In the more remote areas, you will have to depend upon a tape deck and a selection of tapes. You can spend a lot of money on "marine" stereo equipment, but an inexpensive auto tape deck will provide excellent sound at a fraction of the cost. Speakers may be flush mounted or, if you prefer, boxed so they can also be used on deck. Weatherproof speakers are also available. Whichever type speaker you select, give preference to smaller magnets and be sure the speakers are always well away from the compass and the autopilot.

A small "ghetto blaster" mounted in a rack below is not a bad choice either. Its unlimited portability means that it can also be used on deck, or even taken ashore. Units with recording capability have the added attraction of being able to capture that *once-a-day* AM radio weather forecast, which you otherwise miss to some momentary distraction, and allowing you to replay it for verification.

For those times when one person wants to read and another wants to listen to music, we cannot recommend highly enough a pair of lightweight stereo headphones. Even though the acoustics inside a boat are usually excellent, they cannot compare with the quality of sound from good headphones. As a reasonable alternative to headphones, you might choose to take a personal stereo aboard.

COMFORT UNDERWAY

The indescribable innocence and beneficence of Nature,—of sun and wind and rain, of summer and winter,—such health, such cheer, they afford forever!

No doubt, Mr. Thoreau, written in the shelter of your snug cabin in the woods. But much of cruising is an outdoor activity. For comfort we require a degree of protection from all three: sun and wind and rain.

The medical world is unusually united on the harmful effects of the sun's ultraviolet radiation. Skin cancer may result from too much exposure to the sun. Long pants, long-sleeved shirts, and wide-brimmed hats are good defense against excessive exposure but they lack the aspect of comfort afforded by shade. Underway, the most satisfactory solution is the Bimini top. Besides shade, it also provides appreciable protection from the rain. Commercially available, a Bimini can be quite expensive. With a bit of ingenuity you may be able to design and construct an inexpensive sailing awning.

The main sheeting arrangement is most often the limiting factor in building a sailing awning. There are two common approaches. On boats fitted with a spray dodger, an awning is attached (with a zipper) to the trailing edge of the dodger. The aft end of the awning is tied to the backstay and held out by a full width spreader. A second approach yields an awning that looks a bit like a covered wagon. An awning roughly the width of the boat, and as long as the design of the boat will allow, is sewn with sleeves on both the forward and after ends. Small diameter PVC water pipe, somewhat longer than the beam of the boat, is slipped through the sleeves. The ends of the pipes are lashed to the lifelines, forcing them to arch up, over the cockpit. The extension of the awning is maintained with a spreader or light lines led fore and aft.

Wind and spray can make going to weather very uncomfortable. When it is cold, the wind alone is sufficient for discomfort. A full-width spray dodger provides protection from both. To further reduce exposure to wind and spray, some cruisers elect to lash weather cloths to the lifelines around the cockpit. The weather cloths also yield additional privacy, but at the expense of reduced visibility and a closed-

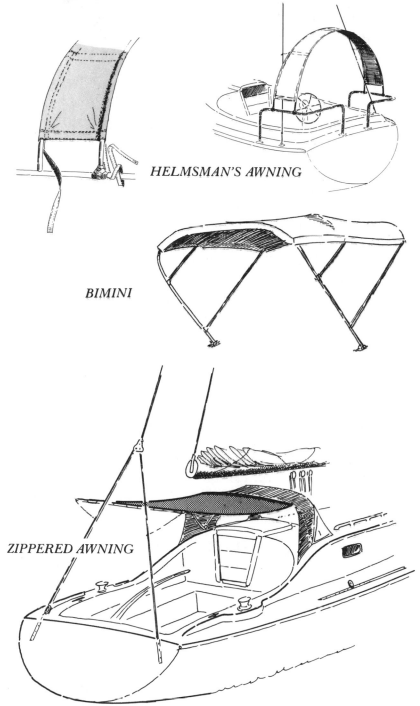

HELMSMAN'S AWNING

BIMINI

ZIPPERED AWNING

Protection from the sun while sailing.

in feeling. Both the dodger and the weather cloths cut down on the cooling breezes at anchor.

THE VERANDAH

"Cooling breezes at anchor"; how nice that sounds.

> *When a traveler asked Wordsworth's servant to show him her master's study, she answered, "Here is his library, but his study is out of doors."*

And so it is also with the cruiser. Much of the time aboard, even at anchor, is spent on deck. We often refer to the cockpit as the verandah, and that is where you will usually find us. Whether we are reading, entertaining, or simply "studying" the world around us ("Did you see how that guy anchored?!"), comfort in the cockpit is as important as below.

COCKPIT CUSHIONS

Our first encounter with cockpit cushions was not a pleasant one. Vinyl-covered polyurethane foam, they soon proved to be six-foot sponges. They never dried out and were as heavy as lead, and just as hard. The zippers corroded and the covers mildewed beyond redemption. We never wanted cockpit cushions again.

Then we discovered closed cell foam. It can be cut and handled like polyurethane but it will not absorb moisture. It is so non-absorbent that we regularly use our closed cell cushions for floats in the water, like air mattresses. The only fault we have ever found with closed cell cushions is that after a long time in the same position, the foam begins to conform to your body shape, making them somewhat uncomfortable for sleeping.

A short time after finding closed cell foam, we discovered the ideal material for cockpit cushion covers. It is an open weave, vinyl-coated material looking more like screening than cloth. You can see it on most new outdoor furniture. It is available in every color of the rainbow, including stripes and patterns, but if you want to be able to sit on the cushions comfortably in the summer, select a light color. Like the foam, this material refuses to absorb water. Add a nylon or plastic zipper (the slides are often metal, so keep them lightly greased for protection) and you have the ingredients of near perfect cockpit cushions.

The material was pure, and his art was pure; how could the result be other than wonderful?

And wonderful they are.

COCKPIT GRATING

The cockpit sole has an annoying habit of harboring a bit of water, wetting the feet when you would prefer them dry. The traditional solution to this is the teak cockpit grating. Unless you have "an uncle in the business," a teak grating is simply too expensive to be sensible. To stay attractive, the grating also requires a lot of maintenance. We have been very satisfied with an alternative solution that is both inexpensive and maintenance free.

For a number of years, a product called Dri-Dek has been manufactured by Kendall Plastics. Originally designed to inexpensively satisfy an industrial need to keep machine operators above the oily floors around their equipment, it has recently been marketed by Kendall for marine use. Interlocking tiles one foot square, Dri-Dek is flexible, resilient, non-skid, and easily trimmed with a razor knife to fit any cockpit. The raised surface keeps feet dry, and the lightweight grating may be easily removed for cleaning the sole. Although offered in several colors, tan provides the most traditional look. Any leftover pieces make an excellent grating for the icebox.

HARBOR AWNING

Without question, a quality harbor awning is the single most important item for a comfortable cruise in the tropics.

It would be well, perhaps, if we were to spend more of our days and nights without any obstruction between us and the celestial bodies.

In some circumstances that may be desirable, but not on a southern cruise. In the daytime, a good awning will provide protection from both the sun's heat and harmful radiation. Keeping the sun off the deck and cabin top will lower the cabin temperature significantly. Night on the water is usually accompanied by a heavy dew. The awning keeps its sheltered area dry, even allowing for comfortable sleeping on deck. In the tropics, thunderstorms are the rule. When it is 90° and raining, confinement in a closed cabin is like enforced time in a sauna. An awning that can stay up in heavy wind gusts will allow both staying on deck during the rain and keeping the hatches open.

There are no absolutes in awning design. The awning for each boat is different. There *are* some absolutes for awning material. Polyester passes UV radiation and is not a proper awning material. We have seen the plastic tarpaulins available in most department and discount stores (usually a bright blue) used as awnings. They provide better shade, but in a breeze they rattle so loudly that you (or your neighbor) will take them down. Acrylic cloth, the stuff most sail covers are made of, is not a bad choice, but not in a dark color. The amount of heat that radiates beneath a dark awning has to be experienced to be believed. Even the striped variety, which looks very festive, is significantly hotter than solid white.

New materials are constantly coming on the market, such as Zefkrome solution-dyed acrylic, with guaranteed color retention, but one that has a long history as a successful awning fabric is called boat-shrunk Vivatex. It is a very strong canvas that is both shrink and mildew resistant. It comes in either pearl grey or natural (an off-white) and in several weights. The weight selected will depend upon the size of the awning. The best choice of color is natural. It is both cool and light yet effectively screens out the harmful UV radiation. Roped or taped around its perimeter, an awning constructed of Vivatex is almost bulletproof and should last a decade or longer.

ETC.

The marine stores and boating catalogs offer an endless list of items that are purported to add to your cruising comfort and pleasure. Some may, but many will not. Be sensible in your evaluation.

> *It is well to find your employment and amusement in simple and homely things. These wear best and yield most.*

We could not have said it as well.

FORMER INHABITANTS;
AND WINTER VISITORS

*In books, that which is most generally interesting is what
comes home to the most cherished private experience of the
greatest number. It is not the book of him who has travelled
the farthest over the surface of the globe, but of him who has
lived the deepest and been the most at home.*

E promised you at the beginning that Mr. Thoreau had
an extraordinary talent for an extravagance of thought
with an economy of words. In only two sentences he has
illuminated perfectly our reason for including this
chapter.

247

There is no shortage of cruising literature. Hundreds of cruising narratives have been published. An equivalent number of technical books on various aspects of cruising have also been printed. There are numerous marine bookstores, a mail-order outlet, even a national book club listing more than 200 titles, devoted entirely to nautical subject matter. There are numerous national and regional magazines that cover cruising, one of the largest devoted entirely to cruising. The body of cruising literature increases every year.

The problem is not acquisition but selection. *Our* choice of titles is not a reflection on those we do not include. In fact, many of our favorite narratives and numerous informative technical volumes do not appear here. With few exceptions, we have selected only "former inhabitants" who exemplify the philosophy of sensible cruising and technical volumes contributing to that objective.

Will you be a reader, a student merely, or a seer?

JOSHUA SLOCUM

The universally accepted patriarch of cruising sailors is Joshua Slocum. His book, *Sailing Alone Around the World,* was first published in 1900 and is still in print today. In 1895, Slocum left Boston aboard the 36-foot *Spray* bound around the world. In 1898 he returned to Boston becoming the first to successfully circumnavigate single-handed. *Sailing Alone Around the World* is particularly important to us because it has been called the "nautical equivalent" to Walden. Indeed, Slocum's narrative reveals Slocum to the reader as an individualist conducting his own experiment in essential living, as a poet and a philosopher in his own right.

Spray was a derelict Delaware oysterman and already 100 years old when Slocum started to rebuild her. His objective was the cruise, and he did not wait until he could fit her out as a proper yacht. Instead, he rebuilt her of whatever he could find or afford. Consider how much like Thoreau is Slocum's language: "Yachtsmen pleasuring in the 'lilies of the sea' will not think favorably of my craft. They have a right to their opinion, while I stick to mine." Perhaps this similarity was not by coincidence as Slocum embarked with a library of 500 books aboard (and a dollar and a half in his pocket).

Sailing Alone Around the World is not packed with tips for small boat cruisers. There were few other small-boat cruisers in his time. You will not learn from Slocum the best design and proper equipment for a small cruiser. *Spray* was not a particularly notable design, and today's equipment was unimagined in Slocum's time. Slocum's tale is

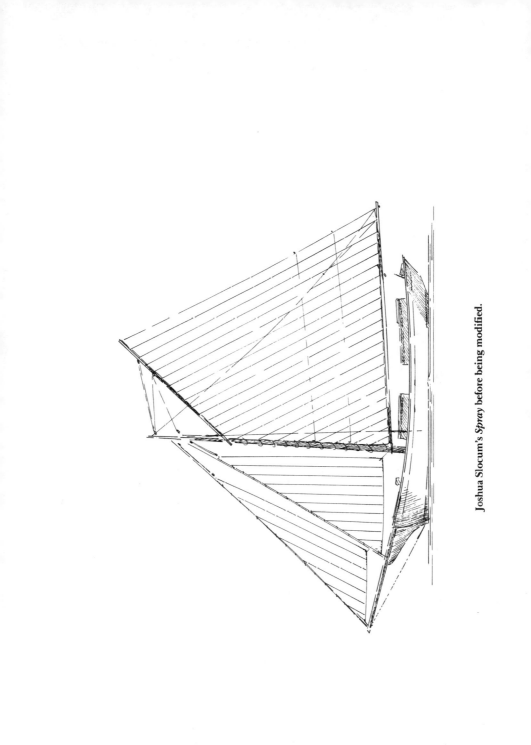

Joshua Slocum's *Spray* before being modified.

important, not for its technical content but rather for its emotional content.

> In literature it is only the wild that attracts us. Dullness is but another name for tameness.

His story has been important to four generations because it is the kind of tale that sets a young person to dreaming. Slocum did not perceive what he had done as extraordinary, beyond the capacity of others. Instead, he wrote, "To young men contemplating a voyage I would say go." For the next 30 years after Slocum's book was first published, young and old sailors alike followed his advice and set out on small-boat voyages all over the world.

IN SOLCUM'S WAKE

One of the first to follow in Slocum's wake was John C. Voss. In 1901, he left Victoria, B.C., bound for Australia. A more unlikely cruising boat could hardly be imagined than his *Tilikum*. *Tilikum* was an Indian war canoe carved from a single cedar tree, 38 feet long, but with a beam of only five-and-a-half feet. Voss reached Australia and carried on around Good Hope to England. Voss' ample self-confidence is apparent in *The Venturesome Voyages of Captain Voss*.

Harry Pidgeon built the 34-foot yawl, *Islander,* and in 1921 set off on what was to be his first of three circumnavigations. Pidgeon's *Around the World Single Handed* is a classic voyaging narrative.

In 1932, Fred Rebell sailed the 18-foot sloop, *Elaine,* from Sydney, Australia to Los Angeles. Rebell narrates the uphill (against wind and current) voyage in *Escape to the Sea*.

In 1924, French tennis champion (and winner of the Davis Cup that year) Alain Gerbault sailed quietly from Cannes on what was to be a six-year cruise. His narrow English cutter, *Firecrest,* had a waterline length of 30 feet and no engine. Gerbault wrote two books about his travels, *The Fight of the Firecrest* and *In Quest of the Sun*. Both were reprinted in 1981 in a single volume titled *Firecrest Round the World*.

Another early narrative that has been reprinted more recently (1971) is *The Saga of Cimba*. Richard Maury's 1933 cruise aboard the 35-foot schooner, *Cimba,* is considered a classic among early cruising narratives.

The best known of those in Slocum's wake is surely William A. Robinson. In 1928, he circumnavigated in the 32-foot ketch, *Svaap,* recounting the cruise in *Ten Thousand Leagues Over the Sea*. (The

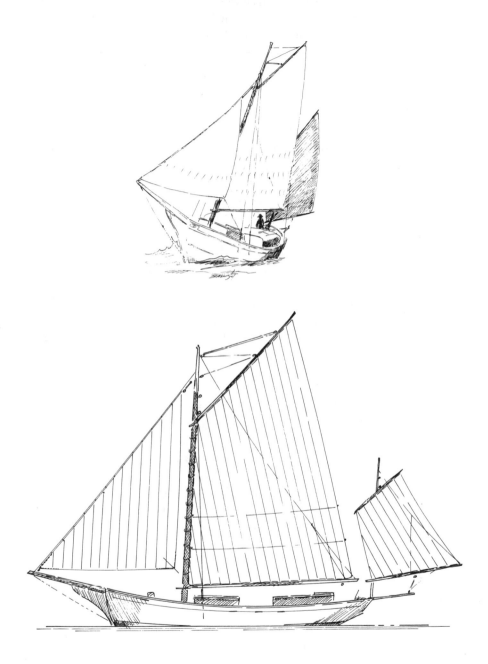

Spray after modifications by Slocum.

British edition was titled *Deep Water and Shoal.*) Robinson was possessor of the most famous appendix in cruising literature. While visiting the remote (even today) Galápagos archipelago in 1933, his appendix ruptured. This incident and subsequent events make *A Voyage to the Galápagos* tense reading.

POST-WAR PASSAGES

Argentinean swimming champion Vito Dumas did not wait for the end of the war, sailing in 1942 aboard the 31-foot ketch, *Lehg II*, on a 12½ month circumnavigation, *Alone Through the Roaring Forties.*

German U-boats were scarcely out of the English channel before Briton Edward Allcard set out in the 34-foot yawl, *Temptress.* Allcard's cruises are documented in *Single Handed Passage, Temptress Returns,* and *Voyage Alone.*

Frenchman, painter, dishwasher, but mainly sailor, Jean Gau left New York in 1947 aboard the 30-foot Tahiti ketch, *Atom. To Challenge a Distant Sea* (by Tazelaar and Bussiere) is the story of Gau's life as a cruiser, including 11 Atlantic crossings and two circumnavigations.

Peter and Ann Pye bought the 29-foot *Moonraker* in 1932, but it was 1949 before they were able to cruise her extensively. The Pyes cruised *Moonraker* for more than a quarter of a century, recording their experiences in *Red Mains'l, A Sail in a Forest,* and *The Sea is for Sailing.*

"Two good dry bunks, two stoves, toilet, chart table, plenty of stores. What more could any sailor want?" So commented Patrick Ellam about the 19-foot sloop, *Sopranino,* that he and Colin Mudie cruised from England across the Atlantic. Before Ellam completed the cruise alone, to Cuba and up the east coast of the United States to New York, their cruise had taken them to Spain, Portugal, North Africa, the Canaries, Barbados, Venezuela, and through the Caribbean. The story of their 1951 cruise is the subject of their book, appropriately titled *Sopranino.*

Al Peterson won the Cruising Club of America's Blue Water Medal in 1952 with a single-handed circumnavigation aboard the 33-foot cutter, *Stornoway.* After their marriage, Al and his wife Marjorie cruised in *Stornoway* for more than 20 years. Marjorie tells their story in *Stornoway East and West.*

Another recipient of the prestigious Blue Water Medal was John Guzzwell. Between 1955 and 1959, Guzzwell cruised his 20-foot yawl and wrote about it in *Trekka Around the World.* He and his wife Maureen subsequently cruised *Trekka* in British Columbia, Hawaii, and California. Under new ownership, *Trekka* later made a second circumnavigation.

Sea Gypsy is an apt title selection for Peer Tangvald. Peer sailed the engineless 32-foot *Dorothea* for five years and 40,000 miles. About half his cruise was solo; the other half included his petite wife, Simonne. Tangvald had previously sailed the 45-foot *Windflower* and found his passages in *Dorothea* consistently faster. Consider his observation:

Tinkerbelle.

"While the maximum speeds of larger boats are obviously higher than that of the smaller, they do not necessarily reach port faster. The smaller one will go faster in light airs, and unless there is a large crew on the big ship she will generally be under much shorter canvas than the little one, which is so much easier to handle."

It is a rare qualification to be able to state a fact simply and adequately, to digest some experience cleanly, to say "yes" and "no" with authority . . .

To the pocket cruiser, Tangvald says *yes*.

Not true cruises, but important because of their effect on the perception of a 30-foot cruiser, are the voyages of Kenichi Horie and Robert Manry. In 1962, Horie sailed 5,300 miles from Osaka, Japan to San Francisco aboard the 19-foot sloop, *Mermaid*. Three years later, Robert Manry took the 13-foot *Tinkerbelle* from Massachusetts to England, a 3,200-mile voyage. They tell their stories in *Kodoku: Alone Across the Pacific* and *Tinkerbelle*.

THE CONTEMPORARIES

The 1970's was an explosive decade for cruising. No longer an oddity, literally thousands of individuals, families, and couples bought small boats and set off on cruises of varying ambition. A vast library of books were published.

This sudden growth in popularity was in part due to the remarkable cruise of Robin Lee Graham which was completed in 1970. In 1965, Graham had departed southern California on a cruise that would take him around the world. What made his cruise remarkable was that Graham was 16 years old and his sloop, *Dove*, was 24 feet in length. What gave the cruise its impact on so many was the fact that *National Geographic* brought the story into millions of American homes. People unfamiliar with sailing or cruising were given a glimpse of it for the first time. The story appeared in three parts, twice as the cover story, and was so popular that it brought in more reader response than any other feature in the prestigious magazine's long history. Graham also told his story in a book, *Dove*, which was later made into a movie with the same title.

Tristan Jones was born on a British ship off the coast of the remote South Atlantic island, Tristan da Cunha. At thirteen, he returned to the sea and a life filled with adventure. It was more than 30 years later when Jones decided to share those adventures in a book.

I cannot afford to be telling my experience, especially to those who perhaps will take no interest in it. I wish to be getting experience.

His first book, *The Incredible Voyage*, was indeed incredible. Determined to make the longest (tallest?) *vertical* sailing voyage in history, he sailed in the world's lowest waters, the Dead Sea, then rounded Africa to South America where he overcame great hardships sailing hundreds of miles up the Amazon. Turned back, he eventually reached the world's highest waters, Lake Titicaca, by hauling the 20-foot *Sea Dart* over the Andes. From the lake, he traversed the continent by river to Buenos Aires.

Jones' second book, *Ice!*, is an even more fantastic tale of an earlier voyage; the events and hardships he endured are nothing less than unbelievable. But whether you believe him or not, he is a real person and knows the sea well, having logged more sea miles than any other small-boat sailor. A talented and prolific writer with a seemingly inexhaustible supply of hair-raising adventures, he has also written *Saga of a Wayward Sailor, Adrift, A Steady Trade, Heart of Oak,* and a single-hander's manual, *One Hand for Yourself, One for the Ship.* Despite the loss of a leg, he continues to sail and write.

As an encouragement to go cruising, Jones' books may send you scurrying for *terra firma.* But there are no other sailors like Jones, no other cruises like his. And like Slocum, Jones' yarns stoke the fires of adventure.

At the opposite end of the spectrum are Herb and Nancy Payson. Just entering middle age and living the Southern California lifestyle, they decided to make a change: "Why don't we give up all this nonsense, buy a boat, and sail around the world?" Fourteen months later, the Paysons had purchased the 36-foot *Sea Foam.* In a few more months, they were off on their cruise; from conception to reality in less than two years. Herb recalls a quote carved in the deck beam of a friend's yacht: "BETWEEN THE DREAM AND THE DEED LIE THE DOLDRUMS." Lethargy is the greatest danger to any cruise. The Paysons will never be accused of being lethargic. Herb Payson's first book, *Blown Away,* is undoubtedly the most humorous account of cruising ever written, and one of the very best. You will not learn the nuances of sailing from Herb Payson. By his own admission, they did very few things in the traditional manner.

How can a man be a wise man, if he doesn't know any better how to live than other men?

We didn't say they do not know better how to *live*. They do. *Blown Away* is a wonderful account of a couple living the cruising dream and proof that a seafaring heritage is not required. Their continuing saga is told in *You Can't Blow Home Again.*

The Voyage of Kristina by Wayne Carpenter is one of the more recent narratives. It is notable because it clearly conveys the feeling of a happy ship even though the *Kristina* was only 27 feet and carried a crew of five. Carpenter, with daughters 14 and 15 years old, wanted a *family* adventure. He and his wife Kristina (of course) elected to purchase a boat that they could afford and that would get them cruising before passing years robbed them of the opportunity to share it with the girls. Kristina's mother rounded out the crew. After three years and 15,000 miles of cruising, they found few faults with the sloop *Kristina.*

THE GURUS

During the sixties and seventies, out of the mass of sailors going quietly around the waterways of the world, three couples have left an indelible mark on the cruising world. They are from three different generations, fly three different ensigns on three different vessels, and have sailed three different routes to many different ports. In common, they have all chosen the cruising life, all pursued it safely and efficiently, and have all written skillfully of their experience. Their names are familiar to all cruisers, revered by most. They are the quintessential cruisers; the cruisers new cruisers emulate.

ERIC AND SUSAN HISCOCK

No cruising couple is better known than Eric and Susan Hiscock, and for good reason; they have probably logged more cruising miles than any other cruising couple in history. Eric first began cruising more than a half century ago, and he and Susan have been cruising's "first couple" for more than 40 years. Perhaps more important than such vast experience is Eric's even greater talent in sharing that experience. Eric Hiscock reminds us of Thoreau's friend, Minott:

> *If a common man speaks of Walden Pond to me, I see only a shallow, dull-colored body of water without reflections or peculiar color, but if Minott speaks of it, I see the green water and reflected hills at once, for he has been there. I hear the rustle of the leaves from woods which he goes through.*

Hiscock's boats have all been named *Wanderer*. Eric acquired his first boat in 1934, an 18-foot sloop built in 1898. He cruised aboard her for three-and-a-half years. *Wanderer II* was a 24-foot cutter which Eric and Susan cruised until 1951. Eric wrote of his early cruises in his first book, *Wandering Under Sail.*

In 1952, their most famous boat, *Wanderer III,* was launched. She was 30 feet overall, sloop rigged. Aboard her, the Hiscocks cruised for the next 15 years. Their two circumnavigations and numerous other cruises are recorded in *Around the World in Wanderer III, Beyond the West Horizon,* and *Atlantic Cruise in Wanderer III. Wanderer III* was the model for numerous cruising boats built in the 1950's.

In 1967, after more than 30 years of cruising which always led home, the Hiscocks decided to sever all permanent ties with land. The house they had owned for 20 years was sold. They commissioned a steel yacht which they hoped would be large enough for permanent living aboard. *Wanderer IV* was 49 feet long, displacing more than 20 tons and requiring almost seven feet of water to float her. Launched in 1968, the ketch-rigged *Wanderer IV* carried the Hiscocks from Holland to New Zealand and later on their third circumnavigation. *Sou'west in Wanderer IV* and *Come Aboard* record their cruises aboard *Wanderer IV.*

Although the Hiscocks had cruised or lived aboard *Wanderer IV* very successfully for twelve years, they were often dissatisfied with the maintenance required of steel construction and never totally comfortable with such a large boat. Spending "more and more time maintaining our 49-foot steel ketch, *Wanderer IV,* and less and less time sailing," the Hiscocks decided in 1980 that it was time to replace *Wanderer IV* with "something smaller, less demanding in upkeep, and easier and a little more fun for the pair of us to sail coastwise." *Wanderer V* was conceived. Launched in New Zealand in 1982, the 39-foot wooden sloop with the Hiscocks aboard is already cruising in the South Pacific. Hiscock writes about her in his most recent book, *Two Yachts, Two Voyages.*

A discussion of Eric and Susan Hiscock is not complete without mentioning Eric's two instructional texts. *Cruising Under Sail* was first published in 1950 and appeared in second edition in 1965. The companion volume, *Voyaging Under Sail,* was printed in 1959, a second edition in 1970. They were the undisputed definitive works on cruising at the time of their publication. Although some of the material is out-of-date, there is still much to be learned about cruising in a small boat from both of these volumes. A great deal of the material they contain is, like the Hiscocks themselves, ageless.

HAL AND MARGARET ROTH

In 1971, Hal and Margaret Roth were honored with the Cruising Club of America's Blue Water Medal "for a circumnavigation of the Pacific Ocean Basin . . . including south and west Pacific island groups, the Japanese Islands, the Aleutian Islands, Alaska, the Queen Charlotte Islands, beginning and ending in California." They made their Pacific voyage in 1967 and 1968, sailing more than 18,000 miles. Unlike Eric Hiscock, Hal Roth did not come to sailing in adolescence. Only five years before their cruise, Hal Roth had no experience with sailing yachts. A sail with a friend piqued his interest. He and Margaret chartered a captained yacht in the Caribbean and the following year a second one in Greece. A dinghy sailing course rounded out their experience when they bought their first boat, a 36-foot steel sloop.

Conceiving their dream cruise, the Roths began searching for a suitable boat. They selected a 35-foot fiberglass sloop built in Vancouver. They christened her *Whisper* when she was launched in 1966. Fifteen months later they were in the Pacific, living the dream. Upon their return, Hal wrote of their cruise in *Two on a Big Ocean*.

There is absolutely nothing remarkable about the Roth's first cruise. They simply went quietly and competently about realizing their dream. Perhaps the great popularity of *Two on a Big Ocean* is due to the tranquility of their narrative, their joy and wonder at the experience, and their satisfaction with the voyage.

> *I wish to communicate those parts of my life which I would gladly live again myself.*

When you cruise vicariously with the Roths, you also become convinced that you need no nautical background, no inherent talents; the cruising alternative is available to the common man.

There is nothing at all mundane about the Roth's second cruise. They elected to challenge Cape Horn. Departing San Diego, they sailed to the Galápagos, called at ports in Peru and Chile, then passed through the Strait of Magellan to Tierra del Fuego. There, only 24 miles from Cape Horn, *Whisper* and the Roths were shipwrecked. Rescued by the Chilean navy after nine days, the Roths were helped by navy personnel to salvage *Whisper*. After extensive repairs in Chile, the Roths sailed south a second time. They were successful this time in rounding the Horn and sailed on up the east coast of South America, carrying on to Bermuda and Nantucket. This extraordinary story is told in *Two Against Cape Horn.*

The Roths continue to cruise aboard *Whisper.* After visiting the east coast of the United States, the Roths returned to the Pacific via the Panama Canal and continued to chase the sun, recently completing a 31,000-mile circumnavigation. Influenced early in his cruising by Hiscock's cruising and voyaging texts, Hal Roth has also compiled a nuts-and-bolts book titled *After 50,000 Miles,* reflecting his own experiences.

LIN AND LARRY PARDEY

While the Roths were circling the Pacific, *Seraffyn of Victoria* was taking shape in Newport Beach, California. The construction took three-and-a-half years. Only four months after launch, Lin and Larry Pardey left California with nothing more concrete in mind than "heading south." Nine years later, they paused in Spain long enough to collaborate on their first book, *Cruising in Seraffyn.* It was a great success.

What makes the Pardey's story so compelling is not the cruise, but the participants. Larry had already decided on the cruising lifestyle while still in high school. He had significant sailing experience, had owned several boats, and was working as a charter captain when he decided to build *Seraffyn.* In sharp contrast, Lin "had barely heard of cruising before the day I met Larry." Nevertheless, she became so infected with Larry's dream that she soon became a full partner in the enterprise. The third participant was *Seraffyn.* Engineless, and only 24 feet long, the little cutter was the kind of vessel that a lot of other dreamers could identify with.

After seven years of cruising, their satisfaction with their lifestyle and with the boat that gave it to them was evident in their book.

> *A man is worth most to himself and to others, whether as an observer, or poet, or neighbor, or friend, where he is most himself, most contented and at home. There his life is the most intense and he loses the fewest moments.*

Because it worked so well for them, they are enthusiastic advocates of keeping the boat small and simple.

After England, the Pardeys continued to cruise through Europe *(Seraffyn's European Adventure),* through the Mediterranean *(Seraffyn's Mediterranean Adventure),* and through the Orient *(Seraffyn's Oriental Adventure),* before returning to Newport Beach.

The "small and simple" theme is consistent throughout the series of narratives.

Their first cruise lasted more than 11 years. Besides the narratives, they wrote two additional books. One on provisioning and food preparation is titled *The Care and Feeding of the Offshore Crews.* The second, *The Self-sufficient Sailor,* is essentially a compilation of many of their numerous magazine articles on a wide range of cruising topics.

During their cruise aboard *Seraffyn,* they formulated definite ideas on what they would like in their next cruising boat. Upon their return to California, they began the process of converting their thoughts and ideas into reality. Three-and-a-half years later, the 29-foot *Taleisin* was launched. Built by Lin and Larry, *Taleisin* remained true to their creed. She is small, strongly built, simply rigged, and simply outfitted, still without an engine. In her the Pardeys are once again cruising, where "life is the most intense." They will undoubtedly continue to share that life with all who are interested.

THE PROFESSORS

Since old Joshua Slocum first wrote of the inadvisability of long overhangs on an offshore boat, of the self-steering qualities of *Spray's* hull shape, or of placing tacks around the deck to repel unfriendly natives in the dark of night, other cruisers have sought cruising knowledge from the printed page. Much can be gleaned from the numerous narratives that have been published. However, a few sailors with extraordinary comprehension and organization have put together true cruising textbooks.

> . . . *I am conscious of the presence and criticism of a part of me, which, as it were, is not a part of me, but spectator, sharing no experience, but taking note of it . . .*

Their purpose was not to tell a story but to share their knowledge and to answer all those questions for which they had answers.

For more than two decades, Hiscock's *Cruising Under Sail* was the definitive work on cruise preparation; *Voyaging Under Sail* the perfect companion for those with more adventurous plans. Since Hiscock, other sailors have emerged to carry on his tradition, their works encyclopedic. In keeping with our original premise, a third sailor merits inclusion in our group of professors because his approach, solutions, and views are peculiarly suited to the "sensible cruiser."

DONALD STREET

In 1973, *The Ocean Sailing Yacht* by Donald Street was published. It was immediately recognized as an indispensable text for anyone contemplating a cruise. In Street's own words, the book was written "for the person who . . . wishes to cruise. This book is designed to enable him to pick a good cruising boat, to equip her, and to cruise with safety, enjoyment, comfort, and also a fair degree of speed." Thirteen years later the book is still in print and still contemporary.

Street was uniquely qualified to write such a book. He had grown up around sailboats. He had lived in the West Indies for almost 20 years (more than 30 years now), chartering his own boat and operating as a delivery skipper on a wide variety of boats belonging to others. He was thus exposed to a broad array of designs and equipment. He brought to the project with him an ability to evaluate his experience and draw useful conclusions.

Street is not quick to abandon a boat or equipment simply because it is old or out of style.

> *When I ask for a garment of a particular form, my tailoress tells me gravely, "They do not make them so now," not emphasizing the "They" at all . . .*

"They" have not made a boat like his own *Iolaire* in 80 years. In Street's eyes, her age has little to do with her suitability as a cruising boat. Built of wood in 1905, *Iolaire* has served as a floating laboratory for Street's endless experiments with rig and equipment. She has had half a dozen different rigs and both her interior and her deck layout have been extensively altered. Those methods and equipment that have been the most successful are the ones Street recommends.

Street's study of cruising did not end with the publication of *The Ocean Sailing Yacht*. To the contrary, he became even more involved in the study of safe and competent cruising. Five years later the *Ocean Sailing Yacht, Volume 2* was published. A companion to the earlier book, it amplified or clarified some of the original material, offered an altered viewpoint in some cases, and contained a quantity of totally new material. Between the two books, Street provides you with *his* viewpoint on virtually every aspect of cruising that you might imagine.

Street continues to live in the West Indies, continues to sail the venerable *Iolaire,* continues to experiment, and continues to write about what works and what does not in regular contributions to sailing magazines.

STEVE AND LINDA DASHEW

Between the moment of decision (with no boat) and the moment of departure was less than 18 months for Steve and Linda Dashew. Their cruise lasted three-and-a-half years. Steve Dashew is an engineer by vocation—and by inclination. During their cruise, he analyzed and evaluated every aspect of their enterprise. He compared their choice of a cruising boat with others they encountered along the way. He and Linda asked other cruisers what equipment they were happy with and what they were not. They were fascinated by the variety of solutions different cruisers conceived to similar problems, were always looking for better solutions to the problems and compromises that accompany cruising. *The Circumnavigators' Handbook* is the compilation of their findings.

Unfortunately for those who have just stepped up to a used Catalina 22, the Dashews began their cruise aboard a 50-footer. In South Africa they commissioned a custom-built, 62-foot aluminum cruiser with every imaginable feature. Their particular perspective allows them, when discussing optional equipment, to use $1,600 and inexpensive in the same sentence. By accident or by choice, their book is insensitive to the financial realities of most would-be cruisers. Many of their recommendations are beyond the means of the "common" man.

Perhaps it sounds as though we are being deprecatory toward the Dashews. Not at all.

He is my contemporary and neighbor. He is one tribe, I am another, and we are not at war.

To the contrary, *The Circumnavigators' Handbook* is surely the best and most comprehensive cruising text in a decade. It is literally packed with information of value to every cruiser regardless of the ambition of his cruise. It is just that the Dashews are fortunate enough to have the means to cruise in any style they choose, and they choose a style which only few can emulate.

The Dashew's motivation in undertaking to write a 500-page book is one of sharing the incomparable pleasures of cruising. They want you to sail with them, to see how it is done, to do it yourself. But the kind of monetary commitment represented by the Dashew's fantastic *Intermezzo II* and by their selection of gear and equipment may have just the opposite effect. The *Circumnavigators' Handbook* can be intimidating.

Do not be intimidated. You do not need a 62-footer to go cruising, nor do you need much of the special equipment selected by the Dashews. It is the cruise itself that is important, as they will tell you: "On the other hand luxuries can be expensive. If that means waiting additional years, forget them . . . Go cruising now!" If you can take the Dashew's advice and look beyond the preponderance of high price tag items in this book, you will encounter something of value on almost every page.

Steve and Linda Dashew quickly followed their first book with *Bluewater Handbook*. Subtitled *A Guide to Cruising Seamanship,* it is applicable to cruising boats of every size. The two books together represent an enormous amount of information and clearly distinguish the Dashews from their peers.

TONY GIBBS

Tony Gibbs epitomizes the small-boat cruiser. He is easy to identify with. He has neither sailed around the world nor spent years in "the islands." He has a family, a house, and a "regular" job. Yet he has always found time for cruising. He has owned six cruising sailboats, five of them under 30 feet.

What distinguishes Gibbs from other experienced cruisers is his profession. Author of numerous sailing books, he has been an editor of *Motor Boating & Sailing* and of *Yachting.* This has given him a critical eye for successful designs and the opportunity to cruise and sail aboard a wider array of yachts than most of us will experience in a lifetime.

Drawing on both personal and professional experience, Gibbs has written *The Coastal Cruiser*. It is a comprehensive treatise of the pocket cruiser. Gibbs defines the small cruiser as no larger than 30 feet. *The Coastal Cruiser* is not a book about cruising but about the cruising *boat*. In it Gibbs provides a wealth of information about both selection and outfitting; a 48-page design portfolio is included. His observations about cruising are contained in a companion book titled *Cruising in a Nutshell.*

THE CRAFTSMEN

Regardless of what size boat we select, few of us can resist the temptation to make changes—enhancements we always call them. It may be something as simple as screwing a teak binocular box to the bulkhead or as complex as a completely new interior. For many, working on the boat, preparing her for the cruise, is a way of expanding the joy of cruising. It keeps us *physically* in touch with our goal, each completed project visible evidence of progress.

The quality of our "enhancements" depends upon our skill level, how well conceived the idea is, and our understanding of the steps required. If you have the requisite skills (and you undoubtedly do), there are two sailors who can provide excellent help with the ideas and the process.

FERENC MATÉ

In the early 1970's, Ferenc and Candace Maté built a 32-foot Westsail. *Warm Rain* emerged as a yacht of such quality and beauty that the Westsail Corporation commissioned Maté to write a book about the project. *From A Bare Hull* resulted. Before we talk more about Maté, allow us a small digression.

If you have entertained the thought of constructing your own cruiser, perhaps you have wondered why we have not mentioned this course of action. It is because this is a book about cruising, about *beginning* cruising. "Building your own" kills more first cruises than it enables. The number of unfinished hulls sitting around in boat yards and back yards attest to the fact that you stand a good chance of running out of time, money, or interest before the project is finished. The greatest risk is that in the time required for construction, the dream will wither and die.

> *The youth gets together his materials to build a bridge to the moon, or perchance a palace or temple on the earth, and at length the middle-aged man concludes to build a wood-shed with them.*

Buy your first cruiser. You can consider building the second one.

Back to the Matés. No wood-shed for them; their boat had the finish of an Eastern temple. The craftsmanship and the unique and innovative ideas of Ferenc Maté single him out as the very best contemporary source of enhancement ideas and instructions. Specifically, his book *The Finely Fitted Yacht* is without peer. Containing over 200 projects, it will also serve as an effective catalyst for the conception of original enhancements to fit your particular need.

DAN SPURR

Dan Spurr is the senior editor of *Cruising World*. Perhaps more to the point, for several years Spurr owned and lived aboard a 1967, 28-foot Pearson Triton. Despite regular encounters with a variety of naval architects and myriad new designs, *Adriana* was Spurr's choice for *his* cruising boat. Enamored though he may have been, he was not blind to her shortcomings nor to the charms of others.

Over the years Spurr made numerous modifications to *Adriana*, incorporating many new ideas. More important to us, he evaluated hundreds of enhancements with *Adriana* in mind. These evaluations are valid for any pocket cruiser and are clearly documented in *Spurr's Boatbook: Upgrading the Cruising Sailboat.*

Maté's projects, although always functional, place a heavy emphasis on aesthetic appeal; you are likely to be working with teak or mahogany. Spurr has a more nuts-and-bolts approach, covering a far wider range of subjects. Aside from those enhancements you might make, Spurr also evaluates those you might buy. *Spurr's Boatbook* is the best single source of enhancements to the pocket cruiser.

AND YOU

Each of the eight sailors (or couples) that we have reviewed is pursuing his (or their) chosen course. It is different for each of them. They differ in approach, in the boat chosen, in philosophy; but their choices have served to get them all cruising. We can learn much from all of them, but keep in mind that all they can tell you is what led *them* to elect the course *they* have chosen.

> *If you wish to know how I think, you must endeavor to put yourself in my place. If you wish me to speak as if I were you, that is another affair.*

Only *you* can determine *your* proper course.

WINTER ANIMALS

I feel more like a citizen of the world at the sight of the palm-leaf . . .

HE United States is blessed with a climate that allows wonderful summer cruising along all of its coastline. One can easily spend a summer exploring the Chesapeake, enjoying the rugged beauty of the Maine coast, or sampling the variety of Puget Sound.

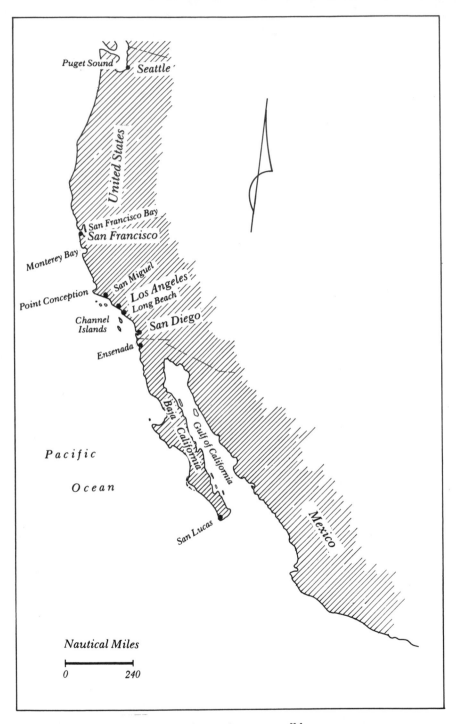

Along the West Coast, going south means an offshore passage.

WINTER ANIMALS

There are those who prefer to go north in the summer, enjoying cold weather cruising. Certainly there is spectacular beauty in pictures we have seen of a tiny yacht sailing beneath the vast face of a glacier. White sails against the translucent blue of the ice have an undeniable artistic quality. Those choosing to cruise the high latitudes must get great satisfaction from their extraordinary independence, must find solace in isolation. We respect them, admire them, but we are not likely to share an anchorage with them.

Why? Because the rest of us equate cruising with swimming, diving, and sunbathing; with shorts, not parkas; with bikinis, not long johns. A sensible cruise, specifically a first cruise, is a warm climate cruise. It will be more comfortable, more fun, less demanding, and safer. If you sail in an area with warm summers, plan on a summer cruise. If you want to cruise in a season other than summer, or if you want to cruise for longer than a summer, you will probably find yourself considering going south.

Every fall the migration of the winter animals begins. It is heralded by red maple leaves and blue northers. As winter approaches, the northern sailor has only two choices: haul out or head south.

The north wind stepped readily into the harness which we had provided, and pulled us along with good will. Sometimes we sailed as gently and steadily as the clouds overhead . . .

Along the West Coast, going south means an offshore passage. From the Canadian border to the tip of the Baja peninsula, inlets are widely spaced. There are few places to seek safe refuge so weather is of prime importance. As the season progresses, storms coming in from the Pacific increase in intensity and frequency. Waiting too late in the season exposes boat and crew to a much greater risk. Even in benign weather, the exposure leads most skippers to get south as rapidly as possible.

In contrast, the East Coast is as close to perfect for a winter migration as a cruiser could hope for, thanks to God and the U.S. Army Corps of Engineers.

THE INTRACOASTAL HIGHWAY

The Intracoastal Waterway (ICW) officially runs from the Annisquam River, north of Boston, to Brownsville, Texas. It allows the cruiser to transit north or south through bays, sounds, and protected channels. It is travelled at all times of the year, but ice can restrict the northern reaches in winter. Typically cruisers travel south along the Waterway in the fall and return in the spring or summer.

Unlike sailing south along the West Coast, unless the cruiser has waited until bitter cold has gripped the northeast, there is little weather urgency to hurry south. If a storm approaches, a snug anchorage or marina is never far away. The people who keep track of such things say that on the average there is a marina or good anchorage every 20 to 25 miles. With security rarely more than three hours away, one can choose a relaxed pace going south.

Sure you are headed to the land of palm leaves. But as you travel the ICW, you will pass through some of the best cruising grounds in America. America's great history lies along her waterways, particularly along the East Coast. If you are going south, go early enough that encroaching winter does not hurry your passage. There is much to see.

Yet we should oftener look over the tafferel of our craft, like curious passengers, and not make the voyage like stupid sailors picking oakum.

Actually, the trip itself down the Intracoastal Waterway can be (and often is) a good choice for a first cruise.

Some people do not care for the ICW. The opportunities to sail can be limited. It is not difficult to find yourself aground in some of the narrow channels. There is commercial traffic as well as a lot of power yacht traffic. From the Chesapeake to South Florida, you have to pass through more than 100 opening bridges. They think about all of these things and simply *endure* the trip south.

That is too bad. The Blue Ridge Parkway or the Pacific Coast Highway are not exactly a pleasant drive for motorists either. It is what lies alongside the highway, the history, the vistas, the people, that makes the drive worthwhile. The same is true for the Intracoastal.

What does lie alongside the ICW? There is: physical evidence of our earliest history and our most current events; the concrete and glass towers of our largest city and the flower boxes and picket fences of our smallest villages; the marble mansions of some of our richest citizens and the clapboard shacks of some of our poorest; evidence of development and evidence of conservation. A cruise along the ICW provides the fortunate mariner with a view of a cross-section of America.

I was daily intoxicated, and yet no man could call me intemperate.

Sailing from historic Boston, the ICW takes the sailor past Plymouth and into Cape Cod Bay. Passage through the Cape Cod Canal leads into Buzzards Bay. To port is Woods Hole, once home to whalers, now the sight of the renowned Woods Hole Oceanographic Institution. Just below Woods Hole are the Elizabeth Islands, behind which lies Vineyard Sound and Martha's Vineyard.

Across the bay is the Acushnet River. Few whaling ports are better known than New Bedford, near the mouth of the Acushnet. From here Herman Melville sailed aboard a whaling ship, providing the foundation for *Moby Dick*. Across the river, in Fairhaven, Joshua Slocum rebuilt *Spray* before setting off on his famous voyage.

Passing Cuttyhunk Island, the ICW leads out of Buzzards Bay. To the east is Narragansett Bay and Newport, Rhode Island, the sight of

the America's Cup Race until the successful Australian challenge. Past the 1816 lighthouse at Point Judith and the northern tip of Block Island, the ICW transits Block Island Sound and into Long Island Sound; Long Island provides one shore, Connecticut the other. On the Connecticut shore at Mystic is the maritime museum of Mystic Seaport. Further along, at New Haven, is venerable Yale University, there since 1716. A thirst for classic theatre can be slaked at Stratford, home of the American Shakespeare Festival Theater.

Through the East River and the notorious Hell Gate, the ICW runs between Queens and Manhattan, literally in the afternoon shadow of New York City. Down the Hudson River, between Staten Island and Coney Island, the ICW leads around Sandy Hook and offshore along the New Jersey coast.

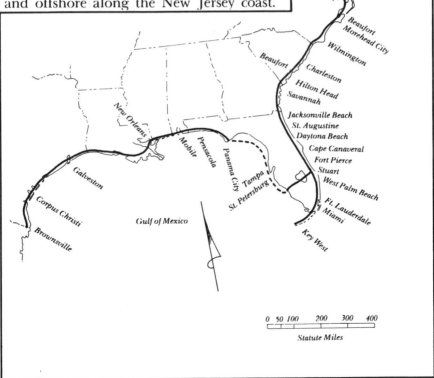

The Intracoastal Waterway offers passage through bays, sounds, rivers and protected channels.

272

Ducking in the Atlantic City inlet, the sailor can take a stroll on the famous boardwalk or try his luck at the casinos.

Around New Jersey's southern tip, Cape May, the ICW takes a northwesterly course up the Delaware Bay to the C & D Canal. After transiting the canal, for the next 200 miles the Intracoastal runs the length of the Chesapeake Bay. Cruising on the Chesapeake is legendary.

> . . . and they shall see teal—blue-winged, green-winged—
> sheldrakes, whistlers, black ducks, ospreys, and many other
> wild and noble sights before night, such as they who sit in
> parlors never dream of.

There are other attractions besides the Bay's great natural beauty. The sailor can visit Baltimore, a city riding a crest of revitalized pride. Annapolis exudes historic significance, beginning with being the meeting place of the Continental Congress. It is the home of the Naval Academy and the epicenter of East Coast sailing. On the Eastern Shore is the Chesapeake Bay Maritime Museum at St. Michaels. St. Michaels was the setting for Michener's historic novel, *Chesapeake*.

With a shoreline of more than 7,000 miles, and with 150 rivers and creeks emptying into it, cruising possibilities in the Bay are limitless. The largest of the rivers is the Potomac, on which the cruising sailor can sail right up to our seat of government. The museums and galleries in Washington, D.C. are among the best in the world.

Leaving the Chesapeake at Hampton Roads, Virginia, the ICW enters the Elizabeth River. Here the cruiser may encounter a vast array of water craft, including Jacques-Yves Cousteau's famous *Calypso* (when not on some adventure) and the wind ship *Alcyone*. At Milepost Zero, Waterside at downtown Norfolk, Virginia offers sailors a festive and inviting atmosphere. From Norfolk to Miami, the ICW is known as "the ditch." Leading through a series of rivers, canals, and sounds, the ICW slips behind notorious Cape Hatteras, past the sailing fleet at Oriental, and between Morehead City and Beaufort, North Carolina. Historic Beaufort, founded in 1709, is today a growing sailing center and a major offshore departure port (for Bermuda or the Caribbean); and nearby Cape Lookout is a favorite stop of many cruisers.

Further south on the Waterway is Wrightsville Beach, where the sailor will find warm hospitality and easy access to the Atlantic Ocean. Passing behind banks and sandspits and the "other" cape, Cape Fear, the Waterway enters South Carolina near the new inlet to Little River, a good seafood stop. The ICW follows Pine Island Cut past Myrtle Beach and into the enchanting Waccamaw River, lined on either side by huge brooding cypress trees laced with Spanish Moss. A few miles further south is Charleston, with an air of stately southern elegance. Across the Waterway from Charleston is Fort Sumter, where the Civil War began.

Skirting beautiful and exclusive Hilton Head, the ICW crosses into Georgia at the Savannah River. Savannah is a Deep South city of antebellum homes and magnolia trees. Beyond Savannah, the Waterway follows a course behind the barrier islands of Georgia, including well-known St. Simons and Cumberland Islands.

Florida at last, land of palm trees and winter sun. Miami is still almost 400 miles away, but there is much to see first. Passing Jacksonville Beach, the Waterway runs through St. Augustine. Founded in 1565, St. Augustine is the nation's oldest city and proud of that distinction. Past the famous beach of Daytona Beach, the sailor on the Waterway soon arrives at Cape Canaveral and the John F. Kennedy Space Center. Frequent shuttle launches may be viewed close at hand from several anchorages near the Space Center.

At Stuart, the mariner (with a mast height not exceeding 49 feet) may choose to follow the Indian River west, transiting Lake Okeechobee and the length of the Caloosahatchee River to the west coast of Florida and the Gulf of Mexico, and negotiating five locks on the passage.

The sailor continuing south on the ICW enters Florida's "Gold Coast." Finally palm trees become common, the warm Gulf Stream maintaining the tropical climate. Through the opulence of Palm Beach and the Venice-like canals of Ft. Lauderdale, the ICW leads into the international city of Miami. Beyond Miami is Biscayne Bay and the Florida Keys, a 150-mile long cruising ground offering warm, clear water and sunny skies, even in the winter. Quaint old Key West is the end of the line on the ICW, the final destination on a southerly cruise down the Intracoastal Waterway.

THE BAHAMA ISLANDS

In our opinion, the best nearby winter cruising ground is the Bahama Islands. Less than 50 miles from Florida, it is a sailor's heaven. A 700-mile-long archipelago, it has friendly people, adequate facilities, infinite skies, and deserted beaches but it is the water that makes the most lasting impression on the cruising sailor. Nowhere else will you encounter water as clear nor of such beautiful colors.

A cruise of the Bahamas is not a difficult one. The only obstacle is the Gulf Stream and, if you choose settled weather, it should present no problem. Entry requirements are also easy. U.S. citizens need only proof of citizenship (passport, voter's registration, or a birth certificate) and the vessel will be issued a cruising permit good for six months.

Departing Miami or Ft. Lauderdale, the cruiser clears customs at either Bimini or Cat Cay. Approaching either of these islands on the western edge of the Great Bahama Bank from off soundings is a visual treat as the water changes from cobalt to sapphire to sky blue, the bottom visible a hundred feet below. Through a series of transparent greens, the water becomes colorless at about a fathom. Navigational aids are almost nonexistent in the Bahamas; navigation is by sight, depths judged by the color of the water.

There is a certain aura about sailing in "foreign" waters. Removal seems more complete, relaxation deeper. This is especially true in the laid-back atmosphere of the sun-washed Bahamas.

While I sit here listening to the waves which ripple and break on this shore, I am absolved from all obligation to the past, and the council of nations may reconsider its votes. The grating of a pebble annuls them.

The Abaco Cays are the northern-most group of the Bahamas. They are normally approached by departing the United States at Palm Beach and clearing into the Bahamas at West End, Grand Bahama, then crossing the Little Bahama Bank to the northern islands in the chain. With marinas, boat yards, supermarkets, restaurants, laundromats, and a large charter fleet, the Abacos are among the most popular island groups. You will seldom have an anchorage to yourself.

In sharp contrast, the Berry Islands are rarely cruised extensively. Approached across the Great Bahama Bank from Cat Cay, only Chub Cay at the south end and Great Harbour Cay at the north end have any facilities. The other islands in the group are either private or uninhabited.

South of Chub Cay is Andros, the largest of the Bahama Islands. Heavily forested, Andros is unlike the other islands. It has several settlements and offers superb diving along its 120-mile-long barrier reef. The reef also makes the sailing more difficult and Andros sees few cruising boats.

Only 20 miles away is New Providence Island, where Nassau is located. The center of government (and everything else), about 80% of the nation's population lives on New Providence. Nassau is a historic city with numerous forts and other interesting sights. It is also a modern city with ample stores, shops and markets. Casino gambling and high glitter entertainment are available. Cruise ships call daily at

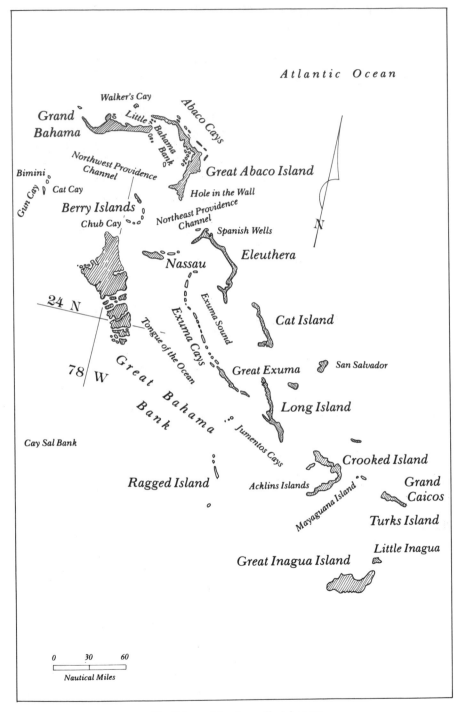

The Bahama Islands, a sailor's heaven.

the Prince George Wharf. Nassau has an excellent harbour and all yachting services are available.

To the east of New Providence, a string of cays leads to Eleuthera Island. The eastern-most is Spanish Wells. Settled by Eleutherian Adventurers in 1648, and expanded after the American Revolution by British Loyalists, it is one of the most picturesque settlements in the Bahamas.

Eleuthera is a big island, 90 miles long, and has several interesting settlements. Among them is Governor's Harbour, the oldest settlement in the Bahamas. The Eleutherians settled there in 1647 on Cupid Cay. The Bight of Eleuthera offers excellent sailing in the prevailing winds.

Surely the best cruising ground in the Bahamas is the Exuma Cays. Only 35 miles from New Providence, the Exumas stretch for 90 miles, providing the most perfect anchorages and the most beautiful waters that one can imagine.

> *I look down into the quiet parlor of the fishes, pervaded by a softened light as through a window of ground glass, with its bright sanded floor the same as in summer; there a perennial waveless serenity reigns as in the amber twilight sky, corresponding to the cool and even temperament of the inhabitants. Heaven is under our feet as well as over our heads.*

Facilities are limited but fuel and a few basic staples are available at Highborne, Sampson, and Staniel Cays. Water is limited and expensive. George Town is located on Great Exuma at the southern end of the chain. Host to the annual Family Island Regatta, George Town is the cruising headquarters for the southern Bahamas. Blessed with excellent protected anchorages, pristine beaches, and lovely reefs, most necessary supplies are available.

Only 20 miles from Exuma, Long Island is frequented by cruisers, but is an inhospitable island. With only two difficult harbors on its windward side and extensive shoals to leeward, it offers natural beauty but little protection. An annual regatta at Salt Pond has, in recent years, attracted more cruisers.

Farther east is Cat Island, the highest in the Bahamas, yet still reaching a height of only 204 feet above sea level. Continuing east is San Salvador, where Columbus first set foot in the New World in 1492. There is disagreement about where Columbus landed, and no less than three monuments have been erected in separate locations to mark "the spot." San Salvador has no safe harbor and should be visited only in

277

settled weather.

The southern Bahamas include the Jumentos Cays and Ragged Island, Crooked and Acklins Islands, Mayaguana Island, and Great Inagua. Here the trade winds are stronger, the seas rougher, the distances between anchorages greater. Except for those passing through to and from the Caribbean, few choose to cruise these more remote islands.

THE CARIBBEAN

There are two approaches to the Caribbean from the eastern United States. One is an offshore passage. The other is an island-hopping passage. In the first, the cruiser sails far enough east to clear the Bahamas, then shapes a southerly course, typically directly to the Virgin Islands. In the second, the sailor cruises south through the ICW (or along the coast), through the Bahamas and the Turks and Caicos Islands, along the northern shore of Hispaniola, along either the north or south coast of Puerto Rico and to the Virgin Islands. Following this route, the longest offshore passage is little more than 100 miles. Unfortunately, it is almost all to windward.

Both Hispaniola and Puerto Rico offer excellent cruising. The Virgin Islands are perhaps the best known. They are a compact cruising area offering endless summer and great variety. They are divided into U.S. and British ownership. On the U.S. side are the neighboring islands of St. Thomas and St. John and, separated by 40 miles of open water, St. Croix. The British islands include Tortola, Virgin Gorda, Anegada, and Jost Van Dyke. A huge charter fleet operates in the Virgin Islands. Although it is very crowded, it is still quite beautiful.

> . . . for a long time, nature overlooks the encroachment and profanity of man.

The Anegada Passage is a notorious chunk of ocean, usually the worst you will encounter during a Caribbean cruise. Once across it, you are in the Leeward Islands. Here the islands are more mountainous. Rarely more than 20 miles apart, most of the islands have good harbors. Anguilla is under British rule while her nearest neighbor, St. Martin is split between French and Dutch rule. St. Barts is also French. Brooding Saba is Dutch. So is Statia, the Dutch colony that, in 1776, saluted an *American* warship. This was the first time a foreign power formally recognized the Continental Navy, and Britain razed the island

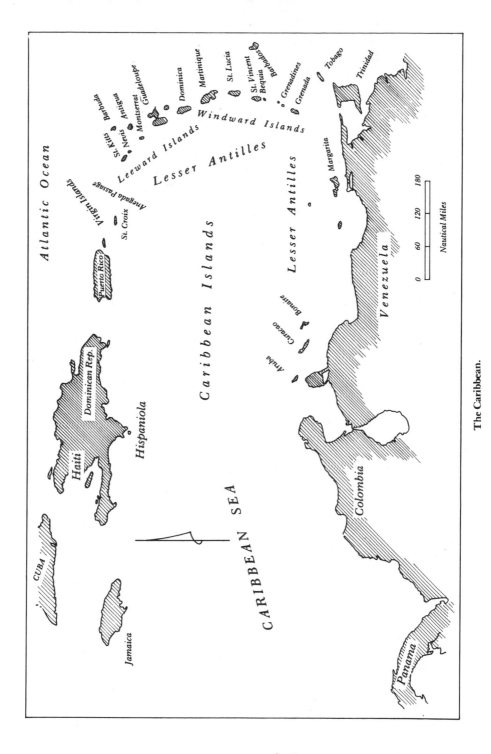

The Caribbean.

College of the Ouachitas

in response.

No such ill will exists today. Nearby St. Kitts and Nevis have close ties to the United Kingdom, as does Barbuda and Antigua. Arguably, the best harbor in the Caribbean is English Harbor at Antigua. Harbour Captain here in the 1780's was Trafalgar's Admiral Nelson. Nelson's Dockyard has been carefully restored, today catering to charter yachts rather than frigates.

Guadeloupe is a department of France, governed by Paris. The French flavor is unmistakable in its bustling cities. The last of the Leeward Islands, it is also the highest, the volcanic peak of Soufriere towering more than 4,800 feet above the ocean.

The first of the Windward Islands is independent Dominica. Next is another French department, Martinique. A jewel in the Caribbean, Martinique is the birthplace of Empress Josephine. It is also where a volcano called Pelée erupted in 1902, killing 30,000 people. Cruising around Martinique, you will encounter the H.M.S. Diamond Rock, a stone pinnacle saluted even today by ships of the British Royal Navy as a commissioned sloop of war.

Continuing south, the sailor finds St. Lucia and St. Vincent. More than 100 miles to the east (windward) is Barbados. Barbados is often visited by yachts arriving in the Caribbean from a trans-Atlantic passage, but only the hardiest beat out to it from the Windwards, against the trade winds.

Some of the best Caribbean cruising is found south of Bequia, among the islands called the Grenadines. At their southern tip is Grenada, traditionally known as the "Isle of Spice," but now familiar to millions as the sight of the American invasion in 1983. A hundred miles of open water separate Grenada from Trinidad and Tobago, the southern-most of the Caribbean Islands. Trinidad is just ten miles from the coast of Venezuela; further cruising is limited only by the imagination.

As long as possible live free and uncommitted. It makes but little difference whether you are committed to a farm or the county jail.

MEXICO

The East Coast sailor is fortunate to have three distinct warm weather cruising areas reachable without requiring lengthy offshore passages. The West Coast sailor really has only one choice: Mexico. Not to worry; Mexican cruising is among the best.

Like the Caribbean, there are two ways to arrive at the most popular

Mexican cruising area, the Sea of Cortez (Gulf of California). The departure point for either is usually San Diego. One way is to stand offshore until you can round the southern tip of the Baja peninsula. This is a distance of more than 700 miles. The other is to cruise down the west coast of the peninsula.

The first Mexican port is Ensenada, an overnight sail from San Diego. Often imagined as a sleepy little town, Ensenada is actually a large city; the next one is nearly 1,000 miles away. A lack of facilities is the primary problem with Mexican cruising. It may be a substantial distance between reliable sources of supplies, including fuel and water.

> . . . *the voyageur will do well to replenish his vessels often at the uncontaminated sources.*

The west coast of Baja offers some unique cruising. A few good anchorages will be found, but more often the anchorages will be plagued with an uncomfortable swell. Most cruisers daysail between anchorages, staying only one night at rolly anchorages such as Colonet or San Martin. The next anchorage is rarely more than 50 miles away. Stopping to sample the Mexican atmosphere is saved for the more protected and comfortable anchorages like San Carlos or Bahia San Bartolome. From Bahia Magdalena, the next anchorage is Cabo San Lucas, 150 miles away. This is the longest required passage from California to the Sea of Cortez.

Once around Cabo San Lucas, the cruiser enters the Sea of Cortez and turns northward. It is less than 150 miles to the city of La Paz, with two anchorages to break up the passage. From La Paz north, the eastern shore of the peninsula and numerous off-lying islands provide a plentiful supply of smooth anchorages. La Paz, a city of more than 100,000, is the capital of Baja California Sur and a good base for cruising the southern part of the Sea of Cortez.

Continuing north brings the cruiser to Puerto Escondido, the center of an ancient volcano and an all-weather anchorage. Just north is the town of Loreto. Good anchorages continue to be plentiful beyond Santa Rosalia. The sailor might also choose to cruise on the mainland side of the Sea of Cortez.

From the Sea of Cortez some choose to continue down the Mexican coast into Costa Rica, ultimately through the Panama Canal to sample Caribbean or East Coast destinations. Others head offshore for the legendary South Pacific. Many find Baja sufficiently close to paradise, leaving only when it is time to go home.

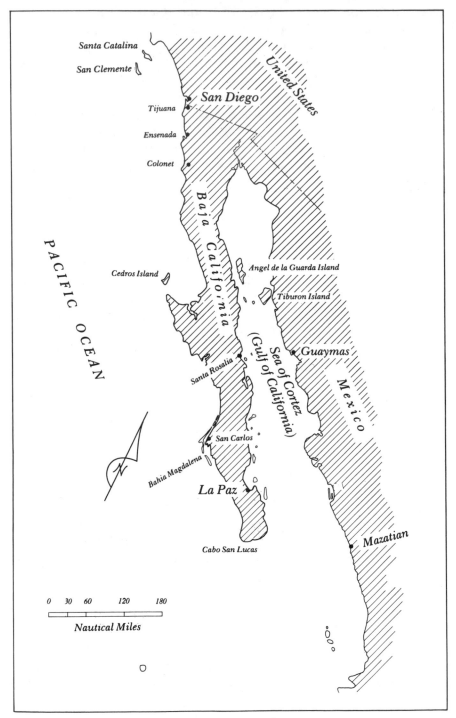

Baja California & Mexico.

WINTER ANIMALS

> *It matters not where or how far you travel . . . but how much alive you are.*

Thoreau's wisdom is not lost on them.

TIERRA DEL FUEGO

There are, of course, infinite destinations. You may want to join a racing fleet to Bermuda. A passage to Hawaii might be your dream. Why not a Mediterranean cruise, or a Polynesian one? Why these four?

Because they are the easiest to reach. They are particularly suited to the pocket cruiser. They offer some of the best cruising to be found anywhere, regardless of distance. And they can be experienced without totally disrupting your life.

> *If you are chosen town clerk, forsooth, you can't go to Tierra del Fuego this summer.*

For a first cruise, they are the sensible choices.

THE POND
IN WINTER

There is life, an experiment untried by me, and it does not avail me that you have tried it.

HAT is a cruise really like, a winter cruise to an area of warm skies, clear waters, and palm trees? Much of it is an individual experience, a mixture of images, sensations, and emotions. You will only know what it is like for you if *you* try it. It will not be exactly as you imagine it; rigid expectations are almost always a mistake. Sometimes it will be better, sometimes worse. Anticipate only a unique experience and you will not be disappointed.

Perhaps it will help if you share our images, our sensations our emotions. Come with us on an imaginary first cruise, imaginary only in the sense that it did not actually unfold the way we have chosen to tell it.

AWAY AT LAST

The dock lines came *aboard*—already a new experience and we had not even cleared the slip. Always before they stayed on the pilings, ready for our return tomorrow . . . or next week. This time we would not be back tomorrow . . . or next week.

Magic is 27 feet long, an old Alberg design. Cris and I had owned her for three years when we decided on a cruise about a year ago. The last six months have been a whirlwind of activity. We seemed so organized at the start. We went through old sailing magazines, reading all the cruising articles. We read all the cruising books in our public library (there were only five). We made a list of everything that needed to be done to get *Magic* ready for a six-month cruise. It was only three pages! No problem.

Then we actually started getting ready. The more we did, the more we found to do. After three months, the list was up to eight pages. We set November 1 as the departure date, but in October we still had five pages of unfinished items. November 1st, we were back to three. With full time application, and some culling, we were down to a page by the end of the week. It was time to go; we would finish the list on the Waterway.

Before we could finish last minute arrangements, the Siberian Express blew in bringing high winds, low temperatures, sleet and snow. We had delayed too long. When the temperature climbed above freezing, we put $400 worth of groceries aboard, gave Cris' dad the keys to the house and car, slipped the dock lines off the pilings, and pointed the bow south.

A NEW COMMUNITY

The next norther caught us south of Coinjock, North Carolina. We shared the small anchorage to the left of the Waterway with six other sailboats. Slashing rain and gusty winds kept us below. The first two days were not bad; we got two more items off the list and re-stowed everything, trying to empty the three remaining boxes of groceries on the bunk. We had planned to keep a narrative log of our cruise but had thus far failed to start it.

> *It is not easy to write in a journal what interests us at any time, because to write it is not what interests us.*

Exactly. With other activities limited, we started a journal and brought it up to date, both resolving to write in it daily. As the rain continued, we read a little, studied charts and cruising guides, listened to tapes, and even played Trivial Pursuit. I enjoyed the forced relaxation.

> *As a man grows older, his ability to sit still and follow indoor occupations increases.*

By the third day, Cris had cabin fever.

The rain stopped. I bailed the dinghy and we rowed around the anchorage. As we passed astern a graceful trimaran named *Swan*, her owners hailed us, inviting us aboard. Jim and Sally had taken a year sabbatical from teaching and, having cruised the Chesapeake all summer, were now headed for the Bahama Islands. *Swan* was only 30 feet and accommodations were compact, but the cockpit where we sat was entirely enclosed with zippered panels of clear plastic.

Another couple, Rob and Li, soon joined us. We had seen them going out in the rain to take their dog ashore twice a day, and wondered at the wisdom of cruising with a pet. Mickey, a huge Labrador retriever, was the third crew member aboard *Pisces*, their Tahiti ketch. They would not consider cruising without him. There was a degree of inconvenience, but they never worried about leaving the boat unattended with Mickey aboard, they really liked the welcome they always got when returning to the boat, and besides, he was part of the family.

Before the wind moderated four days later, we had been aboard every boat in the anchorage, had *been* dinner guests two nights and had *had* dinner guests the other two.

> *One man proposed a book in which visitors should write their names, as at the White Mountains; but, alas! I have too good a memory to make that necessary.*

Our memory was not so good, and we began what was to become on this cruise a fat Guest Log.

Friendships sprang up; we found ourselves especially drawn to Jim and Sally. Finally, on a sunny day with a light northeasterly, six of the seven boats weighed anchor and headed for dreaded Albemarle Sound. We expected a drubbing but were surprised with a very pleasant sail. Four of us stopped early, anchoring in the Little Alligator River. We all spent the evening together aboard the 41-foot *Faire Wind*.

All the way to Miami, it was much the same. Usually three or four boats travelled together. We ran aground in the Waterway twice, but were able to get off quickly, once with the help of the big diesel in *Faire Wind*. When the weather deteriorated, we holed up in a secure anchorage, enjoying the camaraderie among the cruisers. When we could anticipate the weather, we would stop where there were shoreside attractions. Often several crews would go ashore together. We made a fine picture, ten of us walking through elegant southern towns, all of us in bright yellow foul weather gear. Before the cruise, we had worried about bad weather, but some of our best times were in the worst weather.

> *From the right point of view, every storm and every drop in it is a rainbow.*

It seems right that a cruising community should be fluid. We left some behind, some went on ahead, but we met new cruisers daily. Our circle of cruising friends continually expanded. Soon it was the rare anchorage or marina where we did not meet "old friends" when we stopped.

SUNNY FLORIDA

We arrived in Daytona Beach, Florida, three days before Christmas. There were decorations everywhere. Many of the boats in the marina strung with lights. Jim and Sally were making all the preparations for Christmas aboard, complete with a tree and a turkey. It was 80°; Christmas to us required cold weather. More than that, it required family. We locked the boat, asked Jim and Sally to keep an eye on it, and rented a car. It only took a day (a long one) to drive what we had taken six weeks to sail.

Lured by our descriptions of palm-lined beaches and warm temperatures, Cris' dad returned with us a week later to join *Magic* for the run down the Florida coast. When we got to Daytona, it was 37°! We were soon underway again, but only went 50 miles before we decided to stop—for two weeks. When we arrived in Titusville, *Swan* was there. Jim and Sally were waiting to watch the space shuttle launch in two weeks. It seemed like a good idea to us. It was an

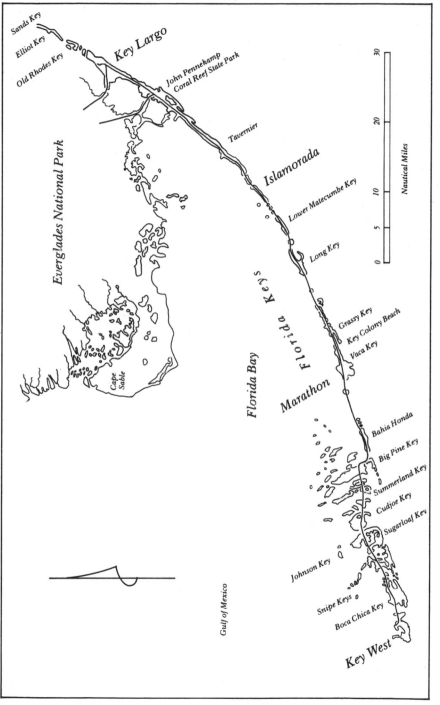

The Florida Keys.

unexpected treat and an incredible experience. We envied those aboard.

Thus we sailed, not being able to fly, but as next best, making a long furrow . . .

Warm weather returned and held all the way to Miami. Cris' dad flew home and we cruised the Florida Keys all the way to Key West. At Boot Key, in Marathon, we found almost a dozen of our friends settled in for the winter. Some had taken jobs to fatten the kitty. After a week of visiting, we left Marathon, sailing up the Keys on the ocean side in Hawk Channel. We planned to anchor in Angelfish Creek, north of Key Largo, and from there across the Gulf Stream to the Bahamas.

A SINKING FEELING

Ten miles from the mouth of Angelfish Creek, the automatic bilge pump began to run every two minutes. By the time we reached the creek, it was running every 20 seconds. The water was coming from a through-hull fitting and when I twisted it to see if the hose was loose, the threaded tail-piece sheared and the ocean rushed in. The seacock was frozen, one of the items still on "the list." Like the little Dutch boy, I held out the ocean with my hand—

To insure health, a man's relation to Nature must come very near to a personal one . . .

—while Cris rummaged through the cockpit locker looking for the tapered plugs we had aboard for such an emergency. Eventually the plug was driven in place to stop the leak.

The next day, we sailed back up to Miami where we found a yard that could haul us the following day. The faulty seacock was replaced and all the other seacocks were serviced. A tapered emergency plug was *attached* to each. As long as we were out of the water, we got the yard to pressure-wash the bottom and we put on a quick coat of bottom paint. We had spent $300 in two days. The yard accepted VISA.

A NEW COUNTRY

It was the third week in February when a front stalled over central Florida, swinging the normally southeasterly wind on around to south. With dew-laden decks, we slipped out of No-Name Harbor at 4:00 a.m. to cross the Gulf Stream.

THE POND IN WINTER

In each dewdrop of the morning
Lies the promise of a day.

Anticipation, combined with the motion, had us both sick by 6:00 a.m. We both wanted to turn back, but neither brought it up. Two hours later, Cris was feeling better and handling the helm; I was staying close to the rail. Schools of flying fish (or are they flocks when they fly?) scattered in front of us, skimming over the cobalt blue of the Gulf Stream. Cris was excited; I was miserable.

I was miraculously cured a little after eleven when Cris (whose head was higher than mine) spotted trees on the horizon. We soon identified it as North Bimini. As we came off soundings, the water was unbelievable. Everyone had told us that the water was clear, but we didn't know it could be this clear. We were so impressed with the colors that it came as a sudden shock to us that we were looking at brain coral and sea fans. Cris rounded up while I jumped for the depth sounder. Twenty-eight feet! I didn't believe it and used the lead line. Twenty-eight feet! It looked like six.

With the depth sounder flashing, we closed with Bimini. Monster sportfishermen were all around. I was congratulating myself on perfect navigation—we had held the same course all the way from Cape Florida—when we turned too soon and ran aground on the bar at the entrance to Bimini Harbour. The next wave lifted us clear and swept us into the channel that runs along the beach. By 1:00 p.m., we were anchored. In the Bahamas.

LESSONS LEARNED

Clearing took less than ten minutes but the Immigrations Officer was not very friendly. In fact, Bimini did not seem very friendly. We were a little put off. Weather kept us in Bimini Harbour for five days. After two sleepless nights while *Magic* seemed to sail all over the harbor, we learned to cope with the strong tide through the harbor using a properly set Bahamian moor. It was how we anchored 90% of our time in the Bahamas.

With an easterly breeze, we entered the Great Bahama Bank at Gun Cay and started across, looking for a single light structure 65 miles away. The water was rarely more than 12 feet deep and so clear we were in constant fear of running aground. "Fish muds," opaque areas caused by vast schools of fish feeding on the bottom, were especially disconcerting. So were shadows from the clouds.

The Bahamian moor.

At mid-day, I became aware of a difference in sound. Looking around, I realized that the dinghy was no longer astern; the light weight painter had chafed in two. We quickly reversed our course and soon found the errant boat. The new painter was three times larger, but still small compared to some we later saw.

Tacking across our charted course, by nightfall we were short of the half-way point. We anchored and spent a miserable night rolling and pitching, sleeping on the cabin sole to keep from being tossed out of the bunk. We dreaded a second night on the Bank. Dawn brought a wind shift to the southeast and we could lay our destination. Before noon we passed the Northwest Channel light and off the Bank.

At Chub Cay we watched an old motorsailer use a second anchor to hold the boat beam to the wind. No seaman here, we thought smugly. After dark, a swell began to round the point and run through the anchorage. We were rolling so badly that sleep was impossible. At first light we could see our mast sweeping a 40° arc across a roseate sky. The motorsailer sat quietly, pitching only slightly, its bow pointed directly into the swell. We didn't know as much as we thought.

THE POND IN WINTER

When we should still be growing children, we are already little men.

As we entered Nassau Harbour, our outboard quit with an expensive sounding crunch. The breakwater was terrifyingly close. All sails were neatly furled and covered. I could not help but think how "nice" we were going to look on the rocks with our bright blue sail covers. I removed the main cover in record time and hoisted the sail. The incoming tide had sucked us right into the harbor and we sailed to an anchorage. It was the last time we entered a harbor without a sail up or ready for instant hoist.

The motor was irreparable. We couldn't believe it! Then we discovered that a new outboard would cost about $400 less than in the States! We rationalized that the engine was old and we would have soon replaced it anyway—for a lot more money. The blues went away.

DOWN TO BUSINESS

Meanwhile, we enjoyed the hustle and bustle of Nassau. Huge cruise ships lined Prince George Wharf, colorful island freighters at Potter's Cay. Captain Nemo's yellow "submarine" made daily trips to the reef, loaded with sunburned tourists. Hundreds of small boats constantly crisscrossed the harbor. We visited historic forts, the chaotic straw market, and the casinos of Paradise Island. We explored shops, mailed post cards, went to a movie, and sampled several restaurants.

Sated and over budget, we sailed for the Exuma Cays. At Allan's Cay, Cris refused to get out of the dinghy while huge, prehistoric iguanas raced down to the beach to see if we brought food. At Hawksbill Cay we climbed the high hill and looked down at *Magic*, agreeing that the water could never be more beautiful than here; we were wrong. At Bell Island we found *Swan*. Jim and Sally were delighted to see us.

It is long since a human friend has met me with such a glow.

We felt the same way.

Together we gorged on plentiful fish, conch, and lobster. We swam and snorkeled and lay in the sun. We went hiking on the islands, exploring in the caves, and shelling on empty beaches.

We soon discovered that all the cruisers in the Exumas were working south, planning to attend the Family Island Regatta at George Town in mid-April, a sailing series among traditional Bahamian work boats. It is a classic Bahamian social event and we quickly decided to be there. When we sailed into beautiful Elizabeth Harbour, we could not believe how many cruising boats were there, how many we already knew from the trip down, how many we had yet to meet, and how many different nations were represented. For two weeks, the activity never stopped. There were beach parties, dinghy races, excursions to colonial ruins around the harbor, and evening get-togethers. An informal windsurfing school was always in session. There were dances in town, and cookouts. And, of course, the official events.

We had intended to take advantage of our stay in George Town to complete a few more items on the list and to do some cosmetic maintenance. It did not happen that way.

> *There were times when I could not afford to sacrifice the bloom of the present moment to any work, whether of the head or hands.*

A REASSESSMENT

A week before Regatta, *Pisces* sailed into the harbor. Enthusiastic divers, Rob and Li soon had Cris and me joining them every day. In their fast inflatable sport boat, we could zip out to good diving locations in a few minutes. Boarding the inflatable from the water was also easy. We began to have second thoughts about our own rigid, rowing dinghy.

Henry, off the 51-footer, *Duchess,* offered us an old inflatable at a very good price. We took it. Three days later we sold our rigid dinghy for the same price. By mounting *Magic's* new outboard to the inflatable, the outboard did double duty and we found our horizon expanded at every anchorage. We were wildly enthusiastic, until we sailed for Cat Island towing the dinghy. It took a full knot off our speed. We learned to partially deflate it and take it aboard. Later, in the open anchorage at Spanish Wells, I would try and fail to row an anchor out in a building wind. It would have been easy in our old rigid dinghy. Unwilling to leave *Magic* without power, even momentarily, the solution was to float the anchor on a life jacket and swim it out. Our enthusiasm was also dampened.

TIME FLIES

Suddenly it was May and we needed to be back in July. Jim and Sally had continued south for a quick visit to the Caribbean. *Pisces* was sailing up the coast of Cat Island and Eleuthera with us. In the smooth waters in the lee of these islands, we had some of the best sailing we have ever experienced. Some days we raced *Pisces* to the next anchorage; other days we just laid back and watched the sail.

> *. . . the play of its pulse so like our own lives, so thin and yet so full of life, so noiseless when it labored hardest, so noisy and impatient when least effective; now bending to some generous impulse of the breeze, and then fluttering and flapping with a kind of human suspense.*

At Little Harbour, Abaco, Cris was astonished to find the studio of world-renowned sculptor Randolph Johnston. As a devotee of art, Cris was fascinated by Johnston's works and we stayed several days, watching while a bronze piece was cast at Johnston's foundry.

Short on time, the month we had planned to spend in the Abaco Cays was reduced to ten days. The numerous charter parties we met were invariably amazed at the clarity of the water. Having come up from the southern Bahamas, we found the clear Abaco waters "murky" by comparison. We wondered what we would think of our home waters now.

EXPANDING HORIZONS

At Allan's-Pensacola Cay, we had a decision to make. We could turn west across the Little Bahama Bank to West End, then cross the Gulf Stream to Florida and return home via the Inland Waterway, or we could leave the Bahamas at Walker's Cay and sail offshore almost due north to Beaufort, North Carolina. We had not even spent a single night offshore although we had been cruising for more than six months. We had not planned an offshore passage, but now we wanted to do it though we were both frightened by the prospect. Then Rob and Li told us that they would be leaving us in two or three days to sail to Bermuda. From Bermuda, they were going to Europe for a year of cruising there. That pushed us off the fence. If they could cross the Atlantic, surely we could sail to Beaufort with the coast never more than a couple of hundred miles away.

Three days later, after carefully checking everything aboard, we sailed through the reef in tandem with *Pisces*. In a matter of hours, they had disappeared over the eastern horizon and we were alone. I held my breath for 24 hours. On the second day I breathed twice. By the third day we were talking; on the fourth beginning to feel confident. Then a black cloud loomed on the horizon. We doused all sail before the squall hit. It was not nearly as bad as we had expected. When it passed, it left us on a heaving but windless sea.

Nightfall brought a sky packed with stars.

I just looked up at a fine twinkling star and thought that a voyager whom I know, now many days' sail from this coast, might possibly be looking up at that same star with me. The stars are the apexes of what triangles!

We thought about *Pisces,* halfway to Bermuda; about *Swan,* still in the Caribbean. We thought of all the people we had met, all the places we had seen, and of the thread of the cruise that held them together.

The following night found us at a marina in Beaufort, calling family to let them know where we were. It was six more days before we reattached our dock lines in our home slip, but the cruise seemed to be over when we reached Beaufort. As we covered the requisite miles to reach home, we relived the cruise, reminding each other of special moments, often reading to each other from the log.

Perhaps this is the main value of a habit of writing, of keeping a journal—that so we remember our best hours and stimulate ourselves.

A MEASURE OF SUCCESS

We had conceived the cruise, planned it, prepared for it, gone on it, and incredibly it was over. We had sun and rain, wind and calm, ecstasy and terror, good and bad. It was all part of the experience, the way cruising is, and now we knew.

Your greatest success will be simply to perceive that such things are, and you will have no communication to make to the Royal Society.

You will not discover the satisfactions of cruising in the *Journal of the Royal Society.* You will find them only in your own journal.

SPRING

. . . with our wings spread, but never lifting our heel from the watery trench; gracefully plowing homeward with our brisk and willing team . . .

FTER a winter cruise comes spring. The time allotted for this enterprise has expired. Some cruises are open-ended, but most are not; spring eventually arrives (regardless of the actual season) when you return to the "real world," a world that has continued on even without you. The cruise has followed its course from dream to reality, and now, inevitably, to memory. The boat has returned to a home mooring, you to the life you left behind.

In previous chapters we have concentrated on adjusting to cruising; such things as learning to anchor properly, selecting crew, and conserving water. This chapter is about the adjustments that are required *after* a cruise. Perhaps it seems ludicrous to suggest problems in returning to the familiar. We assure you that it is not. After the liberty of a cruise, the constraints of society stand out in sharp contrast.

The life you left behind.

> *It is an unfortunate discovery certainly, that of a law which binds us where we did not know before that we were bound.*

You may find the adjustment process far more difficult than you had ever imagined.

There are two likely scenarios when the cruise is over. The first is that you absolutely loved cruising and have stopped only because you ran out of time or money. The lifestyle that you must return to is, in your mind, inferior to cruising. It is easy to see that in this circumstance returning may be difficult. The second scenario is that the cruising experience was not as good as you had fantasized and you are ready to return to a lifestyle with which you are more comfortable. Perhaps less severe in this case, adjustment problems will exist nonetheless.

RETURNING TO THE REAL WORLD

> *With a bending sail we glided rapidly by Tyngsborough and Chelmsford, each holding in one hand half of a tart country apple pie which we had purchased to celebrate our return, and in the other a fragment of the newspaper in which it was wrapped, devouring these with divided relish, and learning the news which had transpired since we sailed.*

The first hint of trouble may come from your friends. Do not flatter yourself that they have pined away for your return. They have not. Although perhaps not as rich, their lives have been as full as yours, with no more time for you than you have had for them. Like yours, their lives have gone on. Unlike yours, theirs has remained intertwined with the community.

> *He cannot see any such motives and modes of living as I; professes not to look beyond the securing of certain "creature comforts." And so we go silently different ways . . . while the same stars shine quietly over us. If I or he be wrong, Nature yet consents placidly.*

Having chosen a divergent path, you no longer share common experiences. You are unaware of the Smith's divorce or the Jones' new addition, do not know who got promoted at the company, have not kept abreast of current events, have not seen the latest movie. And your initial interest in such things is, at best, nominal.

If their interest in your adventure is more than politeness, they will ask about pirates or storms. Perhaps they are looking for adequate calamity to reaffirm that they spent their year more wisely than you. More likely, they simply do not understand the cruising experience. You will be unable to share it with them.

> *Perhaps the facts most astounding and most real are never communicated by man to man. The true harvest of my daily life is somewhat as intangible and indescribable as the tints of morning or evening.*

In both cases, previously easy communication becomes difficult. Much common ground has eroded during your absence. Your difficulties are especially pronounced in contrast with the array of common interests and concerns that you have just shared with other members of the cruising community. A previously familiar environment may seem foreign, with you, in a sense, unable to speak the language. As a result, you may experience an overwhelming sense of isolation. Keep in mind that your friends have not changed, you have. It is up to you to make any adjustment.

One other warning about your friends: if you grieve over the end of the cruise, do not expect a great deal of sympathy. Remember that while you have been off yachting in a land of palm trees, your friends and associates have been holding their own noses to the grindstone, perhaps shoveling snow in their spare time. They are not likely to feel truly sympathetic toward your readjustment problems.

ROSE-COLORED RECOLLECTIONS

Only when you return will you realize how unprepared you may be for the required adjustment. While noise, traffic, and the general hustle and bustle will at first be disconcerting, it takes only a few days to adapt to the quickened pace. Adjustment difficulties will be much more deep-seated than handling noise pollution or dodging kamikaze dump trucks. The experience of the cruise alters your perceptions and dispels certain illusions, illusions that we sustain to comfortably exist in modern society.

One of those illusions is the cruising experience itself. Perhaps this sounds like double talk, but bear with us. Before a trip, you may often compare your current lifestyle to your concept of cruising. We are not discussing escapism here, so we will assume that your current situation is not uncomfortable. Still, since you are reading this book, we can also assume that, for you, cruising appears to be the more desirable of the two; it is also the more uncertain. It is this uncertainty that allows you to justify settling for second choice rather than risk time, money, and "momentum" to try cruising. If you actually go, the situation changes—all doubt is removed.

For most, the experience exceeds even expectations, confirms the appeal of cruising. Perhaps there were moments of terror as weather deteriorated, frustration at a chronic engine problem, or discomfort on a hot, still night. By spring, those recollections have faded into the background, have become pleasurable themselves as challenges met.

> *If the day and the night are such that you greet them with joy, and life emits a fragrance like flowers and sweet-scented herbs, is more elastic, more starry, more immortal—that is your success.*

The certainty of a more satisfying lifestyle can make a previously comfortable situation difficult to re-embrace.

Cruising may also be so seductive that your desire to cruise has not been satisfied but intensified instead. Many return from a first cruise with only one thought in mind: How and when can I go again? There is little doubt that the various pleasures of cruising can be addictive. This can be a disconcerting discovery for those planning a cruise as a kind of ultimate vacation, little more than a pleasant pause in their quest for upward mobility.

Even if you return feeling that the experience did not match up to its press, there are still aspects that will impact your ability to re-enter mainstream society.

A QUESTION OF SIGNIFICANCE

Your perception of the world around you will have changed. In a world where airliners fly in multiples of the speed of sound, you cannot avoid examining the world more closely when you travel at five knots. You cannot live as closely with nature as cruising requires without redefining terms. Infinity is more than an abstract concept in a math class; it describes the night sky. Aground on a falling tide, you fully comprehend unrelenting. Full water tanks define wealth; a storm at sea, fury, and perhaps fear.

> *When we are unhurried and wise, we perceive that only great and worthy things have any permanent and absolute existence, that petty fears and petty pleasures are but the shadow of the reality.*

When physical safety depends constantly upon the ability to competently navigate or anchor, the importance of navigating the shoals of social *faux pas* are significantly diminished. Even more important, upon returning many experience a feeling of a relative lack of significance of daily shoreside decisions or activities, particularly those within the framework of the business organization. This can seriously impact their ability to function effectively within the organization.

So can the effect cruising has on the illusion of your own significance. A small boat afloat in an immense and indifferent ocean is a miniature kingdom. Your decisions determine the fate of your world and all its inhabitants. When you return, you quickly realize what a tiny cog you really are in this incredible machine we call civilization. Such a realization can be devastating, robbing you of all conventional aspirations. It is a very real problem and can make returning to prior employment extremely difficult. However, it is likely to be no more than the darkest hour before the dawn. Most eventually come to grips with this issue of significance, appreciating their new perception of the world around them, and finding the cruising experience to have been one of life's most valuable lessons.

Our ecstatic states, which appear to yield so little fruit, have this value at least: though in the seasons when our genius reigns we may be powerless for expression, yet, in calmer seasons, when our talent is active, the memory of those rarer moods comes to color our picture and is the permanent paint-pot, as it were, into which we dip our brush.

Life seems much richer when painted with the vivid colors of a cruise.

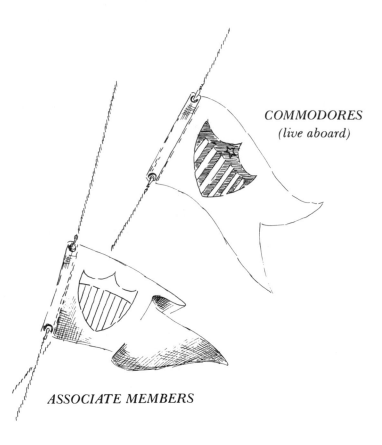

COMMODORES
(live aboard)

ASSOCIATE MEMBERS

Burgees for Seven Seas Cruising Association.

FULL TIME CRUISING?

If cruising is so great, returning so difficult, why not cruise full time, adopt it as a lifestyle? Why not, indeed? Some do cruise perpetually; most do not. There is a family to raise, a class to teach, a business to run, a book to write, other things to experience.

> *Perhaps it seemed to me that I had several more lives to live, and could not spare any more time for that one. It is remarkable how easily and insensibly we fall into a particular route, and make a beaten track for ourselves.*

A cruise can be a satisfying experience for many; full time cruising is for relatively few. Perhaps it is the lifestyle for you. That is for you to decide. We advocate only a sensible approach.

Without experiencing cruising, both the good and the bad, a decision to adopt cruising as a lifestyle is a roll of the dice. Do not tell everyone that you are off to sail around the world and spend years in preparation for such a lofty undertaking. Try a limited cruise first. If you find it is indeed all you ever want to do, then trade in your shore life. If it is not, you can return in the spring without embarrassment, without any sense of time wasted or of failure, and without unduly complicating your life.

MAKING THE ADJUSTMENT

Returning from an extended cruise, regardless of the length, requires some adjustment. With varying severity, this is a common problem among cruising sailors. A six-month cruising interlude to add contrast to a promising career in suburban America might not turn out as you plan. It may simply whet your appetite for more distant horizons and your current aspirations may pale in comparison. There is a real risk that you cannot easily pick up where you left off.

> *As for the complex ways of living, I love them not, however much I practice them.*

Your perspective on "living" may have changed so drastically that the secure situation you left behind may be untenable upon your return.

We know executives and engineers with tremendous earning potential who are bussing tables and painting boat bottoms, interested only in earning enough to continue cruising a little longer. The motivations they once had no longer exist. Before they sampled cruising, they could not imagine themselves accepting a two-thirds cut in pay. Now they cannot imagine themselves again as willing participants in office politics, struggling for the next promotion.

Are we warning you against going cruising? Absolutely not! The risk of hitting a reef is minimized if you are aware that it is there; the risk of foundering from a failed through-hull fitting minimized if you are prepared to stem the flow. Neither risk should prevent you from cruising. Similarly, the risks at your return are minimized with knowledge and preparation and should not keep you from going.

Is there a solution? None that we know of. Nor do we seek a solution. We want only to make you aware of the fact.

Let us not underrate the value of a fact; it will one day flower in a truth.

Indeed it will. And that may be that the life you discover fits you better than the one you left behind.

CONCLUSION

*How many a man has dated a new era in his life from the
reading of a book!*

UR purpose in compiling this book has been to provide
both a philosophic and a practical approach to cruising
that we hope will lead the reader to the recognition that
cruising is possible for anyone with the desire. Many
books have already been written that provide practical

guidance, although almost without exception they are intended to prepare the cruiser for unlimited cruising. We think a sensible approach to cruising recognizes that most cruises are not unlimited.

It is the around-the-world voyage, or at least the crossing of an ocean or two, about which cruising narratives are written; the long distance voyager who shares with us his preparation and the lessons learned. Yet far more cruisers take to the water for a matter of only weeks or months, challenge the oceans with no more than a daysail in fair weather. Where is the logic in putting windvane steering aboard when no blue-water sailing is planned, in seeking a boat with cavernous stowage when cruising is limited to six weeks, in being influenced by advertising copy reading "world cruiser" when planning only to winter in the Bahamas?

The practical aspects of this book differ from others in that we define the "proper" cruising boat as that one with only the features and equipment necessary to accomplish the planned cruise, *and no more.*

> *Simplicity, simplicity, simplicity! I say, let your affairs be as two or three, and not a hundred or a thousand . . .*

Cruising gear is often a misnomer, the associated complexity and expense inhibiting cruising rather than facilitating it. Cruising dreams are too often thwarted by the enormity of the recommended preparations.

The other reef upon which many would-be cruisers are wrecked is a jaundiced perception of values. If "as soon as" follows "cruising" in your sentences, you are in dangerous waters. "I am going cruising *as soon as* we buy a bigger boat." "We are going cruising *as soon as* business improves." "We are going cruising *as soon as* I can retire." It is called procrastination and is fatal to the cruising dream. This book is about cruising now, not someday. It is about adopting an attitude, a philosophy, that cruising is not simply prolonged uselessness but a worthwhile endeavor, an opportunity to sample some of life's finer fruits. It deserves the same dedication, perhaps more, that we accord to more traditional goals.

> *The life which men praise and regard as successful is but one kind. Why should we exaggerate any one kind at the expense of the others?*

It is our hope that this book, punctuated with the profound, poetic, and succinct comments of Thoreau, provides the reader with both the determination and the information necessary to achieve a goal of cruising.

THE DECISION

Perhaps you have sat for hours on a freeway-turned-parking-lot on your way home from a job-turned-drudgery and asked yourself, "Is this all there is?" Perhaps you have read of the cruises of others in books and magazines and imagined yourself in that happy circumstance, at least for a while. Perhaps you suspect that the life for you is that of a carefree vagabond blowing around the South Seas but have the acumen to recognize that you should at least interview the cruising lifestyle before you adopt it. Whatever the circumstance, it is the imagination that launches every cruise.

> *If you have built castles in the air, your work need not be lost; that is where they should be. Now put the foundations under them.*

That foundation is a decision to go. "Someday" is not a decision; it is little more than a wish. Forget "someday I am sailing to Polynesia"; try "November we are going to Baja." Then make whatever other decisions are necessary to achieve that goal.

In America, how we use our time is at our discretion.

Money is often cited as an obstacle. Generally the object is to achieve a parity between the money available and the money required. If you cannot increase the money available, you must reduce the money required. That means a smaller boat, less equipment, a shorter cruise.

Time is also perceived as an enemy of cruising, a curious perception indeed. There is not a single person with one minute more time in a day than you have. In America, how we use that time is totally at our own discretion. Those cruising are not doing so because they have more time; they are cruising because that is how they decided to use their time.

> *I confess that I am astonished at the power of endurance, to say nothing of the moral insensibility, of my neighbors who confine themselves to shops and offices the whole day for weeks and months, aye, and years almost together.*

To take the time for cruising, you must exchange the time required for other activities. It is fundamental to the cruising decision—your decision.

THE BOAT

Marinas, moorings, and private docks are littered with seaworthy little boats capable of accomplishing almost any cruising goal; meanwhile their owners struggle and save, or merely harbor the dream, to someday own a "real" cruising boat. When someone tells you that a real cruising boat is at least 40 feet in length, pay no attention. Length has little to do with it. A 40-foot "world cruiser" getting oohs and ahhs at the marina but never leaving the slip is no cruising boat at all. A real cruising boat is the boat that takes you cruising—period. In almost every instance, the pocket cruiser will do that as well as the world cruiser, and sooner.

Aside from a bit of extra comfort, and a bit of extra space if required, the 40-footer is not the sensible choice.

> *As the time is short, I will leave out all the flattery, and retain all the criticism.*

The larger boat is going to cost three times as much to purchase, twice as much to maintain. It will bar you from shallow cruising areas, confine you to deep (and perhaps crowded) anchorages. Sails will be more difficult to hoist and to trim, ground tackle more difficult to retrieve. The world cruiser will be more difficult to handle in a confined space, harder to bring to the dock, and the consequences of an error in judgement will be much more serious.

Faced with adversity, the short-handed world cruiser is more likely to get into trouble. In storm conditions, the sails are more difficult to douse or reef, additional ground tackle more difficult to deploy. Grounding is a more serious lapse. Gear failure, such as a dismasting, may be impossible to effectively deal with. Even the potential for superior speed may not materialize due to the need to manage sails conservatively.

In any case, the higher speed has more of a sensual impact than a practical one where passage lengths are limited, probably no impact at all on the essence of cruising.

The universe constantly and obediently answers to our conceptions; whether we travel fast or slow, the track is laid for us.

A sensible cruising boat facilitates cruising; it does not hinder it. It should not be too large to handle, too complex to maintain, or too expensive to afford. For the majority of cruising objectives, and for most cruising couples, that translates into a boat of less than 35 feet; for many, significantly less. Cruising is far more at risk from selecting a boat too large than from getting one too small.

THE EQUIPMENT

We have devoted a major portion of this book to the examination of a wide array of cruising equipment. To go cruising requires only sails and ground tackle, minimal navigational equipment, a handful of essential safety items, and a galley stove and a pot. Everything else is optional.

There is an almost overwhelming tendency to load a cruising boat with an extensive inventory of extra equipment. Loaded may be a positive term for a luxury car, but a "loaded" cruising boat simply sits lower in the water. When considering the addition of any equipment, the question to ask is not, "Can I use it?"; the sensible question is, "Do I need it?"

. . . for my greatest skill has been to want but little . . .

When evaluating the desirability of each equipment item, there are two considerations. The first is contribution. How will the item contribute to the cruise? Will it make the cruise safer? More comfortable? More enjoyable? Is it certain to provide the contribution promised, or is it prone to failure? Would that failure be a minor inconvenience or a major disaster?

The second consideration is cost. Is the item a good value in dollars and cents? Does the money spent on the item impact the cruise? Shorten it? Delay it? If funds are available, does this item offer the most contribution to the cruise for the dollars spent? Does it add unnecessary complexity to the boat? Will maintenance and repair require time, reduce your liberty?

When outfitting a boat for a cruise, you would do well to always think in terms of how little is required, not how much.

> *In proportion as he simplifies his life, the laws of the universe will appear less complex . . .*

The simpler the boat and its equipment, the less you will be insulated from the cruising experience.

THE ARRANGEMENTS

Once the decision has been made, the boat acquired and equipped, there are arrangements to consider. What is to be done about the life you are leaving behind? The sensible approach is to arrange the cruise in such a manner as to minimize the disruption of the normal flow of your life. That means burning as few bridges as possible.

If at all possible, take an extended leave or a sabbatical from your employment; if not, try to leave the door open for re-hire. If you own a home, do not sell it to finance a first cruise. Find another way. Rent the house to someone, or borrow against it, but make all arrangements reversible. Only after you have accumulated ample cruising experience can you properly evaluate the wisdom of trading your home for a boat.

We are not suggesting taking so conservative an approach that you have to wait until retirement to go cruising.

> *There is no more fatal blunderer than he who consumes the greater part of his life getting his living. All great enterprises are self-supporting.*

To the contrary, we advocate cruising now. The cost of a cruise need not require drastic measures. A small cruiser need not cost more than the average new car. With equipment limited to the basics, it is possible to go cruising with nothing riskier than a car-payment-turned-boat-payment. Lowering the cost in no way devalues the cruise.

CONCLUSION

Unless you plan to cruise alone, crew arrangements will be necessary. Enough friends and family are usually available to satisfy crew requirements for an initial cruise. In fact, most cruising is done by couples. If you are a couple and you are both committed to cruising, you already have crew. If only one is committed to cruising, you already have a problem. The solution is to structure the cruise so that it satisfies some expectations of both partners, i.e., sightseeing, diving, shell collecting, or whatever. The cruising couple must share the commitment or the cruise is in jeopardy. A compromise cruise is a far better alternative than no cruise at all.

Guests are distinguished from crew by a lack of responsibility for the handling of the boat. Sharing a cruise with guests can be one of the highlights of a cruise. It can also be calamitous. If guests are planned, early and thorough preparation will improve the odds.

THE DESTINATION

Cruising destinations are as varied as cruising boats and those who sail them. To some extent, the destination is limited by the time available. If a cruise is planned for a month or two, it will be planned for waters not very far from home. Such a cruise is in no way second class. Nearby cruising grounds invariably offer delights and experiences every bit as enjoyable as those areas beyond the far horizon.

> *Such is beauty ever—neither here nor there, now nor then, neither in Rome nor in Athens, but wherever there is a soul to admire. If I seek her elsewhere because I do not find her at home, my search will prove a fruitless one.*

When more time is available, many will elect to sail beyond the horizon, to sample the pleasures of a new environment. The choice of which horizon to sail beyond is a personal one; we suggest the southern horizon. It is not our intention to disparage northern cruising grounds or to deter those inclined to visit them. It is simply that we find that warm-climate cruising showcases all of the best aspects of cruising: swimming, diving, sunning, windsurfing, stargazing, beachcombing, and others.

The American east coast offers innumerable cruising opportunities. The Intracoastal Waterway passes through most of them, and the cruiser can follow the season south, cruising in a warm climate virtually year-round.

Less than 50 miles offshore of the east coast of Florida lie the first of the Bahama Islands, a nation of islands and shallow banks that stretch southeastward for more than 700 miles. The waters of the Bahamas are like none other in the hemisphere.

> *It is a mirror which no stone can crack, whose quicksilver will never wear off, whose gilding Nature continually repairs; no storms, no dust, can dim its surface ever fresh;—a mirror in which all impurity presented to it sinks, swept and dusted by the sun's hazy brush,—this the light dustcloth,—which retains no breath that is breathed on it, but sends its own to float as clouds high above its surface, and be reflected in its bosom still.*

In contrast to the low islands and the homogeneous people of the Bahama Islands are the high and varied islands of the Caribbean. There the cruiser will encounter a half dozen different languages, a dozen different nations, including Britain, France, and the Netherlands. These legendary West Indies have long been a favorite winter cruising ground.

West Coast sailors have only one "nearby" cruising ground, but it is a jewel. The Sea of Cortez and the eastern shore of Baja peninsula offer much for the cruising sailor. Rarely visited fifteen years ago, these Mexican waters are now enormously popular with American cruisers.

THE EXPERIENCE

Experience is what a first cruise is all about. If all you can manage is a month, do not despair at those you read of who are cruising for a year. Take your month and make the best of it.

> *For it matters not how small the beginning may seem to be: what is once well done is done for ever.*

If the cruising life captivates you, you will find a way to go again and you will have a far better understanding of the preparation required.

Regardless of the length of your cruise, and regardless whether you ever go on another cruise, it will still be an experience that you will think of often. And it will be one that will alter your perceptions of life and the world around you.

> *I went . . . because I wished to live deliberately, to front only the essential facts of life, and see if I could not learn what it*

had to teach, and not, when I came to die, discover that I had not lived.

If you are comfortable with your current perceptions, you may find that you will return with some new ones that are, at least initially, disconcerting. Ultimately, your life will be richer for the experience.

We have done our very best to outline a philosophical attitude and a practical approach to cruising that puts it within the grasp of the common man. We can do no more. The rest is up to you. Your determination will be the difference between dream and reality. For one final time, we defer to the wisdom and poetry of Thoreau:

. . . if one advances confidently in the direction of his dreams, and endeavors to live the life which he has imagined, he will meet with a success unexpected in common hours.

Hold tenaciously to the dream and follow a sensible course and your success is assured.

BIBLIOGRAPHY

Allcard, Edward. *Single-Handed Passage.* New York: Norton, 1950.

—. *Temptress Returns.* New York: Norton, 1953.

—. *Voyage Alone.* New York: Dodd, Mead, 1964.

The American Practical Navigator, originally by Nathaniel Bowditch (issued by the U.S. Naval Oceanographic Office), Washington, U.S. Government Printing Office, periodically revised.

American Radio Relay League. *Radio Amateur's Handbook.* Newington, Ct.: American Radio Relay League.

Baader, Juan. *The Sailing Yacht.* New York: Norton, 1979.

Beiser, Arthur. *The Proper Yacht.* Camden, Me.: International Marine, 1978.

Blewitt, Mary. *Celestial Navigation for Yachtsmen.* New York: de Graff, 1967.

Bode, Carl (ed.) *The Portable Thoreau.* New York: Viking, 1947.

Borden, Charles A. *Sea Quest.* Philadelphia: Macrae Smith, 1967.

Bottomley, Tom. *The Boatkeeper's Project Book.* New York: Motor Boating and Sailing Books, 1972.

Bowker, R.M., and Budd, S.A. *Make Your Own Sails.* New York: St. Martin's Press, 1959.

Brown, Larry. *Sailing on a Micro-Budget.* Newport, R.I.: Seven Seas, 1984.

Buckley, William F. Jr. *Airborne: A Sentimental Journey.* New York: Macmillan, 1976.

—. *Atlantic High.* Garden City, N.Y.: Doubleday, 1982.

Burke, Katy. *The Complete Live-Aboard Book.* Newport, R.I.: Seven Seas, 1982.

—. *Managing Your Escape.* Newport, R.I.: Seven Seas, 1984.

Carpenter, Wayne. *The Voyage of Kristina.* Annapolis, Md.: Azimuth, 1983.

Chapman, Charles F., et al. *Piloting, Seamanship and Small Boat Handling*. New York: Motor Boat and Sailing Books.

Chichester, Francis. *Alone Across the Atlantic*. New York: Doubleday, 1961.

—. *Atlantic Adventure*. New York: de Graff, 1963.

Coles, Adlard. *Heavy Weather Sailing*. New York: de Graff, 1981.

Colgate, Stephen, *Fundamentals of Sailing, Cruising, and Racing*. New York: Norton, 1978.

Colvin, Thomas E. *Coastwise and Offshore Cruising Wrinkles*. New York: Seven Seas, 1972.

—. *Cruising as a Way of Life*. New York: McKay, 1979.

Cornell, Jimmy. *Modern Ocean Cruising*. London: Adlard Coles, 1983.

Dashew, Steve & Linda. *Bluewater Handbook*. Ojai, Ca.: Beowulf, 1984.

—. *The Circumnavigators' Handbook*. New York: Norton, 1983.

Davison, Ann. *My Ship is So Small*. New York: Sloan, 1956.

Desoutter, Denny M. *Small Boat Cruising*. London: Faber & Faber, 1972.

Dumas, Vito. *Alone Through the Roaring Forties*. New York: de Graff, 1960.

Eastman, Peter F., M.D. *Advanced First Aid Afloat*. Cambridge, Md.: Cornell Maritime, 1972.

Ellam, Patrick, and Mudie, Colin. *Sopranino*. New York: de Graff, 1958.

Gerbault, Alain. *Fight of the Firecrest*. New York: de Graff, 1955.

—. *In Quest of the Sun*. New York: de Graff, 1955.

Gibbs, Tony. *The Coastal Cruiser*. New York: Norton, 1981.

—. *The Coastal Navigator's Notebook*. Camden, Me.: International Marine, 1982.

—. *Cruising in a Nutshell*. New York: Norton, 1983.

Gilles, Daniel, and Malinovsky, Michel. *Go Cruising*. St. Albans, England: Adlard Coles, 1978.

Graham, Robin Lee. *Dove*. New York: Harper & Row, 1972.

Griffith, Bob and Nancy. *Blue Water: A Guide to Self-reliant Sailboat Cruising*. New York: Norton, 1979.

Groene, Janet. *Cooking on the Go*. Boston: Sail Books, 1980.

—. *The Galley Book*. New York: McKay, 1977.

Guzzwell, John. *Trekka Round the World*. New York: de Graff, 1963.

Hackler, L.R. *The Complete Sailor's Log*. Colonial Heights, Va.: Seascape, 1985.

Hayden, Sterling. *Wanderer.* New York: Norton, 1977.

Henderson, Richard. *Choice Yacht Designs.* Camden, Me.: International Marine, 1979.

—. *The Cruiser's Compendium.* Chicago: Henry Regnery, 1973.

—. *Sea Sense.* Camden, Me.: International Marine, 1972.

—. *Singlehanded Sailing.* Camden, Me.: International Marine, 1976.

—. *Better Sailing.* Chicago: Henry Regnery, 1977.

Herreshoff, L. Francis. *The Compleat Cruiser.* New York: Sheridan House, 1956.

—. *Sensible Cruising Designs.* Camden, Me.: International Marine, 1973.

Hiscock, Eric C. *Atlantic Cruise in Wanderer III.* London: Oxford University, 1968.

—. *Around the World in Wanderer III.* London: Oxford University, 1956.

—. *Beyond the West Horizon.* London: Oxford University, 1963.

—. *Come Aboard.* Oxford: Oxford University, 1978.

—. *Cruising Under Sail.* London: Oxford University, 1965.

—. *Sou'west in Wanderer IV.* London: Oxford University, 1973.

—. *Two Yachts, Two Voyages.* New York: Norton, 1985.

—. *Voyaging Under Sail.* London: Oxford University, 1970.

—. *Wandering Under Sail.* Oxford: Oxford University, 1977.

Horie, Kenichi. *Kodoku: Alone Across the Pacific.* Rutland, Vt.: Tuttle, 1964.

Howard-Williams, Jeremy. *Sails.* New York: de Graff, 1971.

Jones, Tristan. *Adrift.* New York: Macmillan, 1980.

—. *Heart of Oak.* New York: St. Martin's, 1984.

—. *Ice!* New York: Avon, 1980.

—. *The Incredible Voyage.* Fairway, Ks.: Sheed, Andrews & McMeel, 1977.

—. *One Hand for Yourself, One for the Ship.* New York: Macmillan, 1982.

—. *Saga of a Wayward Sailor.* Fairway, Ks.: Andrews & McMeel, 1979.

—. *A Steady Trade.* New York: St. Martin's, 1982.

Kemp, P.K. (ed.) *Oxford Companion to Ships and the Sea.* New York: Oxford University, 1976.

Kinney, Francis. *Skene's Elements of Yacht Design.* New York: Dodd, Mead, 1973.

Kline, Harry. *Yachtsman's Guide to the Bahamas,* Coral Gables, Fl.: Tropic Isle Publishers, published annually.

Kotsch, William J. *Weather for the Mariner.* Annapolis, Md.: Naval Institute Press, 1977.

Lane, Carl D. *The Boatman's Manual.* New York: Norton, 1979.

—. *Go South Inside: Cruising the Inland Waterway.* Camden, Me.: International Marine, 1977.

Leone, Nicholas C., M.D., and Phillips, Elisabeth C., R.N. *Cruising Sailors Medical Guide.* New York: McKay, 1979.

Letcher, John S. Jr. *Self-steering for Sailing Craft.* Camden, Me.: International Marine, 1974.

Maloney, Elbert S. *Dutton's Navigation and Piloting.* Annapolis, Md.: Naval Institute Press, 1981.

Manry, Robert. *Tinkerbelle.* New York: Harper, 1966.

Maté, Ferenc. *The Finely Fitted Yacht.* New York: Norton, 1979.

—. *From a Bare Hull.* Vancouver: Albatross, 1976.

—. *Shipshape.* Vancouver, Albatross, 1985.

Maury, Richard. *The Saga of Cimba.* New York: de Graff, 1973.

Miller, Conrad. *Engines for Sailboats.* New York: Ziff-Davis, 1978.

Miller, Conrad and Maloney, Elbert. *Your Boat's Electrical System, 1981-82.* New York: Motor Boating and Sailing Books, 1982.

Mixter, George W. *Primer of Navigation.* New York: Van Nostrand Reinhold, 1967.

Moeller, Jan and Bill. *Living Aboard: The Cruising Sailboat as a Home.* Camden, Me.: International Marine, 1977.

Moffat, Alex W., and Porter, C. Burnham. *The Galley Guide— Updated.* New York: Dodd, Mead, 1977.

Norgrove, Ross. *The Cruising Life.* Camden, Me.: International Marine, 1980.

Pardey, Lin and Larry. *The Care and Feeding of the Offshore Crew.* New York: Norton, 1980.

—. *Cruising in Seraffyn.* New York: Seven Seas, 1976.

—. *The Self-sufficient Sailor.* New York: Norton, 1982.

—. *Seraffyn's European Adventure.* New York: Norton, 1979.

—. *Seraffyn's Mediterranean Adventure.* New York: Norton, 1981.

—. *Seraffyn's Oriental Adventure.* New York: Norton, 1983.

Payson, Herb. *Blown Away.* Boston: Sail Books, 1980.

—. *You Can't Blow Home Again.* New York: Hearst, 1984.

Petersen, Marjorie. *Stornoway East and West.* New York: Van Nostrand, 1966.

318

Pidgeon, Harry. *Around the World Single-Handed*. New York: de Graff, 1955.

Pye, Peter, *Red Mains'l*. New York: de Graff, 1961.

—. *A Sail in a Forest*. London: Rupert Hart-Davis, 1961.

—. *The Sea is for Sailing*. New York: de Graff, 1961.

Rebell, Fred. *Escape to the Sea*. London: Murray, 1951.

Robinson, William A. *Deep Water and Shoal*. New York: de Graff, 1957.

—. *A Voyage to the Galápagos*. New York: Harcourt, 1936.

Roth, Hal. *After 50,000 Miles*. New York: Norton, 1977.

—. *Two on a Big Ocean*. New York: Macmillan, 1972.

—. *Two Against Cape Horn*. New York: Norton, 1978.

Rousmaniere, John. *Annapolis Book of Seamanship*. New York: Simon & Schuster, 1983.

—. *The Sailing Lifestyle*. New York: Simon & Schuster, 1985.

Searls, Hank. *Overboard*. New York: Norton, 1977.

Shepard, Odell (ed.) *The Heart of Thoreau's Journals*. New York: Dover, 1961.

Sleightholme, J.D. *Cruising*. London: Adlard Coles, 1979.

—. *Fitting Out*. London: Adlard Coles, 1977.

Slocum, Joshua. *Sailing Alone Around the World*. New York: de Graff, 1952.

Smeeton, Miles. *Once is Enough*. New York: de Graff, 1960.

Spurr, Daniel. *Spurr's Boatbook: Upgrading the Cruising Sailboat*. Newport, R.I.: Seven Seas, 1983.

Street, Donald. *The Ocean Sailing Yacht*. New York: Norton, 1973.

—. *The Ocean Sailing Yacht, Volume 2*. New York: Norton, 1978.

Stuermer, Gordon and Nina. *Deep Water Cruising*. New York: McKay, 1980.

—. *Starbound*. New York: McKay, 1977.

Tangvald. Peter. *Sea Gypsy*. New York: Dutton, 1966.

Taylor, Roger. *The Elements of Seamanship*. Camden, Me.: International Marine, 1982.

—. *Good Boats*. Camden, Me.: International Marine, 1977.

—. *More Good Boats*. Camden, Me.: International Marine, 1979.

Tazelaar and Bussiere. *To Challenge a Distant Sea*. Chicago: H. Regnery, 1977.

Thompson, Chris. *The Care and Repair of Small Marine Diesels*. Camden, Me.: International Marine, 1982.

Thoreau, Henry David. *Walden and Civil Disobedience*. New York: New American Library, 1980.

Voss, John C. *The Venturesome Voyages of Captain Voss*. New York: de Graff, 1955.

Warren, Nigel. *The Outboard Book*. New York: Motor Boating & Sailing Books, 1978.

INDEX

ABOUT THIS BOOK:

Cover design by Mark Smith.
Illustrations by Bobby Basnight.
Book design by Lew Hackler.

The cover photograph by Carolyn Alexander
was taken offshore near Diamond Shoals at Cape Hatteras.

The text type is 11 point Baskerville, leaded two points.
Quotations are in Baskerville Italics.
Headline type is Baskerville Bold.

Baskerville is classified as a Traditional typeface
bridging the Old and the Modern. It was created by
John Baskerville in 1757.

Typography by Type Time/Boardwalk, Inc.
The text was electronically converted from word
processing diskettes to digital type using
an Epics/6400 phototypesetting system.

Art style is appropriate to the period of Thoreau's life.
PMT reductions of the line art were by Keith-Fabry.
Text paper is an off-white, sixty pound, offset paper,
supplied to Seascape's specifications.

Printed and bound in the USA.